Silence and Sound

Silence and Sound

Theories of Poetics from the Eighteenth Century

Richard Bradford

Rutherford • Madison • Teaneck
Fairleigh Dickinson University Press
London and Toronto: Associated University Presses

© 1992 by Associated University Presses, Inc.

All rights reserved. Authorization to photocopy items for internal or personal use, or the internal or personal use of specific clients, is granted by the copyright owner, provided that a base fee of $10.00, plus eight cents per page, per copy is paid directly to the Copyright Clearance Center, 27 Congress Street, Salem, Massachusetts 01970. [0-8386-3435-4/92 $10.00+8¢ pp, pc.]

Associated University Presses
440 Forsgate Drive
Cranbury, NJ 08512

Associated University Presses
25 Sicilian Avenue
London WC1A 2QH, England

Associated University Presses
P.O. Box 39, Clarkson Pstl. Stn.
Mississauga, Ontario,
L5J 3X9 Canada

The paper used in this publication meets the requirements of the American National Standard for Permanence of Paper for Printed Library Materials Z39.48-1984.

Library of Congress Cataloging-in-Publication Data

Bradford, Richard, 1958–
    Silence and sound : theories of poetics from the eighteenth century / Richard Bradford.
      p.   cm.
    Includes bibliographical references (p.) and index.
    ISBN 0-8386-3435-4 (alk. paper)
    1. English poetry—History and criticism—Theory, etc. 2. Poetics. I. Title.
PR502.B66   1992
821.009—dc20   90-56225
                                                                                   CIP

PRINTED IN THE UNITED STATES OF AMERICA

To Jan Elliott

Contents

About the References, Notes, and Bibliography	9
Acknowledgments	11
Introduction	13
1. The Prosodic Background	19

Part One: Silence

2. Visualist Reading: Woodford to Sheridan	33
3. The Critical Debate: The Eighteenth versus the Twentieth Century	50
4. Shape and Identity: Milton, Wordsworth, and Literary History	72

Part Two: Sound

5. The Voice of Form	103
6. Rhyme	133

Part Three: Silence and Sound: The Modern Perspective

7. Fenollosa and the Silence-Sound Conflict	161
8. The Spoken Word Unheard: Silence and Sound in Modern Poems	180
Codebreaking: Conclusions for Criticism	201
Notes	210
Bibliographical Essay—Further Reading	216
Bibliography	218
Index	229

About the References, Notes, and Bibliography

I have attempted to limit the number of notes by placing most of the page references within the main text. The date of the first edition will be given in the main text and the date of the edition cited will, unless otherwise indicated, be found in the bibliography. Phrases such as "Rice argues that . . ." or "Say states . . ." relate to the single work of the author listed in the bibliography.

Where a cited critic quotes from another work, I have not attempted to correct any spelling, punctuation, or substantive variants in accordance with more reliable texts. For example, Sheridan's quotations from *Paradise Lost* are copied verbatim, but my references to the poem are taken from the edition cited in the bibliography.

The "Bibliographical Essay—Further Reading" refers mostly to works not cited in the main text or bibliography, but which are connected with the themes and issues dealt with in the study.

The following abbreviations will be used in the main text:

Hooker   *The Critical Works of John Dennis*, ed. E. N. Hooker, 2 vols. (Baltimore, 1939).
Ker   *Essays of John Dryden*, selected and edited by W. P. Ker, 2 vols. (New York, 1961).
Smith   *Elizabethan Critical Essays*, ed. G. Gregory Smith (Oxford, 1904). Reprinted 1937–71.
Spingarn *Critical Essays of the Seventeenth Century*, ed. J. E. Spingarn, 3 vols. (London, 1909). Reprinted 1957.

Acknowledgments

I first became interested in the lost voices of eighteenth-century criticism when doing doctoral research at Oxford and I would like to thank my supervisors, The Rev. Graham Midgley of St. Edmund Hall and Miss Anne Elliott of St. Hilda's College, for their encouragement and assistance. I am grateful also to the University of Wales for awarding me a postdoctoral Research Fellowship and to St. David's University College, Lampeter, for providing me with the time and resources to conduct my investigations into the relationship between seeing and hearing poetry. The Humanities Faculty of the University of Ulster provided me with the funding and resources to prepare this study for publication. At various times and in various ways the following people have played an important part in the realization of the *Silence and Sound* project: David Skilton, Geraldene Mangan, Dai Howells, Louie and Bill Bradford, and Jan Elliott.

Permission to reprint material has been granted by the following copyright holders:

Professor Geoffrey Hill for a section of his BBC Radio 3 interview on "The Composed Voice," July 1981.

Longman Group UK for Milton's note on "The Verse" from their edition of *Paradise Lost*, edited by Alastair Fowler.

Andre Deutsch Ltd., for a section of Geoffrey Hill's "Funeral Music" from *King Log*.

Seymour Chatman for a section of Samuel Levin's "The Conventions of Poetry" from *Literary Style: A Symposium* (ed. Chatman).

Faber and Faber Ltd., for lines from W. H. Auden's "Look Stranger" and "Musée des Beaux Arts"; from T. S. Eliot's *The Waste Land, Ash Wednesday,* and *Four Quarters;* and from Marianne Moore's "To a Chameleon."

Collins/Grafton Ltd., for "57" from e. e. cummings's *73 Poems*.

Random House Inc., for lines from W. H. Auden's "Look Stranger" and "Musée des Beaux Arts."

New Directions Publishing Corporation for lines from William Carlos Williams's "The Corn Harvest" and "The Red Wheelbarrow," and for a section from Charles Olson's "Projective Verse."

Introduction

I should first of all explain the title, Silence and Sound. My thesis is that it is wrong to assume that seeing, speaking, and hearing a poem are parallel coordinates of the same experience. Conventional opinion would have it that the printed text is merely a prompter to a variety of oral performances, and that the definitively poetic effects of textual depth and intensity are a consequence of oral delivery. I shall show that reading silently and reading aloud involve two separate dimensions of understanding; that unless we grant what I shall call silent poetics an equal status to that held by spoken performance and accept that a multidimensional experience is vital to our understanding of a number of important poems, we will perpetuate an inaccurate perception of how poetry works.

Such a challenge to the traditional communicative priorities of speech and writing is probably familiar to readers of concrete poetry and those with interests in the currently fashionable practices of deconstruction and poststructuralist linguistics, but it occurred, with startling consequences, in the work of a number of eighteenth-century critics of poetic form. Their names and their work have made brief and unremarkable appearances in bibliographies of linguistics and histories of English prosody, and it is their accepted status as prosodists, granted according to modern conceptions of what poetic form is and of how it influences meaning, that clouds our awareness of their most intriguing critical achievements. Paul Fussell expanded on work already done by T. S. Omond in *English Metrists* (1921) and by George Saintsbury in *History of English Prosody* (1906–10); and his *Theory of Prosody in Eighteenth Century England* (1954) is generally regarded as the most comprehensive documentation of theories of form in the Restoration and eighteenth century. But Fussell is precise about the scope of his work: "Limitations of space have prevented me from treating (1) the controversy over the nature of accent and quantity; (2) the eighteenth century theory of the nature of rhyme; (3) the theory of line integrity; and (4) the theory of the caesura: no consideration of eighteenth-century prosodic theory can of course pretend to completeness which is obliged to neglect these four topics" (pp. vi–vii). The omissions are, to say the least, unfortunate because the theories of rhyme and of what the poetic line actually is are crucial to the significance of eighteenth-century criticism. These writers found themselves dealing with a poetic "tradition" that was barely a hundred and fifty years old, and they lacked a single methodology or code of interpretation through which they might deal with the complex relation between structure and effect. The sense of uncertainty was further intensified by the appearance of *Paradise Lost*, a poem that fractured the fragile conventions of interpretation of the late seventeenth century.

The most valuable critical work of the period has been marginalized by modern literary history because of its peculiarity, its ability to move beyond any established interpretive precedent. It is valuable because critics such as Samuel Woodford, John Walker, Thomas Sheridan, and Joshua Steele constructed critical methods according to their own individual experience of reading, with no concessions to theoretical abstraction or to a priori notions of correctness. Their work thus transcends what we comfortably accept to be the aesthetic circumstances of "the eighteenth century." Some came to the conclusion that meaning could be generated independently from within the silent configurations of the printed text, a process that could operate as a threat both to the logic of sequential language and to the ideal of oral transparency; some found that classical expectations of form—metrical feet, regular and predictable line structure—were irrelevant and even restricting in our understanding of English metrical form—they created a manifesto for free verse. The point of divergence for these very often conflicting theories exists in the question of what happens when we see and hear poetry, and thus their work is divided into two parts, Silence and Sound. The third part, The Modern Perspective, explores the intriguingly close correspondences between the productive uncertainties of the eighteenth-century theorists and the equally complex questions offered to the reader of twentieth-century poetry.

Criticism, in its role as a code of expectations, can establish preconditions that narrow and limit our repertoire of responses. The familiar methodological duo of form and meaning operates most effectively when we can distinguish form from formless contingency, but for the eighteenth-century critics structural keystones such as the poetic line were recognized as shifting and elusive phenomena. This condition of instability threatened not only the reliable equations of form and meaning, but also the validity of discrete interpretive categories. To regard these critics simply as prosodists or linguists, in the modern understanding of these words, is inaccurate; and, as its title implies, the opening chapter will examine prosodic issues as the "Background" that the new methods of reading would eventually both displace and transcend.

Silence and Sound

1
The Prosodic Background

Poole's Parnassus

Any study of eighteenth-century ideas of poetic form should, most properly, begin with the publication of Joshua Poole's *English Parnassus* (1657). The author of its preface, the mysterious "J. D.,"[1] should have been heir to the conflicting prosodic theories and the chaotically varied technical vocabulary of the late sixteenth and early seventeenth centuries, but his preface is precise and assured, and he gives emphasis to stylistic and interpretive issues that would effectively dominate writing on poetic form for the next century and a half.

> This harmony in *prose* consists in an exact placing of the *accent*, and an accurate disposition of the words; such as delighting the ear, doth in a manner captivate the passions and the understanding.... In Poesie it consists besides the aforesaid conditions of Prose in, *measure, proportion* and *Rhime*. All we have to say relates only to the latter, and in that, confining ourselves particularly to *English* Poesie. (sigs. A2v–A3r)

His dismissal of attempts to adapt the form and structure of classical, quantitative prosody to English is complete and unambiguous. He attacks those who find the vernacular, accentually based prosody, "savage and barbarous" and asserts that in comparison with Greek and Latin, "it is much more excellent. To which may be added the advantages, in point of poetry, accrewing by *Rhime*, and consequently that the Languages are enriched by it, are the most susceptible of Poesie" (sig. A3r). He cites as his mentors in this matter, Sidney, Puttenham, and Daniel, all of whom represent a resistance to quantitative ideals and attempted adaptations, but he is more precise than his predecessors on the available alternatives. He states that although some writers had "vainly attempted to write a Heroic poem in imitation of the *Greeks* and *Latines* . . . without regard to rime . . . all kind of

Historical Poesie [was], performed by most of the *European languages*, till of late, by way of *Stanzas*" (sig. A4r).² By "till of late" he refers to the increasing popularity of the rhymed couplet. Later in the preface he quotes a sequence of loose, heavily enjambed couplet poetry, very similar to Donne's *Elegies* and *Satires*, and harshly condemns "the poet" who has "here imitated the *Greek* and *Latine*, presumed on to dismember and *disjoyn* things that should naturally march together" (sig. A6v). Two essays published in the 1930s by Ruth Wallerstein and George Williamson³ document the pre-Restoration emergence of the heroic couplet as a vehicle for different poetic genres, and examine how in the hands of Fairfax, Sandys, Jonson, and Waller a tendency toward iambic regularity and rhetorical parallelism and balance gradually replaced the formal convolutions of the metaphysicals. J. D.'s preface represents a perceptive, contemporary critical record of these developments.

J. D. is also the first proponent of the syllabically limited iambic pentameter. He does not speak of iambs or trochees because in 1657 such terms still connoted the discredited optimism of a classical system. His system of "accent," "measure," "proportion," and "rhyme" is part of an attempt to move beyond the conditioned expectations of foot terminology, but his 'corrections' of lines in which there is a "misplacing of the accent" make it clear that his ideal is of a syllabically limited unit with a regular succession of unstressed and stressed syllables. For example:

> Though death doth presume, yet vertue preserves

becomes

> Though death doth ruine, vertue yet preserves.
>
> (sig A5v)

He is, in effect, constructing a theoretical framework for the Augustan closed couplet, a form that virtually controlled the idiom of poetry in the age of Dryden and Pope. This new prosody would move beyond foot patterns; stress and accent would depend as much upon rhetorical and syntactic position as upon lexical fixity—"exact placing of accent and . . . accurate *disposition* of the words." Rhyme would divide rhythmic units equally and the impression of order conveyed to the listener would depend less upon the oblique apprehension of fixed time sequences overlaid upon syntax and more upon syntax generating its own formal units, structurally emphasized by grammatical closure and rhyme.

J. D.'s model would within two decades become part of a critical orthodoxy led by John Dryden, and it should be noted that his treatment of rhyme promotes the device to the status of a formal keystone that preserves the identity and structure of the line. Blank verse, whose first English manifestation in Surrey's *Aeneid* had been followed by a small group of imitations by men such as Gascoigne, Grimald, Turberville, and even Spenser, is consequently dismissed as a poetic form. It is only referred to indirectly in connection with the "Dramatick": "In these the poet is not strictly obliged to rhime, but only to measure, being such as are principally intended for the stage, the main graces here consist of representation and action" (sig. A4v). This judgment accurately preempts the later equation of unrhymed metrical structures with the contingent stress values of speech, a form that falls below the artifice of poetic writing and is more closely related to the realism of "representation" and "action."

Dryden

John Dryden's critical work on prosody is probably the most important of the period. He was the first to establish the polarity between the couplet and blank verse as central not only to dramatic writing but also to the future debate on the nature of English poetic form.

In the dedication of *The Rival Ladies* (1664) are to be found the origins of his early theory of versification. Dryden used the publication of this play as a convenient platform for making public his views on formal structure, which are applicable to all poetry rather than specifically related to drama.

The most important point made in the preface concerns rhyme. It is seen not merely as a metrical device but as capable of compelling and directing the poet's creative faculty. The separation and contrast of the functions of the fancy and the judgment are often regarded as merely a Hobbesian obsession and are sometimes condemned as superfluous freight when grafted onto the theory and practice of the Restoration writing. But in Dryden's treatment of the balance between the accuracy and clarity of judgment and the creative refractions of the fancy, we find that these abstractions of theory receive their most vivid practical application in the sphere of poetic form.

> But that benefit which I consider most in it, [rhyme], because I have not seldom found it, is, that it bounds and circumscribes the fancy. For imagination in a poet is a faculty so wild and lawless, that like a high ranging spaniel, it must have clogs tied to it, lest it outrun the judgment. The great easiness of blank verse renders the poet too luxuriant; he is tempted to say many things which might better be omitted, or at least shut up in fewer words; but when the difficulty of artful rhyming is interposed where the poet commonly confines his sense to his couplet, and must contrive that sense into such words, that the rhyme shall naturally follow them, not they the rhyme; the fancy then gives leisure to the judgment to come in, which, seeing so heavy a tax imposed, is ready to cut off all necessary expenses. (Ker, I, p. 8)

This much quoted and discussed passage holds the key to our understanding of the issues and controversies of contemporary theories of form. Rhyme has become not merely a unit of metrical form, but the crucial axis between form and meaning. Meter in the abstract, classical sense of measurement had been replaced in English by accent and rhyme, both of which are produced from the syntactic and rhetorical structure of the lines. Thus, poetic form has become inextricably tied into the structures of grammar and meaning.

The "assistance" that rhyme gives to the poet is mirrored by its effect upon the reader.

> I mean the help it brings to memory, which rhyme so knits up, by the affinity of sounds, that, by remembering the last word in one line, we often call to mind both verses (Ker. I. p. 7)

Again there a sense of Dryden attempting to reconcile the conflict between classical expectations of artifice and the linguistic condition of English: for the formal status of accent and rhyme to be discernable and productive, it must become almost a grammar of writing distinct from the conventions of rhythmic prose. Thus, blank verse, which lacks the essential keystone of rhyme, is not really poetry.

> Shakespeare . . . , invented that kind of writing which we call blank verse, but the French, more properly, *prose mesuree;* into which the

English tongue so naturally slides, that, in writing prose, it is hardly to be avoided. (Ker, I, p. 6)

The *Essay of Dramatic Poesy* (1668) contains the summation of Dryden's most important work on prosody and its conclusions represent the first comprehensive declaration of the Augustan prosodic ideal. The structure of the work itself reveals the importance of the debate on rhyme and blank verse. The dramatized colloquy centers upon three basic areas of concern: the relative value of ancient and modern writers, the relationship between French and English drama, and the argument over rhyme and blank verse. As the piece develops, Lisideius and Eugenius drift almost imperceptibly out of the mainstream of the debate leaving Crites, as the defeated champion of the ancients, and Neander, as the patriotic defender of English drama against the French, to embody antithetical positions in the ultimate and most topically immediate debate on what poetic form actually is and how it can be distinguished from the contingent patterns of prose. Dryden, through Crites, carefully rearticulates the arguments of Sir Robert Howard's Preface to *Four New Plays* (1664), but in the essay Dryden makes sure that Howard's/Crites's defense of blank verse is sown with the seeds of its own destruction, allowing Neander (Dryden) to win the argument and extend it into a formal manifesto for nondramatic poetry.

Crites is here defending his mimetic theory that writing which is least removed from the spontaneous patterns of speech is most suitable for impassioned verse.

> For this reason, says Aristotle, 'tis best to write tragedy in that kind of verse which is the least such [constrained], or which is nearest prose: and this amongst the Ancients was the iambic, and with us is blank verse, or the measure of verse kept exactly without rhyme. (Ker, I, p. 9)

Neander picks up Crites's Aristotelian reference and turns it upon him. Aristotle, he says, specifies that it must be a form of verse which is nearest prose, but, as Neander goes on to show, Crites's definition of measure kept exactly without rhyme is not verse at all but "measured" or typographically arranged prose. Crites's comparison of the classical, quantitative iambic with blank verse is vital to this denouement, because he fails to point out that an iambic sequence based upon relative stress values will not establish its own metrical identity without the assistance of grammatical closure or rhyme. Having identified the weakness of Crites's argument, Neander goes on to elaborate his own theory not merely of the drama but also of the nature of English versification.

> This new way consisted in measure or number of feet, and rhyme; the sweetness of rhyme, and observation of accent, supplying the place of quantity in words, which could neither exactly be observed by those Barbarians, who knew not the rules of it, neither was it suitable to their tongues, as it had been to the Greek and Latin. No man is tied in modern poesy to observe any farther rule in the feet of his verse, but that they be disyllables; whether spondee, trochee or iambic; it matters not; only he is obliged to rhyme. (Ker, I, p. 97)

So not only is the English accentual structure limited to disyllabic units, it cannot, in itself, create a line of verse. Its "measure" of five feet or ten syllables possesses an insufficient degree of artifice to separate it from rhythmic prose; it must also be marked by the rhyme to indicate the discrete structure of the line.

Dryden seems to be fully aware that these formal prescriptions exercise a form of rhetorical and structural control over poetic writing that is far beyond the classical ideal of measure, because the essay concludes with a debate on the question of how such a tight linguistic formula could hope to discharge or reproduce patterns of spontaneity and feeling that were thought to be central to the poetic use of language. This is Neander's defense.

> Verse 'tis true, is not the effect of sudden thought; but this hinders not that sudden thought may be represented in verse, since those thoughts are such as must be higher than Nature can raise than without premeditation, especially to a continuance of them, even out of verse; and consequently you cannot imagine them to have been sudden either in the poet or in the actors. (Ker, I, p. 102)

The case for rhyme rests: it is arbitrary and artificial but it is essential to the distinction between the "higher thought" of poetic writing and the "sudden thought" of unstructured feeling.

Milton's Note

I have given emphasis to Dryden's prosodic theories chiefly because they raise issues which were to become the central concern of eighteenth-century writing on versification: how could the English poetic line exist as an oral phenomenon without rhyme or full grammatical closure? What effect upon the range and flexibility of poetic effects did the rhymed form have? And, most significantly, did the accentual structure of English predicate a completely new and, so far undocumented, formula for verse structure?

The third question might well have been closed down by Dryden's conception of accent and rhyme, had it not been for a piece of almost theatrical timing. *Paradise Lost* was soon to become recognized as the first substantial attempt to create a form of unrhymed, accentual nondramatic English verse, and it was published in 1667, within months of Dryden's *Essay*. There has been much scholarly speculation on why Milton was urged by his printer Simmons to insert a note on—in effect an explanation of—his verse form, but it would not be implausible to suggest that by the time of the fourth issue of the first edition, Dryden's manifesto for rhymed poetry had been read and discussed. The note appeared in the fifth issue of 1668. The enigmatic terseness of the note could bear witness to this accident of chronology, but since it exists as the only instance of stated authorial intention in what was to become the most intense and wide-ranging debate in the history of poetic form, it is worth quoting in full.

> The measure is English heroic verse without rhyme, as that of Homer in Greek, and of Virgil in Latin; rhyme being no necessary adjunct or true ornament of poem or good verse, in longer works especially, but the invention of a barbarous age, to set off wretched matter and lame metre; graced indeed since by the use of some famous modern poets, carried away by custom, but much to their own vexation, hindrance and constraint to express many things otherwise, and for the most part worse than else they would have expressed them. Not without cause therefore some both Italian and Spanish poets of prime note have rejected rhyme both in longer and shorter works, as have also long since our best English tragedies, as a thing of itself, to all judicious ears trivial and of no true musical delight; which consists only in apt numbers, fit quantity of syllables, and the sense variously drawn out from one verse into another, not in the jingling sound of like endings, a fault avoided by the learned ancients both in poetry and in all good oratory. This neglect then of rhyme so little is to be taken for a defect, though it may seem so perhaps to vulgar readers, that it rather is to be esteemed an example set, the first in English, of ancient liberty recovered to heroic poem from the troublesome and modern bondage of rhyming.

The note says much more by implication and omission than it does by direct statement. His opening comparison with classical verse is vague and unspecific, with no real claim to the reproduction of quantitative form in English, only the safely analogous "as that of." His condemnation of rhyme as "barbarous" and of "no musical delight" is little more than rhetoric, and its popularity for later slogan-mongers prompted R. D. Havens in *The Influence of Milton on English Poetry* (1922) to state that, "it were a weary stale, flat and unprofitable task to try to register all the assaults upon it" (p. 52). Chapter 6 of this study will dispute this claim, but to return to Milton we must regard his brief definition of his new form of writing as the note's most significant and intriguing contribution to literary history: "which consists only in apt numbers, fit quantity of syllables, and the sense variously drawn out from one verse into another." Toil as one might over the significance of "apt numbers" and "fit quantity" one would still have to conclude that they are essentially meaningless concessions to terminology: Milton neither attempted nor succeeded in the reproduction of English quantity, and "apt" can mean nothing more than "apt." It is "sense variously drawn out from one verse into another" that holds the key to his explanation. Here he posits two distinct patterns of form and meaning, the drawn-out sense and the verse line, and this double movement was to become the focus of a critical debate on the nature of form that was central to the most significant aspects of eighteenth-century criticism and which has extended itself into the modern period. If you "draw out sense" you must, by implication, establish a stable unit of form from which to do so, and if, in English, the poetic line was dependent upon the oral signals of syntactic closure or rhyme, how could the "sense" that establishes the identity of the unrhymed line be drawn out beyond it without simultaneously destroying it? In the immediate context of the "Note" this might seem to be a matter of metrical pedantry, but, as the work of the critics to be covered will show, it is the starting point of a much more complex and significant debate: what is the poetic line?; do we see it, or hear it, or both?; and how does its tenuous identity affect the writing form of writing for which it is the central and definitive component?

Early Responses

Most of the early responses—and by early I mean up to the beginning of the eighteenth century—to the formal status of

Paradise Lost were rhetorical statements of partisanship and preference, without depth or interpretive detail. The debate, such as it was, is very accurately summarized in Sir Thomas Pope Blount's *De Re Poetica* (1694). The book is a miscellany of literary biographies, philosophical axioms, and critical remarks produced in the Restoration by its best-known men of letters. The value of the work is barometric, in that Blount takes the trouble to organize his critical references into a form that he thinks will reflect the impact of the blank verse-rhyme debate upon the public imagination. The result shows that although there was a good deal of enthusiasm in some quarters for the experiment, the theoretical weight of the discussion lay firmly with the champions of the couplet. Blount proves immensely astute in emphasizing the aspects of Dryden's criticism that had, in a sense, become codified as a matrix of English prosodic theory. He stresses the fact that Dryden's speculations on rhyme as an aid to memory, a measure of line and syntax, and a balance between judgment and fancy were, by 1694, the conventional wisdom on the matter. On the subject of blank verse, however, he simply praises *Paradise Lost* and *Paradise Regained* as its "two most perfect examples," and his rather vague tone of approval accurately reflects the more general sense of Milton as having succeeding in something but also as having moved beyond the terminology and categories of the established formal canon.

For instance, in his Preface to *Theatrum Poetarum* (1675) Edward Phillips's statement of approval often sounds like a plea for mitigation.

> Let the fashion of the Vers be what it will, according to the different humour of the Writer, if the Style be elegant and suitable, the Verse, whatever it is may be better dispenc't with; and the truth is the use of Measure alone without any Rime at all would give far more ample Scope and liberty both to Style and fancy than can be observed in Rime. (Spingarn, II, p. 266)

In other words style has effectively replaced verse form as the point at which the critic responds to the structural identity of the poem, and Phillips politely admits that Milton, the admirable stylist, has virtually abandoned or "dispenc't with" any formal structure that was, by contemporary standards, recognizable as poetry.

In Roscommon's *Essay on Translated Verse*, Milton is celebrated as returning the "British Muse" to pre-Barbarous days, but in explaining quite how he had done so the Earl reverts to a versified paraphrase of Milton's Note. Thomas Rymer, in 1678, promised to send his dedicatee, Sir Fleetwood Sheppard, "some reflections on that *Paradise Lost* of *Miltons* which some are pleased to call a Poem, and assert *Rime* against the slender sophistry wherewith he attacques it." These reflections never materialized and their absence is an almost eloquent comment upon the state of perplexity into which Milton had thrown the emergent English critical world.[4] And what of its most eminent spokesman, Dryden? He never referred directly to *Paradise Lost*, but in one of the last works to be published in his lifetime, *The Dedication of the Aeneis* (1697), he implicitly acknowledges the entry into the nondramatic canon of a form that he had earlier judged to be unpoetic:

> He who can write well in rhyme may write better in blank verse. Rhyme is certainly a constraint even to the best poets, and those who make it with most ease; though perhaps I have as little reason to complain of that hardship as any man, excepting Quarles and Withers. What it adds to sweetness, it takes away from sense; and he who loses the least by it may be called a gainer. It often makes us swerve from an author's meaning, as if a mark be set up for an archer at a great distance, let him aim as exactly as he can, the least wind will take his arrow and divert it from the white. (Ker, II, pp. 220–21)

The concluding simile seems to be a self-conscious revision of his "wide ranging spaniel" judgment, but outside the qualified tone of approval it is significant that he does not attempt to reconcile the existence of *Paradise Lost* with his earlier definition of what English prosody and poetic form actually are. One might even assume that his promised "English *Prosodia*, containing all the mechanical rules of versification, where I have treated, with some exactness, of the feet, the quantities, and the pauses" (Ker, II, p. 217) did not materialize because of the uncomfortable presence of a work that was by general agreement "heroic" but whose formal identity meant that any precise critical appreciation would also require a rewriting of established metrical codes and expectations.

If imitation is to be regarded as a form of judgment, there is little to suggest that Milton's early followers were any more capable than the critics of assimilating his prosodic technique to their own purposes. Philips's famous parody in *The Splendid Shilling* is in many ways too accurate: he duplicated Milton's tendency toward enjambment and syntactic inversion so well as to throw the attendant ridicule of vocabulary and reference into the foreground. No critic took Philips seriously enough to actually analyze his technique and process of imitation. The small group of early "serious" imitators found themselves caught between the opportunity for experiment and the orthodoxy of theory. A typical case is John Dennis, who simultaneously praised the freedom and variety of blank verse and produced, in pseudo-epics such as *The Monument* (1702), unrhymed couplets. It would not be until the emergence of poets such as Young and Thomson that the creative impact of *Paradise Lost* would begin to be felt, and these will be dealt with in chapter 4.

I have emphasized the rather subdued condition of early commentators on Milton's form for two reasons. First there is an analogy to be drawn. The effect of *Paradise Lost* upon the literary world of the Restoration, was in a number of significant ways, similar to that of the emergence of free verse at the beginning of this century. True, Milton was not part of a broader aesthetic movement and the formal tradition whose rules and conventions he violated was by no means well established. But for criticism, which must be regarded as the official voice of the reader, there are close correspondences. To write about literature even the most imaginative and iconoclastic critic must depend upon a fixed system of terms and conventions with which to compare and contrast a new work. *Paradise Lost* announced itself as a poem, but how could its commentators consider its formal qualities when it manifestly disrupted the tenuous categories of dramatic and nondramatic writing, the identity of the line and the accepted conventions of prosodic form?

It will be argued that the gradual development of critical strategies to deal with uncharted formal territory works as a kind of refractory lens for later readers, not necessarily distorting what is already there, but focusing upon, emphasizing, and naming elements of structure that provide the reader with a frame of reference for the type of appreciative interplay that goes beyond mere understanding. The process by which free verse was, in effect, assimilated into the tradition of English versification was much more complex and wideranging than the absorbtion of Miltonic form, and the most significant correspondences will be dealt with in "The Modern Perspective," but the part played in both processes by critics is both intriguing and illuminating. And this is the second reason for my emphasis upon the early critical background, because two Restoration critics rose above the general state of perplexity, and, in effect, founded what were to become two separate eighteenth-century traditions, traditions that are reflected in the division of the central parts of this book into "Silence" and "Sound."

Samuel Woodford was a little-known country parson whose first publication, the *Paraphrase on the Psalms of David* (1667), betrays, in its preface, a slight interest in the condition of English prosody; but his preface to *A Paraphrase Upon the Canticles* (1679) contains a startlingly original discussion of form that centers upon *Paradise Lost*, and this both preempts a series of adventurous eighteenth-century readings and anticipates analyses of form and criticism of the modern period. His work will introduce us to "Silence."

John Dennis, whose creative excursions in blank verse and rhyme, are, mercifully, forgotten, matches Woodford's interpretive innovations with creative hypotheses and conjectures on the future of English form, which would not find an environment conducive to their full poetic manifestation until the beginning of modernism; and a more detailed examination of his work marks the beginning of "Sound."

PART ONE
Silence

2
Visualist Reading: Woodford to Sheridan

Woodford

A theory of reading and interpreting poetry based upon the experience and condition of Silence would seem to be a contradiction in terms. Practically all of the components of poetic form—rhythm, rhyme, pause, alliteration, assonance—are acoustic phenomena, and poetry itself is regarded as the aesthetic medium that is closest to the immediacy and sincerity of the spoken word. There is a form known as visual poetry, in which typographic shape appeals directly to the eye of the reader and is not deployed merely as a guide to, or record of, oral performance. But this is a rather isolated subgenre that we tend to associate with two specific traditions and periods of literary history: the first being the brief seventeenth-century engagements with typographic pattern; and the second being the modern tendency toward the use of shape as a formal constituent of free verse, a development that has reached its most explicit and self-conscious manifestation in concrete poetry. Both are regarded as interesting yet marginal sidetracks from the more central developments of poetic history, and to claim that either could have drawn anything more than brief and dismissive comments from the theorists and practitioners of poetry of the Restoration and eighteenth century might seem to invite equally brief charges of fantasy.

The two best known critical judgments from this period on the use of typographic shape come from Addison and Johnson. In *Spectator* 58 (1711) Addison considered the influence of the shaped poems of the Greek Anthology upon a number of his fellow countrymen, of which George Herbert is probably best known to modern readers. Addison regards these excursions into visual pattern as a "species of false wit," and we should be reminded here of Dryden's opinion that to "wings display and altars raise" reduces poetic writing to the "torture" of "one word ten thousand ways" (*Mackflecnoe*, ll. 207–8). The subtext of both judgments is that by foregrounding the visual materiality of language such poets move that much further from the, albeit qualified, ideal of poetic clarity and transparency. Johnson's well-known claim that Milton's blank verse "seems to be verse only to the eye"[1] is a consistent extension of Addison's and Dryden's attitudes toward poetic language: *Paradise Lost* does not rhyme nor does it employ other oral signals for the identification of that most vital component of poetic form, the line. It thus appears to be straying into the realm of communication where form, in this case visual form, exerts a dangerous influence upon meaning. But as the following study will show, these critical judgments represent for us the critical orthodoxy only because they have survived in the work of men who are now regarded as, in variety of ways, embodiments of their literary ethos. The critics to be discussed below have largely been forgotten by modern historians of literature, but their absence should not be regarded as token evidence of their dullness, eccentricity, or unpopularity. Thomas Sheridan's work on elocution and poetic writing was as well known and as much discussed in the second half of the century as were the observations of his now more famous contemporary, Samuel Johnson. And the most serious loss to our awareness of the concerns, and in some cases the obsessions, of eighteenth-century criticism becomes evident when we find that these writers return again and again to the problem of how poetry can maintain a unity and consistency of form and meaning when its continued existence is dependent upon the silent configurations of the printed text. We still regard the spoken performance as the ideal realization of a poem's formal effects, but such an allegiance becomes a meaningless generalization unless we consider the attendant problems of precisely how each gap, spacing, and most importantly, each line, can resist the bewildering variety of betrayals, diversions, and tensions that prey upon them in their journey from the page to the ear. These problems were particularly troubling for the eighteenth-century critics because they were the first generation of commentators who found themselves dealing with the still relatively new phenomenon of the printing press and with the related phenomenon of a "reader" whom they might never meet and whose experience of the poetry in question might well be conditioned either by unreliable oral readings or by a confrontation with the silent printed page. One consequence of the emergence of the printing press into the center stage of public life was a gradual shift of critical emphasis away from the writer and toward the reader, a person who might need to have the developing complexities of form and technique explained and interpreted for him. There was an increased sense of distance between the creator of the poem and the person who might find himself faced with the task of disclosing subtle nuances of intended meaning, either in the silent contemplative atmosphere of the drawing room or in the more active context of the public reading. We will thus find that poetic Silence is a phenomenon that operates far beyond its more obvious associations with extravagant typographic experiment, that the "lines" of certain poems maintain a tenacious degree of loyalty to the literal meaning of that word: physical, visual units whose transformation into components of sound is far from straightforward.

The most serious challenge to the early conceptions of what the central component of poetic form, the line, actually is, and consequently to how the attendant repertoire of metrical phenomena affect meaning was made by *Paradise Lost*. Johnson's diagnosis of "verse only to the eye" was no more than a perfunctory acknowledgment of a long-established contemporary attitude toward the unrhymed pentameter as a convention of the printer, an attitude that reaches as far back as Samuel Woodford's Preface to *A Paraphrase Upon the Canticles* (1679).

It is time that Woodford's significance in the history of interpretation were recognized because he both addressed himself to what would become one of the major concerns of eighteenth-century critics and also raised problems of reading that, have reemerged in the early responses to the invention of free verse.

Woodford makes it clear that he regards the experience of reading poetry conditioned and influenced as much by what the reader expects to find in poetic writing as it is by any genuine sense of surprise or disrupted expectation. In a prose oration the mind

> Suffers itself to be imposed upon . . . as long as it perceives no Artifice used, yet when that is once discovered, or but suspected, it grows obstinate and puts a bar to the best that is, or can be said. In verse the Mind is quite otherwise dispos'd and requires naturally another kind of Movement . . . Number also and Harmony, which Prose has, but under another Character, Rhythm in our own Modern Languages, or something equivalent to it, variety of Feet and Measure, which if it want, as the Verse is therefore depriv'd of its greatest and best, and only distinguishing Ornaments. The mind also that came prepar'd to tempt its Charms, and expected them, languishes under the disappointment. (sigs. C1v–C2r)

It should first be pointed out that by "Rhythm" Woodford actually means rhyme.[2] His point is that when told he is reading poetry, the reader will naturally search for a formal keystone, a structural component upon which he might base an equation of "Artifice" and meaning. A problem arises with blank verse because Woodford, like Dryden, believes that English has no means of "differencing [poetry] from Prose, except by Rhythm [rhyme]" (sig. C2v). Where then is the attention of the "disappointed" reader drawn in a poem such as *Paradise Lost,* which seems to have dispensed with any identifiable pattern of artifice? A substitute is, it seems, provided by the visual format.

Woodford admits that *Paradise Lost,* "shall live as long as there are Men left to read and understand it," but of its style he suggests that though Milton might have been in a "Poetic rapture . . . through the Disguise, the Prose appears" (sig. B7r). The "Disguise" is supplied by the printer, and it is the typographical appearance of the poem, "drest up like Hercules by Omphale" that prompts the reader to accept it as poetry. "[W]ere it written as prose usually is, in its just Periods, [it] would both be read, and be, as indeed it is no other than Poetical Prose" (sig. A6v). Woodford goes on to print a section from Book IV (ll. 440–71) as prose.

Up to this point Woodford appears to be a rather adventurous practitioner of the widely held belief that blank verse is, as Dryden's fictional debater Crites put it, "that kind of verse . . . nearest prose," but his next experiment with shape takes him into deeper critical waters. He reprints a section of Milton's prose as verse.

> Then Zeal, whose substance is Aetherial,
> Arming in compleat Diamond, ascends
> His fiery Chariot, drawn with two blazing Meteors
> Figur'd like Beasts, but of an higher Breed
> Than any the *Zodiac* yields; resembling two
> Of those Four, which *Ezekiel* and *St. John* (saw;)
> The one visag'd like a Lion, to express
> Power, high Authority, and Indignation,
> The other of Countenance like a Man, to cast
> Derision, and Scorn, upon perverse
> And Fraudulent Seducers.
> With these the Invincible Warrior Zeal, etc.
>
> (sig. B7v)

Here Woodford both illustrates his point and makes a significant contribution to the poetics of typography. A prosodist would argue that the reprinted prose involves a sufficient number of departures from the regular iambic pentameter to render it unpoetic, but Woodford's experiment goes beyond the recognition of poetry as a traditional metrical sequence to a network of effects, which, until *Paradise Lost,* were without precedent.

The section from the poem that he reprinted as prose contains a number of adventurous run-on lines and enjambments that cut into and intensify the already elaborate syntax, of which the following is an example:

> follow me
> And I will bring thee where no shadow stays
> Thy coming
>
> (IV, 4 69–71)

Milton's modern editor, Alastair Fowler, correctly suggests that "stays" should be read as "awaits" since the sentence moves on to reveal the more substantial presence of Adam, the proper object of Eve's affections. The verb might, in the brief moment it takes the reading eye to adjust to the syntax of the new line, appear to connote "restrains"; and instead of "Thy Coming." "Thy Desire" might be the object.

This reading might seem to depend upon a familarity with the sophistications of modern criticism and the typography of free verse, but Woodford knew exactly how to reproduce the Miltonic visual effect from a sequence of "unmeasured" prose:

> The one visag'd like a Lion, to express
> Power, high Authority, and Indignation,
> The other of Countenance like a Man, to cast
> Derision,
>
> (sig B7v)

When he was "versifying" Milton's prose Woodford must have been as acutely aware of its appearance as he was of its sound, since his isolation of verb/object in "express / Power" and "cast / Derision" is by no means based upon metrical precept.

Woodford's contribution to critical history is significant in a number of ways. His implicit recognition of a tension between the receptive faculties of eye and ear sets the tone for a century of ingenious readings, and his use of *Paradise Lost* was to be repeated and extended to a degree that will, as I shall show, establish that poem as one of the most significant experiments in the history of poetic form.

In a broader critical context, he manages to preempt a number of modern perceptions of the tension between linguistic substance and interpretive convention. He suggests that the rhythms and intonational sequences that we regard as poetic are actually present in a variety of distinct, expressive contexts, including, it would seem, theological prose. And, by implication, it would also seem that our response to such sequences is determined essentially by our *visual* recognition of context. We read *Paradise Lost* as poetry because it *looks* like poetry, and Woodford effectively demonstrates that we would also read the unpoetically titled *Apology in Answer to the Modest Confutation of a Libel intituled Animadversions upon the Remonstrants Defence of Smectymnuus* as a poem if it were also made to look like a poem. In *The Nation* on 24 February 1916, John Livingstone Lowes responded to an apparently new poetic phenomenon in exactly the same way: "Miss Lowell's free verse may be written as very beautiful prose; George Meredith's prose may be written as very beautiful free verse. Which is which?" This question has migrated through the consciousness of poets and readers for three-hundred years and has even found a place in the rarefied spheres of reader-response criticism and poststructuralist theory: Stanley Fish and Jonathan Culler expose the illusion of formal substance by interpreting a philosophical tract and a random selection of surnames as "poems." I shall deal more fully with the modern perspective in due course, but at this point it is sufficient to note that Woodford and Milton raise an issue that forms the axis for these shifting creative and interpretive dilemmas: the operation of the silent, printed text.

Rice and the "Printer's Measure"

In *Licentia Poetica discuss'd* (1709) William Coward also observed that the effect and meaning of loosely textured blank verse owes something to the illusion of its visual format.

> 'Tis true the *Fiction's* wonderfully done,
> And the whole *Clue of Thoughts* completely spun.
> But like an *Image* cast in Curious Mould,
> Tho' 'tis composed of finely polish'd Gold,
> Yet wants the *Breath of Life* do make it live,
> Which should right *Vigour* and true *Spirit* Give.
> For fine Romances may be set the same,

If but the *Printer* please to set the Frame.
And Declamations ty'd to Measur'd Feet,
May yield an Harmony as truly sweet
But how can such Exactness *Fancy* Raise,
More than loose Prose, and undesign'd for Lays?

(pp. 65–66)

To regard blank verse as an "*Image* cast in Curious Mould" and as partly the creation of the "Printer" was by no means an eccentric opinion, and this emphasis upon the effect of the visual format upon the reader's understanding was later in the eighteenth century to become an essential concern of one branch of criticism known as elocutionism. Writers such as John Rice, Thomas Sheridan, Joshua Steele, and John Walker produced extensive guides to the oral performance of written discourse and, though a certain amount of their instruction is directed toward the preacher and public orator, their most intriguing work is concerned with the interpretation of poetry. The sensitive precision with which the elocutionists addressed themselves to the subtle nuances of poetic form preempts the modern ethos of "close reading," but unlike their modern counterparts, the eighteenth-century critics maintained an almost fanatical concern with the printed text as a refractory medium, capable of subverting the ideal of a single oral performance. The relationship between the configurations of the silent poem and its oral identity was so central to their enterprise that another much used modern idiom, "the words on the page," began to resonate with a more literal and thematically disruptive meaning.

John Mason in *An Essay on Elocution* (1749) regarded the "Printer's measure," except where it coincided with rhyme or a grammatical/metrical hiatus, as irrelevant to the interpretation of the poem, but the first attempt to trace the full implications of this problem came in John Rice's *An Introduction to the Art of Reading with Energy and Propriety* (1765).

Rice, like Woodford, is one of the lost voices of critical history. His work features briefly in T. S. Omond's *English Metrists* and Paul Fussell's *Theory of Prosody in Eighteenth Century England* and in both cases he is presented as a confused and inaccurate student of poetic form. The reason for this is that in 1765, the study of poetic form and structure from the reader's perspective was still a new and untried enterprise. The terminology of scansion, feet, and accentual form had not reached the point at which the likes of Omond or Fussell could fit them into the established subdiscipline of "prosody." Rice could approach the poem as a structure that exhibits its own identity as a linguistic artifact outside the conditioned expectations of what its formal presence was supposed to be and do.

Rice effectively abandoned the classical notion of the foot and the regular heroic line, arguing that in English each individual syllable is an almost undocumentable amalgam of "*long* and *short, loud* and *soft, harsh* and *smooth*" (p. 141). His point is that there is an unbridgeable gap between abstract concepts of English prosodic structure, such as the unrhymed iambic pentameter, and the actualities of oral performance. He attacks Lord Kames and Samuel Johnson for their imposition of classical expectations of form upon the more elusive structure of English: "Now I should be pleased to know from what natural Principles it is that they deduce their rule for pausing at some particular Parts of the Verse, in Preference to others?" His reference is not to the relatively stable form of the stanza or the rhymed couplet, but to the movement of Miltonic blank verse, in which an almost endless variation in pause and accentuation can take place outside the illusion of the printed line.

> Thus it is the quick Succession of a few flowing syllables that constitutes the Harmony of our English blank Verse, and not its perfect Coincidence with the arbitrary Rules laid down as a Standard for heroic verse. . . . Blank-Verse, therefore, does not consist in lines of ten Syllables, as the regular Couplet generally does; unless, indeed, we suppose the Standard of Verse erected in the Printing House, and that a Compositor can convert Prose into Verse at Pleasure by printing it in detached Lines of ten Syllables. (pp. 176–77)

Rice regards the printed pentameter line as an outmoded convention against which the perverse expectations of classical prosody have been shored, and a crucial element of this dependency is the influence of the visual text upon the eye of the reader: "The lines drawn up in Rank and File, with a capital Initial at the Head of each, look formidable, and seem to demand a peculiar Degree of Sound and Energy" (p. 16).

We are back to Woodford's recognition of visual form as a component of meaning, but Rice goes on to reverse the experiments of his predecessor by reprinting sections of *Paradise Lost* not as prose but as a form of free verse.

> —on the eastern Cliff of Paradise
> He lights, and to his proper Shape returns

> A Seraph wing'd: Six Wings he wore to shade
> His Lineaments divine; the Pair that clad
> Each Shoulder broad, came mantling o'er his Breast
> With regal Ornament;
>
> (Book V, II, 275–80; original printing)
>
> On the eastern Cliff of Paradise he lights,
> And to his proper Shape returns a Seraph wing'd:
> Six Wings he wore, to shade his Lineaments divine;
> The pair that clad each Shoulder broad,
> Came mantling o'er his Breast with regal Ornament;
>
> (Rice's rearrangement, pp. 178–79)

Rice believed that the rearrangements would offer "common Readers" a truer visual representation of the poem's formal identity "nor do I believe that they [the new lines] would be deprived of any Part of their poetical Beauty."

The question of whether the original format of Rice's redisposition suffers or gains on the audible scale of "poetical Beauty" is a performative dilemma that has been familiar to actors since Shakespeare. But more significantly, Rice has succeeded in changing not only the sound but also the meaning of the verse, without changing the words. In the original, the phrase "A seraph wing'd" is a summation, a completed picture of the process begun "on the eastern Cliff of Paradise," and its visual isolation from the verb "returns" emphasizes this status. In Rice's version another level of stylistic depth emerges and we could paraphrase the new line as, "he returns a wing'd Seraph to his proper shape." Superficially this may well seem to be a point of metrical/syntactic pedantry, but the new transitive resonance of "returns" leaves even the theologically disinterested reader wondering if Raphael possesses a little more autonomy than his angelic status might suggest: does Paradise control his transformation or does he play some part in the process?

The poem would seem to contain two separate metrical and syntactic structures, and it is the attention given by Rice to the visual presence of verse that discloses the essential key to this depth of texture. He never explicitly acknowledges the silent visual poem as a component of meaning, but it is in Rice's work that we begin to find an intriguing diversity in the study and the creative deployment of silent poetics.

First, there is Rice's claim that the traditional formal structure of unrhymed English verse is dependent upon the illusion of its visual appearance. This has implications both for the history of poetry and for attendant developments in the methodology and assumptions of criticism. As I shall show, a large number of Rice's contemporaries shared his belief that the true potential for rhythmic expression and structure lies behind the illusory artifice of forms such as the iambic pentameter, and the sense of the printed text as both a source and restraint for poetic effects run through the poetic and *ex-cathedra* statements of writers as diverse as Blake, Pound, and Olson. These developments will be dealt with in chapter 5, "The Voice of Form," and in "The Modern Perspective."

Equally intriguing was Rice's awareness of the visual format as an axis for often divergent rhythmic and thematic patterns. Rice attempted to neutralize this refractory medium by rewriting *Paradise Lost* in accordance with its true oral identity. But many of his contemporaries pursued alternative strategies.

Thomas Sheridan and Milton's Occular Poetics

Thomas Sheridan's *Lectures on the Art of Reading* (1775) contains some of the most penetrative and illuminating poetic criticism of the eighteenth century, and, as will be shown, his acute awareness of the interplay between form and meaning anticipates and often supersedes the sophistications of twentieth-century analysis.

The second volume on the "Art of Reading Verse" is an extensive critical discourse that imputes Sheridan's theories on the movement of verse to the creative faculty of the poet, and thus draws certain conclusions on the relationship between the formal structure of the verse, the author's intention, and how the verse should sound and be orally performed—but the crucial paradox in his argument is the acknowledgement of Milton as the first poet to fully explore the signifying potential of silent, written language.

In Lecture II on the prosodic basis of the pause he claims that Milton has laboured in vain on the subtlety of his interlineal breaks if the reader does not interpret them as a meaningful component of the verse structure. He sets out to overturn the argument of Woodford, Rice, and others that the Miltonic line is the coproduct of outdated convention and the practices of the typesetter, and goes on to claim that the visual format of *Paradise Lost* is intended by Milton as a series of typographic signals to the reader. Modern readers, who might consign such claim to the prodigious eccentricities of the period, should examine the opening critical maneuver from Donald Davie's "Syntax and Music in *Paradise Lost*" (*The Living Milton*, ed. F. Kermode, 1960).

>   Him the almighty power
> Hurled headlong Flaming from the etherial sky
> With hideous ruin and combustion down
> To bottomless perdition, there to dwell
> In adamantine chains and penal fire,
> Who durst defy the omnipotent to arms.
>
> (I, 44–49)

The effect is kinetic. The placing of "him," "down" and "To" in particular, gives us the illusion as we read that our own muscles are tightening in panic as we experience in our own bodies a movement just as headlong and precipitate as the one described. We occupy in ourselves the *gestalt* for falling. (pp. 70–71)

If this piece is read as prose we find that there is a natural pause between "combustion" and "down" as the connection between the verb "hurled" and its adverb is made, and that "down" becomes syntactically dependent upon the next line. Indeed, the whole institutionalized practice of "reading" from left to right and following the linear sequence of syntax would seem to destroy Davie's suggestion that "him," "down," and "To" are in some way discretely significant: "down" loses some of its resonance to "bottomless perdition" and "To" becomes merely an adjunct of "down." Davie's reading depends upon a form of attention that acknowledges words and phrases as spatially isolated from the grammatical sequences—a perspective that implicitly relies upon a grammar of space and typography not merely as a notational guide to spoken language, but as itself a separate signifying system.

To deal with this potentially confusing amalgam of sound and vision Sheridan preempted Davie and invented what he called the "pause of suspension," which would occur, literally, when and where the line ended on the page. He did not intend this to be an addition to the traditional scale of grammatical breaks: this was to be something particular to the form and texture of the printed poem. Anticipating the title, if not the spirit, of Davie's essay Sheridan establishes it as a "Musical" as opposed to a "Sentential" pause. The sentential pause is necessary for the logical arrangement of language, "the mere meaning of words," but the "Musical" pause is part of a contract between the poet and the reader, "the nobler and more ornamental part of this art, that of moving the soul and charming the ear" (II, pp. 107–8). Sheridan's use of the word "Musical" is probably a matter of convenience since he refers not to the linear sequence of a melody but to the complex texture of something like the fugue. How, we might ask, can the contrapuntal, multi-instrumental texture of music be regarded as analogous to the sequential components of language? Sheridan explains:

> By melody, is meant, a pleasing effect produced on the ear, from an apt arrangement of the constituent parts of verse, according to the laws of measure and movement. By harmony, an effect produced by an action of the mind in comparing the different members of a verse with each other, and perceiving a due and beautiful proportion between them. (II. p. 169)

Note how the appreciation of "harmony" depends not like melody, upon the "ear" but upon the "action of the mind in comparing," a faculty that operates much more effectively in response to the spatial configurations of print. Consider Sheridan's treatment of "harmony" in a verbal arrangement analogous to that tackled by Davie.

>   and durst abide
> Jehovah thundering out of Sion Thron'd
> Between the Cherubim.
>
>   (I, 385–87)

Here again if we read these lines according to, as Sheridan put it, "the mere meaning of the words," the pause between "Sion" and "thron'd" would be the only one acknowledged and the latter word would lose its visual isolation. But supply the "pause of suspension,"

> and what sublime ideas does not a single monosyllable excite by its position? Bounded on one side by a caesural, and on the other by a final pause. And what more exalted idea could have been conceived of by the Deity, than is expressed by that single word? which, after the description of his executing just vengeance on the rebellious and darting his thunders at their heads, shows that this required no unusual exertion in the Godhead; He performed these wonders—thron'd!
>
>   (II, pp. 249–50)

Sheridan's appreciation of the spatial architecture of the verse can in no sense be dismissed as the product of personal ingenuity. It is not Sheridan but the poem itself that foregrounds the visual texture, because there could be no other reason why the same lines should, as we shall see, draw the attention of critics exactly two hundred years apart.

In a brilliant essay called "Sense Variously Drawn Out" (*Vision and Resonance*, 1975) John Hollander comments on how "closure and flow, the opposed features of Milton's verse form, oppose themselves in ways parallel to the opposition of visual and acoustic modes, respectively, of poetic language" (p. 96), and he chooses the following lines to illustrate his point. Satan's ruminative torment,

> wakes the bitter memory
> Of what he was, what is, and what must be
> Worse; of worse deeds worse suffering must ensue.
> (IV, 24–26)

Hollander comments on how "the static pattern of line 25" "frames" the prayer book formula of "now and ever shall be," only to have the reader's sense of stability jolted with the visually isolated "Worse." Sheridan: "What an amazing force does this position give to the word *worse!* and in what strong colours does it paint to us the desperate state of reprobation into which Satan had fallen" (p. 248).

This intriguing two-hundred-year dialogue continued in response to the following lines:

> Thus with the Year
> Seasons return, but not to me returns
> Day.
> (III, 40–42)

Christopher Ricks in *Milton's Grand Style* (1963) remarks upon the surprise caused by the use of "Day" instead of, say, the more predictable "Spring" and adduces the moment as proof that Miltonic structure operates in terms of successive events, "each new sentence a new small action with its sometimes complicated plot" (p. 42), and Donald Davie isolates the effect of surprise as dependent upon the "swing of the reading eye or voice around the line ending" (p. 73). There is a curious sense of ambivalence here because the eye can certainly trace out something that spatially "swings around"; but the voice? Sheridan is less reticent about the spatial resonances: "Here the caesura after the first semipede *Day*, stops you unexpectedly, and strikes the imagination with the immensity of his loss. He can no more see—

what?—Day!—Day and all its glories rush into the mind." (II, pp. 246–47)

There is a tantalizing ambiguity not merely in the poetic material but in the language that Sheridan uses to describe its effects upon the reader. The lines discussed are from the movingly personal sequence at the beginning of Book III, in which Milton compares his own blindness with the spiritual "vision" of "things invisible to mortal sight" (line 55). The implication in his near-soliliquy is that language provides the only link between his mind and physical presence of the world, and we begin to understand why Sheridan places so much emphasis on the physical isolation of the word "Day," which "strikes the imagination" of the reader; and, through Milton's subtle interpolation of the meaning with the material of language, "all its glories rush into the mind." There is a tragic irony in this technique since the effectiveness of Milton's recreation of the "immensity of his loss" depends upon the ability of the reader to *see* the isolation of "Day" on the page.

Sheridan eventually abandoned the premise that his interpretive technique is primarily for the benefit of the oral performer, and there is a tendency for his critical vocabulary to subtly collapse the distinction between language as descriptive of space and objects and the sense in which the actual shape of Milton's verse can describe its own referential function.

> and now his heart
> Distends with pride, and hardening in his strength
> Glories for never since created man
> Met such embodied force.
>
> (I, 571–74)

> Here by the uncommon caesura, which makes the word, *glories*, as it were project from the rest, the insolent vanity, and obstinate pride of Satan, are more strongly painted, then could have been done by the longest description. And yet no poet but Milton would have placed the word in its present situation.
>
> (II, pp. 253–55)

We should note that in his use of the phrase "project from the rest," he describes an effect that surely runs against the linear progression of spoken language; and his analogy with the visual arts recalls his description of the isolated word "Worse," which "paints" the "desperate state" of Satan. In his comment on the syntactic disjunction of,

> and tore
> Through pain up by the roots Thessalian pines
>
> (II, 544–45)

he states that through their positioning, the words, "paint the action . . . the consequence of which the lofty pines of Thessaly lie prostrate in your view" (II, p. 200). And Christopher Ricks, drawn to the same visual configuration of words, states that the "agonised word order," in the separation of "tore" and "up," "*presents* the knotted effort of Hercules" (*Milton's Grand Style*, p. 45, my italics).

It is probable that Sheridan was familiar with the work of William Benson, whose *Letters Concerning Poetical Translations and Virgil's and Milton's Arts of Verse* (1739) contains the first implicit claim that Milton's visual format was intended to play some part in our understanding of the verse texture. Benson did not supply a theoretical premise for his readings but his practice provides an eloquent enough testimony to this. Consider his analysis of the following lines and note how his critical language is entirely dependent upon the visual arts analogy.

> Now at their shady Lodge arriv'd, *both stood*
> *Both turn'd*, and under open sky ador'd
> The God who made, etc.

This artful Manner of writing makes the Reader see them *Stop* and *Turn* to worship God before they went into the Bower. If this Manner was alter'd, much of the Effect of the Painting would be lost.

> And now arriving at their shady Lodge
> Both stood, both turn'd and under open Sky
> Ador'd the God, etc.

This falls very short of the original. (p. 48)

Benson admits that the loss of effect in the reprinted lines is due not to a change in the words themselves but in the "Manner" of "Writing" them—and not, we should note, "hearing" or "reciting" them. It is almost as though their shape on the page creates something like the visual equivalent of onomatopoeia, and Benson's enthusiasm for this form of transparency is born out in his extravagant extension of the pictorial metaphor.

> Over their Heads triumphant Death his Dart
> *Shook*—But refus'd to strike

makes the Reader see Death with his Dart in his Hand, shaking it over the Heads of the unhappy Creatures . . . as if the whole was painted upon a Canvas. (p. 49)[3]

Sheridan and Benson were arguing against what was eventually to become the prosodic orthodoxy, because their visual perspective emphasizes not the balanced, audible structure of the pentameter line but its function as an instrument that cuts into and subverts the linear movement of syntax. The broader implications of their readings for the study of poetic form will be dealt with in chapter 4 but in the meantime it should be made clear why Johnson condemned *Paradise Lost* as "verse only to the eye," unlike those of his contemporaries, who celebrated its occular effects. Much of *Ramblers* 86 and 90 are devoted to an attack upon Milton's capacity to disrupt expectations of balance and linearity, and it is by no coincidence that he chose many of the same lines as Sheridan and Benson to illustrate what he called an "unpleasing diminution of harmony." We should note that his elaboration of the rule against which they offend partakes of the terminology not of painting, but of music

> When a single syllable is cut off from the rest, it must either be united with the line with which the sense connects it, or be sounded alone. If it be united to the other line, it corrupts its harmony; if disjoined, it must stand alone and with regard to music, be superfluous. (*Rambler* 90, pp. 111–12)

Johnson is correct: the effects he describes are indeed "superfluous" to the musical linearity of verse, and they do "stand alone" outside the conventional meaning of "harmony" in an audible medium. But we might compare this judgment with Sheridan's rather different use of the term to introduce his own celebration of silent poetics: "By melody, is meant, a pleasing effect produced by an action of the mind in comparing the different members of the verse"—or as he might have put it "by an action of the eye." It would seem that John Hollander's emphasis upon an "opposition of visual and acoustic modes" in Milton's verse is less a "discovery" and more a restatement of what was in the eighteenth century the subject of an intriguing critical debate. The tension between the critical priorities and criteria that underpin the different attitudes of Johnson and Sheridan to the function and identity of poetic form should not be regarded as if merely historical interest, because they raise the quesitons of *what is* the poetic line. Do we see it or hear it? Can these distinct spheres of appreciation be reconciled only in the mind of the silent reader or can they be conveyed to the listener? And, most significantly, how do these shifting perspectives in the presence of form affect the meaning of poetic language?

All of these questions emerge from the presence of one aspect of poetic form, which, since the eighteenth century, has been systematically marginalized as a central component of critical reading—the silent, printed text. I have already shown how critics such as Sheridan and Hollander, Benson and Ricks, who seem to exist in radically distinct historical and cultural circumstances, can be drawn to ask the same questions about the effect and meaning of the same poetic structures, and in the following chapter I shall explore the extent to which these correspondences can cut very deeply into our assumptions about the relationship between seeing, hearing, interpreting, and understanding poetic form.

3
The Critical Debate: The Eighteenth versus the Twentieth Century

In 1971 Oxford University Press published a collection of papers entitled *Literary Style: A Symposium*. The conference from which the collection was drawn was intended as a forum to explore the bewildering variety of structuralist, poststructuralist, Eastern bloc formalist, and traditional-New Critical schools of stylistic analysis, which seemed finally to have reached a point of conflict. The essay that was given priority of significance both at the conference and by its placing in the collection was Roland Barthes's "Style and its Image." Central to Barthes's overview of the state of literary linguistics is a complaint and a plea.

> Whence, rightfully, two autonomous linguistics: a linguistics of the syntagma and a linguistics of the sentence, a linguistics of the spoken word and a linguistics of the written. . . . We lack, clearly a grammar of the written language. (But is this kind of grammar possible? Wouldn't the very notion of grammar be eliminated by such a division?) (p. 7)

In answer to the concluding questions I would say, tentatively, yes and no. An understanding of the signifying procedures of silent printed poetry is necessary and possible, but it would be wrong to assume that a "grammar" of the visual poem would totally eliminate the rules and conventions through which we respond to the oral, sequential medium. It would threaten their position in the orthodox hierarchy of linguistic responses, but its presence would be complementary rather than destructive. The results of such an alliance for poetic understanding will be considered in due course, but first I shall examine how and why a "linguistics of the written" has been denied a foothold in modern theories of poetic form, and I shall go on to show that the eighteenth-century debates on the oral/visual modes of perception can serve to clarify a number of important problems of interpretation.

Prosody

One of the major turning points in the four-hundred-year history of English Prosodic Studies was marked by the *Kenyon Review* symposium of 1956. This program was founded upon the identification of separate and diverging intonational sequences to account for the full metrical identity of the poetic line. What has since been termed linguistic metrics is essentially a reaction against the traditional, classically based notation of stress and unstress. The revisions began with Trager's and Smith's "discovery" that there are more than two levels of stress in English[1] (they generously decided on four instead), and Seymour Chatman was the first to apply this broader notation to poetry in the special *Kenyon Review* issue, which contained a number of important essays on meter. Chatman envisages a tension between two systems, the abstract, usually iambic, metrical pattern and the more contingent stress, pitch, and pause variations of spoken language. His chief point is that a performance of a line in some way incorporates both.[2]

A very succinct description of this thesis has been given by Roger Fowler in "Structural Metrics" (1967).

> Structural metrics could be said to be concerned with the reconciliation (through phonemics) of two extremes of analysis. On the one hand is the old belief in two fixed degrees of stress alternating with perfect regularity and uniformly disposed in time. At the other extreme is the instrumental revelation that each of the syllables in a line is realised differently by various complexes of intensity, pitch and length; that there is no identity of weight among the stresses; that there is no clear binary distinction between "stress" and "unstress" and that there is no equality of time interval. (p. 156)

We should note that Fowler seeks a "reconciliation" of the two systems rather than a rejection of one in favor of the other. It is in the modern faith in this reconciliation of the two patterns that we find the most intriguing point of conflict between modern prosody and the theorists of the eighteenth century, and Milton's blank verse supplies the battleground.

If Fowler had pursued the full implications of his recognition that "each of the syllables in a line is realised differently by various complexes of intensity, pitch and length," then in some, apparently iambic, verse the "line" would cease to exist. This might seem a somewhat bizarre conjecture, but compare the treatment of the opening lines of *Paradise Lost* by two critics from the eighteenth century and one from the modern period. Sheridan:

> But when we know, that one of the greatest perfections in our blank heroic verse, is, that of continuing the sense from one line to another, I am afraid in that case, if there be no mark to show where the measure ends, it will often be carried away by the sense, and confounded with it, be changed to pure prose. (p. 104)

He goes on to demonstrate what would happen if the reader were to follow the "sense" of the lines without the assistance of the visual format.

> Of man's first disobedience / and the /
> fruit of / that for / bidden / tree
> whose / mortal / taste brought etc.
> But with the final pause,
>
> and the fruit^{||}
> Of that / forbid / den tree / whose mor / tal taste.^{||}
>
> (p. 116)

Thus, in Sheridan's scheme, the line can anchor or underlie the more promiscuous structure of "the various complexes of intensity" only if the reader can actually see it.

John Walker was Sheridan's most immediate contemporary and rival in the sphere of elocutionary writing and lecturing.[3] Walker agreed with Sheridan on the tendency for the rhythmic and intonational movement of blank verse to, in effect, expose the pentameter as an illusion of print, but his solution to the problem was rather different.

> Even if there were no pauses at all at the end of the lines, they would not on this account entirely lose their poetic character; for at worst they might be called numerous or harmonious prose, and that the greatest part of blank verse is neither more or less than this, it would not be difficult to prove. (p. 210)

This is from Walker's *Elements of Elocution* (1781), and he later went on, much in the manner of Rice, to suggest a reprinting of blank verse in lines which would "present to the eye the same union which is actually made by the ear." His version of the first twenty-six lines of *Paradise Lost* appeared in the *Rhetorical Grammar* (1785), with the opening sentence as follows:

> Of man's first disobedience
> And the fruit of that forbidden tree
> Whose mortal taste
> Brought death into the world

Walker's proposals that poems should be reprinted in accordance with their true oral identity were extensive enough to include sequences from Pope, and his primary thesis emerged in the *Elements of Elocution*.

> This arrangement of the words, though exactly classed into those portions in which they come to the ear, seems to destroy the verse, and to reduce it to unequally measured prose: but have we not reason to suspect, that the eye puts a cheat on the ear, by making us imagine a pause to exist where there is only a vacancy to the eye? (p. 212)

Walker's "vacancy of the eye," as Wordsworth's poetry will show, resonates far beyond its critical context, but the most specific and illuminating modern correspondence is to be found in John Hollander's treatment of the same lines in "'Sense Variously Drawn Out' On English Enjambment."

> "Fruit" might well have led to something like "Thereof" in the following line, thus being taken in the figurative sense of "results"; actually, the line which follows thrusts us into the primary literal sense of *that* fruit of *that* tree. "Disobedience" has the importance of staged centrality, "Fruit" the urgency of a terminal place which reveals both its own positional ambiguity and that of the word occupying it. These two impulses—the one towards the systematic static pattern, the other toward periodic flux and articulated paragraphing—are the warp and weft of the verse fabric of *Paradise Lost*. Whenever brilliantly framed and patterned lines occur, they are opened out at their closing to allow their apparent syntactic closure to flow forward. (*Vision and Resonance*, p. 94)

Hollander's synthesis of the Sheridan/Walker disagreement is at once illuminating and perplexing. Note that his own closing sentence shifts between the terms "opened"/"closing," "closure"/"flow": his critical method is clearly dependent both upon

Sheridan's concept of textual intensity *and* upon Walker's disclosure of rhythmic progression. It is a realization in practical criticism of Fowler's ideal of "reconciliation." The question we have to ask is how the modern critic finds no problem in dealing with the simultaneous presence of what his eighteenth-century predecessors regarded as, in effect, two different poems?

The answer is partly, but only partly, supplied by Hollander himself in the same essay. To demonstrate how what he calls the "Miltonic tradition" of poetic writing can incorporate several distinct patterns of rhythm and meaning, he borrows an example of linguistic complexity from Noam Chomsky. The line/sentence, "They don't know how good meat tastes." can discharge at least seven different patterns of emphasis and structure depending upon which word the reader chooses as the rhythmic and semantic center of the message. Hollander goes on to demonstrate how this choice can be determined by the visual shape of the sentence, and reprints the seven meanings with the line break shifting in each case from one word to another.

But what Hollander does not explain is that although this complexity of meaning in Milton and Chomsky is simultaneously present to the eye—what Sheridan has called the "act of comparing"—the oral identity of each pattern and sequence must remain isolated and discrete. To orally convey the complexity of Hollander's reading of the opening lines of *Paradise Lost* the performer would have to recite them twice—an imperative that was made clear by Sheridan's and Walker's emphasis upon two distinct patterns.

In *Milton's Grand Style* (1963) Christopher Ricks never explicitly acknowledges the influece of modern linguistic prosody upon his close readings, but his dependence upon the multiple oral pattern is evident in his reading of the following lines:

> Thus saying, from her Husband's hand her hand
> Soft she withdrew
>
> (IX, 385–86)

Ricks points out that an initial reading of "Soft" as an adverb, "softly" or "yielding," can be modified first by the implication of lines 319–21 and 376–7 that Eve is persistent as well as meek, and second by the possibility that "soft" might contain traces of an adjectival meaning through a typically Miltonic reversal of adjective and noun, "hand/Soft," so that the total effect is "her soft hand softly she withdrew" with *soft* sounded much more quietly than *softly*. And with the delicate fusion of two points of view, since the adverb has the neutrality of an unlooker, while the adjective puts us in the place of Adam as he feels Eve's hand. (p. 90)

Ricks's method produces a number of thematic alternatives from the syntax, and far from creating incoherence, the results are naturalized as components of a single, if more complex, stylistic intention. But there is something rather odd about his implication that the "total effect," the "delicate fusion of two points of view" is something that occurs in the sphere of oral performance—"sounded much more quietly than"—because the production of textual depth depends upon two *separate* oral performances. When the word 'soft" is spoken with its primary signification as an adverb, the "metrical" or "spatial" pause after "hand" corresponds neatly with a rhetorical or performative pause, but in order for an oral performance to convey the secondary adjectival resonance the gap must be closed considerably to move the modifier away from the verb "withdrew" and closer to the substantive "hand." Moreover, although the basic iamb/trochee sequence "her hand / Soft she" is maintained, there would have to be a quite notable shift of stress pattern from "hand" to "soft" in order for the adjective/noun possibility to be recognized. As is the case with the opening lines of the poem, the depth of form and texture is dependent upon at least two separate oral performances, and Hollander's "warp and weft of the verse fabric" must thus be frozen within the silent printed text.

We are faced here with a perplexing problem of critical self-awareness. Despite Barthes's plea there has not since 1971 been a serious attempt to explore the limits and conventions of a "linguistics of the written," yet it seems clear that for two major modern critics, the written text operates as a crucial, though unaknowledged, axis in their discussion of how form relates to meaning. This reluctance to consider the silent perception of the written text as part of the cognitive procedure of close reading becomes clear in Derek Attridge's sophisticated and comprehensive summation of modern prosodic technique, *The Rhythms of English Poetry* (1982).

> Reading a line of metrical verse aloud, therefore, is not simply a matter of choosing one interpretation and rejecting others: the fact of optionality itself is a characteristic of the rhythm, and remains effec-

tive whatever shades of stressing the line receives. . . . If you prefer to emphasize the regularity of the metre, the resolute irregularity of the language will be felt pulling agsint you; if you let speech rhythms have their head, the periodicity of the beat will exercise a counter claim: both readings, however, will register the inherent tension of the line. (p. 313)

This is a disorientating farrago of perspectives. How can an oral reader effectively perform and convey two separate metrical and syntactic patterns of the type already examined from *Paradise Lost*? The reader might be able to feel the pull of the alternative pattern, but how might such a person announce the existence of this without reading the verse twice, and more significantly, how can both readings, "register the inherent tension of the line" if one of them is capable of exposing the illusion of the line as a typographical construct? Attridge comes very close to locating a key to these contradictions, but not quite: "metre by freeing the spoken language from its univocal straightjacket, invests it with a kind of openness and multiplicity that is normally the special prerogative of the written text" (p. 314). Attridge should have stated that in some poetic texts, meter and the line are produced and supported by the written text, that the optionality of form and meaning is contained within the central core of the silent printed poem.

Visual Structure and Reader Response

The one sphere of modern criticism in which the visual structure of the poem has been allowed to emerge into the foreground is reader-response or reception theory.

In *Structuralist Poetics* (1975) Jonathan Culler embarked upon a systematic demolition of earlier twentieth-century, New Critical, attempts to isolate the intrinsic and definitive properties of poetic language. In his attack upon Cleanth Brooks's assertion that "the language of poetry is the language of paradox" Culler sought to demonstrate that the tensions, ambiguities, and ironies of poetic language are as much the products of the reader's interpretive ingenuity as they are of the particular intention of poetic writers. Culler's thesis is interesting enough in itself, but one is even more intrigued by his method of illustration. He reprints a section from W. V. O. Quine's philosophical essay *From a Logical Point of View* as a free verse lyric.

From a Logical Point of View

```
A curious
          thing
    about the
              ontological
    problem
              is
its
          simplicity
```

The typographical arrangement produces a different kind of attention and releases some of the potential verbal energy of "thing," "is" and "simplicity." We are dealing less with a property of language (intrinsic irony or paradox) than with a strategy of reading, whose major operations are applied to verbal objects set as poems even when their metrical and phonetic patterns are not obvious. (p. 163)

Culler's prose resonates with echoes of his eighteenth-century predecessors. His first observation on the release of verbal energy from visually isolated words follows the technique of Sheridan, but his identification of these effects as a "strategy of reading" takes us back even further to the work of Woodford, who performed in almost identical experiment with Milton's theological prose. The central question is of whether these poetic effects are intrinsic to the structure of the text or generated by the reader via a Pavlovian response to the shapes and conventions of print. One aspect of the question conveniently ignored by Culler is the possibility that the poet might *intend* to produce such effects in the mind of the reader by deliberately exploiting the signifying potential of the silent printed text. Culler probably would not claim that the effects of irony generated by the rhythmic parallelism and rhyme of Pope's couplets are "applied" as a "strategy of reading." In this case he would no doubt claim that there is evidence of the poet's intention to draw acoustic phenonomena from the random distributions of language and to arrange them in a series of orderly patterns. Why then, cannot the same criteria of intention be applied to the patterns of visual shape?

Culler's treatment of the visual format as an entry point for reader-centered interpretive strategies has become something of a habit in contemporary theory. Veronica Forrest Thomson in *Poetic Artifice* (1978) performed exactly the same experiment with a newspaper cutting, and in the collection of essays in which Barthes's issued his plea for a "linguistics of the written" we find an essay by Samuel Levin on "The Conventions of Poetry."

> Obviously, the line has typographical identity . . . the typographical groupings (and the concomitant pauses) are not random; some organising principle must be at work behind them. This is the principle of meter. . . . In fact, most meters are not in themselves transparent over the larger span; they provide no recurrent distinctive metrical configuration to mark the end of the line. In such meters the feature that functions to signal the end of the line is usually some sort of sound-euphony-rhyme or assonance. . . . When the line is defined for the hearer it is defined by conventional features of poetry and is thus, itself a convention; it has no linguistic relevance. (p. 177)

There seems to be a contradiction here. Levin implies that the poet is at the mercy of such impersonal systems of conventions as "sound-euphony-rhyme" and is thus limited in the deployment of the resulting formal unit, the line. But what if, as is clearly the case with Milton, the physical identity of the line becomes the determinant of such shifting linguistic features as the relation between its internal structure and the broader movement of syntax? Surely the line then becomes both the instrument of the poet and the focus of the reader's interpretive perspective. Such an instrument would have a great deal of linguistic relevance.

Levin's reluctance to grant the visual format the status of an authorially intended component of poetic design finds a more elaborate and explicit manifestation in the work of the reader-response theorist, Stanley Fish. Fish's collection, *Is There A Text in this Class?*, contains an amusing anecdotal essay on "How To Recognise a Poem When You See One," in which he invites a group of admirably competent English Literature students to criticize and elucidate a modernist religious lyric, which is on the seminar room blackboard. They proceed to do so and employ an impressive repertoire of analytical techniques and scholarly references. The point of this exercise is that the words on the board are actually a list of names left over from the preceding class on linguistics, and that the students are able to make it sound like a poem because their analytical methodology is triggered by the illusion that it is one. The "poem":

> Jacobs-Rosenbaum
> Levin
> Thorne
> Hayes
> Ohman (?)

There is clearly a similarity between the illusion offered by Fish to his students and Woodford's experiment with Milton's prose. In neither case were the words intended as poetry, and in both cases the readers are asked to accept them as poems because of the context in which they appear—a context whose recognition is crucially dependent upon the shape of the words on the page. Fish's students would no doubt find precedents for their critical procedures in the work of e.e. cummings, William Carlos Williams, or, more specifically, in the writings of ideogram poets such as Olson, Duncan, and Creeley, where the typographic isolation of individual words and phrases has come to constitute something of a grammar, a technical tradition. Woodford's readers would be able to compare the typographically arranged prose with the patterns and idioms of dramatic blank verse and with their more recent, more experimental, manifestation in *Paradise Lost*. But there is a difference. Woodford and the critics who followed him regarded the creative potential of visual format with varying degrees of appreciation and scepticism, but they shared an awareness of it as an addition to the formal effects of poetic writing: they regarded the visual effect as an intended strategy of the poet. Fish's opinion, and one that is shared by most of his contemporaries, shifts the creative role towards the interpretive faculties of the reader, and he makes this clear in another essay in *Is There A Text in This Class?*

> I appropriate the notion of the "line ending" and treat it as a fact of nature; one might conclude that as a fact it is responsible for the reading experience I describe. The truth I think is exactly the reverse: line endings exist by virtue of perceptual strategies rather than the other way around. Historically, the strategy that we know as "reading (or hearing) poetry" has included paying attention to the line as a unit (either of print or of aural duration). . . . In short, what is noticed is what has been made noticeable, not by a clear and undistorting glass, but by an interpretive strategy. (pp. 165–66)

The full implications of Fish's thesis for a whole tradition of poetic writing, particularly in free verse, are depressing, since he reduces much of the twentieth-century technique of unmetrical lyricism to the condition of unstructured word play, which will only find coherence with the assistance of fully qualified members of the interpretive community. I shall deal with the visual structure of free verse in Part Three, but for the moment it would be useful to compare the arguments of Culler and Fish with those of a number of eighteenth-century critics, who did regard the visual poem as a "fact of nature" that could be deployed by the poet.

Silent Reading in the Eighteenth Century

In his essay "On Rhythmical Measures" (1786) Walter Young confronted the problem of how critics such as Rice, Walker, and Sheridan could disclose at least two rhythmic patterns in blank verse. He concluded that this double perspective was the result of a tension between the natural movement of the verse and the convention of organizing this movement into "parcels" to "be more readily perceived by the reader" (p. 72). "A very gentle hint will incline a hearer to count off such feet by combinations of the smaller even numbers. For this, little more is necessary than to write them out (for the oral reader) in separate lines" (p. 102). This would seem to explain the problem of rhythm, but the attendant problem of how distinct meanings can be conveyed in a single oral performance leaves Young with exactly the same paradox that Fowler, Ricks, Hollander, and Attridge conveniently ignore.

> The feet indeed mark times, which may be expressed as equal; but there is no circumstance in the rythm [sic] to lead the hearer to form these times into combinations of any one number in preference to another, besides the mere artifice of writing the intended combinations in separate lines. It is impossible to read it, so as to maintain in the hearer the impression of the combination, without often doing violence to the sense, by separating words which ought to be united. One may be easily satisfied of this, by reciting the first sentence of MILTON'S Paradise Lost, in which almost every line terminates in the middle of a clause. In reading such passages, the pauses must often be omitted, and the measure sacrificed to the sense. (p. 104)

So it would seem that Hollander's effect of "closure and flow," which produces the fascinating intensifications and complexities of meaning is, in oral performance, "impossible to read." Young does not adopt the reader-response solution to this since, "these inconveniences" emerge from *within* "our English blank verse, which is exactly of the nature that I have been describing" (p. 103).

A tentative attempt to codify a series of effects that appear to take place in the realm of silent contemplation may be found in the work of William Kenrick, to whom Rice dedicated his *Art of Reading* in acknowledgment of the former's help and advice. In his *Rhetorical Grammar of the English Langauge* (1784) Kenrick preempted Young's disclosure of a double perspective and suggested a solution.

> The harmony of English verse is partly natural and partly artificial. Its natural harmony depends on the distinct articulation, easy flow and spirited intonation of its elements or feet: its artificial harmony on the regular disposition of these feet according to certain arbitrary modes. (p. 78)

The "natural" harmony is clearly the interlineal movement of the verse and the "artificial" and "arbitrary" the structure of the line, but instead of explaining how this contrapuntal tension might be dealt with or, in Fowler's terms, "reconciled" by the reader, Kenrick emphasizes the intention of the poet.

> The difficulty of reconciling the accents of natural or oratorical declamation with the rules of artificial versification, has occasioned innumerable breaches of the latter in our best and most admired poets. In many of these also, the writers have been happy enough to snatch a grace beyond the reach of art, and, by breaking through the regular trammels of artificial harmony, have given us something more pleasing and harmonius. (p. 51)

This "something" "beyond the reach of art" is apparently outside the codifications of formal analysis, because rather than describe it in the language of criticism he quotes Milton.

>   —Harmony
>   So smooths their charming tones, that God's own ear
>   Listens delighted.

The mildly presumptuous irony of a sound audible only to the "ear" of God becomes even more intriguing when he goes on to "define" this effect:

> Might it not be said of the numbers of these, and many other passages in Milton, in the language of Comus,
>
> > How sweetly do they float upon the wings
> > Of silence!
> > At every fall, smoothing the raven down
> > Of darkness, till it smiles—

> Such sounds as these will take th'enchanted soul,
> And lap it in Elysium?
>
> (p. 51)

This is from Comus's aside to the Lady's Song, which no one but himself can "hear", and it can be no concidence that Kenrick has chosen the visually isolated phrase "Of silence" to describe the complex fabric of unrhymed Miltonic verse. In his Introduction to the *Rhetorical Grammar* he provides the premise for this mysterious disjunction of sound and vision.

> The matter of language is of two kinds, vocal and literal; the elements and construction of which are totally different, and should be considered apart, if we should enter into the true spirit, and development of the principles of their connection. The material elements of vocal language are sounds, which speak to the ears; those of literary language, written types, or figures, which speak to the eyes: so that polished nations have in fact two distinct types of language, which may be called oral or occular; the properties of which, though arbitrarily connected by use, have no natural or physical dependence on each other. (pp. 1–2)

This is a remarkable sequence of propositions. He preempts Barthes's evocation of a "linguistics of the written," and in his division of language into the "literary," "written" forms that "speak to the eyes" and the more spontaneous medium of "sounds which speak to the ears," he cuts very deeply into what is still an encoded desire to give ultimate priority to spoken language and idealize the poem as an oral and not as a written artifact. We might compare Kenrick's model of composition and understanding with Hollander's examination of exactly the same themes in his essay on "The Poem in the Eye." Hollander also distinguishes between the interpretive faculties of the eye and the ear, a distinction that he borrows from Ferdinand de Saussure's model of language as a system of components, rules, and conventions *(langue)* which manifests itself in individual speech events *(parole)*[4]: "It is on the second of these axes that I would pose the ear, the individual talent, the voice, the *parole*; on the first are ranged the eye, the tradition, the mask through which the voice sounds, and the *langue*. The ear responds to the dimension of natural experience, the eye to that of convention" (*Vision and Resonance*, p. 248).

The Saussurean hierarchy of speech/writing is designed to support the ideal of immediacy where signifiers—signs, words—

seem to provide access to intelligible signifieds—the element of reality that language articulates (*Course*, pp. 23–24). Just as Saussure created his hierarchy to uphold the presence of individual meaning and intention, so Hollander has to categorize the effects he identifies as the products of speech rather than writing, or more importantly, the products of the author rather than of a system of literary conventions. But what if, like Kenrick, we are to regard writing not as a convention that supports speech, but as an independent communicative medium to be disposed by the poet and interpreted not as a "mask *through* which the voice sounds," but as a mode of signification that effectively challenges the dominance of speech? To accept Kenrick's proposition we would also have to reexamine the process of understanding the connections between the written components of the poem, and this is what Thomas Barnes did in an essay published in 1785, a year after the *Rhetorical Grammar*.

> The musicalness and flow of numerous composition, which charms the ear of every judicious reader, is certainly felt most strongly, where it is *read aloud*, with taste and expression. But when *read with eye only*, without the accompaniment of the voice, there is a fainter association of the sound, the *shadow of the music*, as it were, connected with the words; so that we can judge exactly of the composition as if it were audible to the ear. This habit of associating *sound* with *vision*, is formed gradually of habit. . . . And some Gentlemen are said to have acquired this art of mental combination so perfectly, as to *read*, even the *notes* of a musical composition with considerable pleasure. . . . Surely the verse of Milton is not "verse only to the eye." ("On the Nature and Essential Character of Poetry as Distinguished from Prose," pp. 69–71)

Elsewhere in the essay, Barnes makes it clear that his own "habit of associating sound with vision" is influenced by the work of Sheridan, and the rather ambivalent qualifying phrases, "a fainter association of the sound" and *"shadow of the music"* imply that there is not a direct and unitary correspondence between the level of awareness achieved by silent reading and that disclosed by oral delivery.

The possibility of there being a distinction between the meaning of a silently read text and its effect upon the ear is also raised by William Cockin in *The Art of Delivering Written Language*, published in the same year as Sheridan's *Lectures*, 1775.

> From the words and phrases of *oral language* always necessarily appearing associated with expressive tones and fashionable modula-

tion, both the author of *written language* and the silent peruser of it must have a secret reference all along to these particulars.

> The silent reader . . . cannot often meet with a person who will deliver the matter in a manner which will either coincide with his ideas, or indeed be free from many real and considerable imperfections. Hence the preference often due to a silent perusal. (pp. 131–32)

Without going into any detail as to how the "secret reference" affects meaning, Cockin suggests that the silent realm of interpretation is uniquely capable of synthesizing the disparate and unpredictable levels of oral delivery—thus what for Attridge was "*normally* the special prerogative of the written" becomes for Cockin its specific prerogative.

The most elaborate and adventurous exploration of the distinctions between the silent, visual text and its oral counterpart appeared in its final edition ten years after Barnes's essay, and Peter Walkden Fogg's *Elementa Anglicana* (1792–96) is yet another lost delight of critical history. Fogg reiterates Sheridan's division of poetic language into melody and harmony—the former being the sequential progress of sound and the latter emerging from the more complex interplay of cadences and units. But Fogg goes on to explore the question of why and how the mind of the reader can both separate and reassemble the materiality and the referential function of language. In the following, Fogg considers form as in itself an aesthetic medium.

> The traces of these delightful movements frequently remain in the mind, and serve as a kind of inspiration, allowing them no rest till they have filled up the craving void of these blanks of harmony with compositions of their own. The varied and yet regular maze affords numberless objects of comparison, which to perceive is unspeakably pleasant, though to point them out might seem tedious. Nay, as was before remarked on the melody of pauses, pleasure may be derived from a view of straight lines in the same variety and proportion. (vol. II, p. 198)

One wonders if the phrase "unspeakably pleasant" is an ironic reference to the fact that Fogg has succeeded in detaching the structure of language from its meaning, because he proceeds to, literally, illustrate his point with a poem by William Hayley which he rewrites as "unspoken" music.

> Of humbler mien, but not of mortal race,
> Ill fated Dryden, with imperial grace
> Gives to th'obedient lyre his rapid laws;
> Tones yet unheard, with touch divine he draws,

The Critical Debate

> The melting fall, the rising swell sublime
> And all the magic of melodious rhyme
>
> ___ _____ _____
> ___ _____ _____
> ___ ___ _____ _____
> ___ ___ _____ _____
> ___ ___ ___ _____
> ___ _____ _____ _____
>
> (vol. II, p. 200)

Fogg comments: "Then the mind glances over the whole with a rapidity that enhances the delight; and the more as we suppose many other proportions still unperceived" (II, p. 199). His method is an extravagant and endearingly bizarre extension of a number of eighteenth-century critical perceptions. Lord Kames, Johnson, and Hugh Blair all praised the balance of order and diversity that could be achieved by allowing variations of rhythm and syntactic structure within the more stable framework of the regular couplet line.[5] Fogg's "lines" provide a perfect visual representation of this ideal, and one could regard these images as preempting Fowler's notion of a reconciliation of "various complexes of intensity" with a uniformity of pattern, since each unit of rhythmic intensity is contained within lineal structures of exactly equal length. But Fogg's experiment with shape also leads him to an implicit recognition of one kind of silent poetics that resists any form of categorization as a visual representation of the oral form. The only type of verse to which he finds himself unable to apply his series of shapes is that in which the "traces" of sound are in conflict with sense: "when the idea of continued motion is conveyed, or the sense is suspended" (p. 202). He gives examples of this from *Paradise Lost;* the same lines that drew the attention of Benson, Sheridan, Ricks, and Davie to the productive effects of, in Hollander's terms, "closure and flow." The "mind" cannot "glance over,"

>   to me returns
> Day

or

> Now in loose garlands thick thrown off, the bright
> Pavement

because sound and meaning are put into a state of tension by the visual format. To represent these movements as shapes Fogg would have had to devise a visual pattern where the line both closes *and* continues into the one beneath it, and the same problem of simultaneously conveying two distinct patterns confronts the oral performer. Fogg's confrontation with Milton represents a significant moment in the history of poetic shape, because although George Puttenham, in The Arte of English Poesie (1589) set the only known precedent for the "translation" of form into black lines, he did so to represent "a naturall *simpathie* betweene the eare and the eye" (p. 70). Fogg had come across verse that produced a conflict between the two dimensions of experience.

For the most complete clarification of these eighteenth-century critics' tentative engagements with silent, visual reading as an independent realm of interpretive experience we must return to Sheridan's Lectures. His complex and very radical interpretive model is worth investigating in detail. Here he refers to the problems raised by Milton's blank verse.

> Harmony therefore, in this sense of the word, can never be applied to poetic numbers, of which there can only be one reciter, and consequently the sounds can only be in succession. When therefore I apply this term to poetic numbers, I only use it for want of another word, to express the effect produced by observing the relative proportion which the different members of poetic composition bear to each other. And in this figurative sense of the word, it has been introduced into arts where the ear has no concern. (p. 273)

Thus, in Sheridan's view, the spoken poem "of which there can be *only* one reciter" is more limited in its power to generate meaning than the silent printed text. The most powerful challenge to the preeminence of the spoken form is in his comparison of sounds "only in succession" with the "observing of the relative proportion which the different members bear to each other," because this strikes not only at the ideal of spech, but also raises the possibility of a separate grammar of the eye in which linguistic integers respond to one another outside the successive continuum of traditional syntactic relations. He goes on:

> We say the harmony of colours, the harmony in parts of a building, of the human body etc. And it is only after examining the different degrees of colouring, and their ordonance; the different members of a building, or the human body; and observing their symmetry, that we can pronounce about their harmony. In like manner, it is not till after

we have taken review of the different members of verse—which had before passed in succession, but lodged in the memory are presented to the mind in one view, as a coexistent whole, that we can observe the relative proportion which these members bear to each other; or consequently judge of the harmony of the whole. To define therefore as precisely as possible these terms according to the meaning in which I shall employ them, when I speak of the melody of the verse, I mean only a pleasing effect produced on the ear, by an apt arrangement of its constituent parts, feet and pauses, according to the laws of measure and movement. When I speak of the harmony of verse, I mean an effect produced by action of the mind, in comparing the different members of the verse, already constituted according to the laws of melody, with each other, and perceiving a due and beautiful proportion between them. (pp. 274–75)

This is a quite remarkable statement, because Sheridan claims that there is a pattern of relations between the components of the silent printed text which, like the elements of a visual image or structure, operate independently of the successive, sequential pattern of traditional grammar. To answer the question of how this new system of linguistic relations might actually work we have only to consult Sheridan's interpretations of the visual format of *Paradise Lost*.

what must be
Worse

resonates with intensities and transferences of meaning that take us beyond the sequential pattern of "what must be worse." The implications for meaning of this new perspective upon language will be examined in detail in the next chapter, but for the moment it is necessary to establish that Sheridan's application of silent visualist reading to poetry is in no sense a personal aberration nor particularly inconsistent with a number of contemporary attitudes toward the materiality of language.

James Beattie was a typical writer of the period in that he combined his interests in linguistic philosophy and literature in a way that has again become fashionable in the multi-disciplinary sphere of poststructuralism. In his "Essay on Poetry and Music as they affect the Mind" (1776) he echoes the contemporary belief that "rhyme is requisite to make the measure and rhythm perceptible" to the ear, and in his later work *The Theory of Language* (1788) we find, if not the influence of Sheridan, then at least a shared awareness of the power of written language.

> Words spoken make an immediate impression, but depend for their permanence, upon the memory of the speaker and hearer; and the best memory loses more than it retains: but words written may be preserved from age to age, and made as durable as anything human can be. (p. 108)

This sense of durability and permanence establishes writing as a fixed point in the shifting relation between the mind and its object; with "writing we make them (thoughts) pass and repass in review before us, till we have made them such as we wish them to be" (p. 109). In other words, the written text freezes and incapacitates the individual variations of the oral, and allows the silent reader to act as a kind of casuist in an unstable communicative circuit.

For poetry, such a linguistic model effectively subverts the Hellenic ideal of one person literally speaking to another, and as will be shown in chapter 5, there was an alternative, yet equally unorthodox, theory of form and meaning based upon the poem as a spoken utterance. But for the most incisive comment on these debates we should turn to a work that has certainly not been lost to literary history. The following is from chapter XII, vol. III, of *Tristram Shandy*.

> —And how did Garrick speak the soliloquy last night?—Oh, against all rule, my Lord,—most ungrammatically! betwixt the substantive and the adjective, which should agree together in *number, case*, and *gender*, he made a breach thus,—stopping, as if the point wanted settling;—and betwixt the nominative case, which your lordship knows should govern the verb, he suspended his voice in the epilogue a dozen times, three seconds and three fifths by a stopwatch, my Lord, each time.—Admirable grammarian!—But in suspending his voice—was the sense suspended likewise? Did no expression of attitude or countenance fill up the chasm?—Was the eye silent? Did you narrowly look?—I looked only at the stop-watch, my Lord.—Excellent observer!

This is one example of Sterne jolting the reader out of any comfortable sense of context or continuity—in this case Toby's and Dr. Slop's debate on the birth. However bizarre and incongruous the passage might seem to a modern reader, a 1760s reader with interests in current theories of language and literature would certainly have felt its sharp satirical edge.

The parodic target of the debate is the contemporary concern with how language can maintain a consistency of meaning in its complex and often conflicting manifestations, as writing and speech. Edward Home, Lord Kames, published the third volume of his *Elements of Criticism* in 1672, and, as will be shown in the following chapter, Kames betrayed an almost obsessive concern with how the physical components of language could become grammatically disconnected in the visual poem, and how this subversion of grammatical continuity might threaten the ideal of transparency in oral language. There is no evidence that Sterne had seen an early volume of the *Elements* prior to the publication of vol. III of *Tristram Shandy* in 1761, nor of whether he had heard Kames's lectures, accounts of his lectures, or read his essays. But the emergence of this coldly meticulous "critic," who happens to be a Lord, and the resemblance between Sterne's pastiche and the style and content of the *Elements* take us beyond mere coincidence.

There is also a reference to the voice "suspended" between two grammatical components, and although Sheridan did not publish an account of the interpretive possibilities of the "pause of suspension" until 1775, his *Lectures* were in fact accounts of theories and propositions that he had been developing in his public lectures and readings of verse since the 1750s.

To trace the ripples of contemporary relevance even further, the reader might consult Joshua Steele's *Prosodia Rationalis* (1775) in which Steele, the linguist and prosodist, gives an account of an exchange with Garrick on how a single oral performance of the *Hamlet* soliloquy can convey the fluctuations and complexities of the written text (see chapter 5, below pp. 109–14).

Sterne's keen awareness of the potential for pedantic absurdity in such debates cannot, however, be regarded as dismissive of the importance of language's materiality in a world, which, by the 1760s, had still not come to terms with the full effects of the printing press and the printed text upon the ideals and protocols of human communication. Because throughout *Tristram Shandy*, Sterne returns again and again to experiments with the visual material of language and betrays an interest in writing as more than a temporary stage in the oral circuit. His black pages, marble pages, his extra linguistic account of Corporal Trim flourishing his stick, provide a link between what might appear to be literary eccentricities and a more widespread contemporary interest in visual form as both a subversion and an expansion of language's repertoire of signifying conventions. We have only to turn back to chapter XI of *Tristram Shandy* to find an experiment with black lines, that not only replace words but trace out their relative lengths and proportions, to remind ourselves that Sterne's self-conscious whimsies found their more serious counterpart in Peter Walkden Fogg's "unspeakably pleasant" shapes.

As Sterne's parody suggests, the most perplexing point of conflict for conceptions of speech and writing is the printed poem, because although the line is not supposed to influence grammar, the fact that the first structural component that comes to the reader's attention is the *sight* of the line has serious implications for the ideal of a direct correspondence between the spoken and the silent text.

The work of these eighteenth-century critics make it clear that the process of reading a printed poem is by no means a silent version of an oral performance, and they offer us two challenging perspectives upon modern critical assumptions.

Conclusions

The modern prosodists are united in their reluctance to grant the silent medium the status of an independent signifying system beyond its traditional role as a temporary record of oral delivery, but when the attitudes of the modern and the eighteenth-century critics to the same lines from *Paradise Lost* are compared, we find that the printed text both incorporates and silences variations of sense and structure.

The reader-response critics acknowledge the function of the visual format as an entry point for critical ingenuity, yet they stop short of recognizing the silent material of language as an instrument of composition. One is stunned by Culler's claim that he, the critic, is able to deploy visual triggers to the process of literary reading, whereas the poet would, by implication, remain immune from this interpretive conspiracy. And Fish's personal "appropriation" of the line ending as an "interpretive strategy" becomes questionable when we find that men who are as distant from the modern "interpretive community" as Woodford the country parson, Sheridan the elocutionist, and Kenrick the grammarian are drawn to the same lines of verse of consider the same problems of interpretation.

The two perspectives raise two equally challenging questions. If we accept that the eighteenth-century critics' almost obsessive emphasis upon the Miltonic line as a unique phenomenon is sufficient evidence of authorial intention, then we must also accept that Milton deployed these effects for a specific reason. Why did he choose the "wings / Of silence"? I shall attempt to answer this question in the following chapter, and I shall proceed to examine the influence of these effects upon the work of other poets.

The second question is addressed to the language and preconceptions of criticism. Critical writing of whatever ideological and theoretical base tends to regard itself as a formalization, a clinical documentation of what occurs in the reading and understanding of literture. But when confronted by the printed poem, the eighteenth-century critics betray an interest in the signifying potential of visual language that modern criticism might rely upon in practice, but will rarely acknowledge as a component of its interpretive procedures.[6] For the eighteenth-century critics the form of meticulous investigative attention that has come to be known as "close reading" was accepted as challenge to the traditional concept of conveying and understanding the full complexity of poetic effects purely through the aural medium. Sheridan's "action of the mind in comparing the different members of a verse" was generated by the interaction of his eye with the silent text. And it seems odd that our own very similar practices of interpretive precision have failed to produce what Barthes calls "a grammar of the written" when the likes of Young, Barnes, Kenrick, and Fogg were inspired toward tentative considerations of these forms of meaning. The grammar of the written poem is clearly a unique phenomenon in that the line inserts itself into the sequential continuum; it acts as a visual axis and allows the eye of the reader to move forward *and* backward along the syntactic track, gathering and redisposing linguistic material and producing meanings that are unique to silent reading. It will become clear that the reason for our reluctance to acknowledge the full potential of silent reading is that it forces us to confront the material of language not as a purely transparent medium, but as something that can influence, as well as reflect, our perceptions of the world.

4
Shape and Identity: Milton, Wordsworth, and Literary History

In recent years the debates concerned with the meaning and purpose of literary criticism have become part of a much broader dialogue that centers upon linguistic philosophy and epistemology. Evidence of this interaction may be found in Hollander's use of Saussurean linguistics as the basis for his model of poetic signification and interpretation, and the Saussurean hierarchy of speech/writing has provided a focus for the interpretive conflicts that have come to be known as poststructuralism. Saussure's premise is that spoken language provides a stable point of fusion between signifier and signified, word and meaning, whereas writing is regarded as a secondary, parasitic medium, at the prey of absence and anonymity (*Course*, pp. 23–24). The most penetrating and subversive questionings of this hierarchy occurred in Jacques Derrida's *Of Grammatology*.[1] Derrida regards Saussure's system of priority as common to practically all Western traditions of thought, traditions in which he includes, and examines, the work of Plato, Rousseau, Condillac, Husserl, and Levi Strauss. He traces a tendency in Saussure and others towards phonocentrism, in which speech is regarded as the communicative ideal where words issue from the speaker as the spontaneous and nearly transparent signs of his present thought, and he quotes Hegel on this, "The visible language is related only as a sign to the audible language; intelligence expresses itself immediately and unconditionally through speech," and comments, "What writing itself in its non-phonetic moment betrays, is life. It menaces at once, the breath, the spirit, and history as the spirit's relationship with itself" (p. 25). Derrida claims that the obsessive ideal of speech operates as a guarantee of permanance and existential stability, and he goes on to examine the function of this ideal in a number of texts and to expose it as self-contradictory. His objective in this process, which has come to be known as deconstruction, is to disclose the real function of writing, not as a derivative or secondary mode, but as a factor that preserves speech from a condition of evanescence and formlessness. This is a very simplified summary of Derrida's complex and often inaccessible thesis, but it seems clear that his reversal of the speech/writing priority mirrors the eighteenth-century debate, in which we find critics such as Sheridan, Kenrick, Young, Barnes, and Fogg challenging the same linguistic preconceptions.

In the third chapter of *Grammatology*, "Of Grammatology as a Positive Science," Derrida postulates a "necessary decentring," a "dislocation of the founding categories of language, through access to another system linking speech and writing." This system is not philosophical or linguistic, but poetic. "This is the meaning of the work of Fenellosa (sic) whose influence upon Ezra Pound and his poetics is well known: this irreducibly graphic poetics was, with that of Mallarmé, the first break in the most entrenched western tradition" (p. 92). I shall examine Fenollosa's essay in Part Three, but for the moment, two points can be made about Derrida's observation. First, Sheridan showed that this "break" occurred in poetry long before the emergence of modernism; it occurred in *Paradise Lost* and, as I shall show, Milton's deployment of graphic poetics matches Derrida's recognition of them as disruptive of the balance between language and meaning. Second, it is rather surprising to find that Derrida's own references to poetic language are so brief and marginal to his thesis, since in its broadest definition, poetry is the medium that offers the most explicit challenge to the ordered transparency of speech: the component that unites and validates poetry as a recognizably discrete genre is the line, and the line continuously removes itself from all the other components of linguistic communication that seek both to convey order and stability, and to fuse the medium with the intention of its user. The line is anterior to the structure of the clause and the sentence, and its independence is confirmed by its typographic identity, its displacement by *means* of writing of the constrictions of traditional grammar. If the visual shape of poetry both intensifies and disrupts the communicative circuit between the poet and the reader, the question to be asked is why and how Milton chose to create these effects in the exploration of "things unattempted yet in prose or rhyme."

Eve's Silent Betrayals

In the middle of Book IV of *Paradise Lost* (ll. 440–91) Eve gives an account to Adam of her first memories of existence, and her speech has attracted the attention of Woodford and Hollander, the two visual interpreters who stand at either end of this critical tradition. Woodford chooses this speech as the section to be reprinted as prose and, as became clear, his motive was intriguing: he closed the visual perspective on this section only to tacitly acknowledge his awareness of its signifying power by recreating a very similar texture from a piece of prose. Why did he choose to devisualize this sequence and not others, in which interlineal movements of syntax are equally varied? John Hollander offers a clue:

> From Book IV again, Eve's account of her displacement of narcissistic admiration on to a recognition of Adam as an objectified beauty concludes "and from that time I see / How beauty is excell'd by manly grace" (lines 489–90), where the literal sense of "see" dissolves into a figurative one ("see how" as "understood that"), with a lingering hedging of her commitment. (*Vision and Resonance*, p. 98)

In Hollander's own communicative model, Milton has created Eve's "voice," which sounds through the visual "mask" to be "heard" by Hollander as a "lingering hedging of her commitment." Yet how is it possible for Hollander to "hear" Eve's sense of indecision, when this is not evident to the person to whom the promise of devotion is orally addressed, Adam? What Attridge referred to as the "optionality" of formal, and in this case literal, tension might well be "felt" by Eve and disclosed by Hollander but it cannot be "heard" by Adam.

I would say that it is Hollander's mastery of the text, his ability to see the written signifiers as Eve's words, that allows him to project his reading onto Eve; a reading that is, of course, denied to Adam, who does not have a printed copy of the poem.

The following is another example from Eve's "speech" in Book IV:

> a murmuring sound
> Of waters issued from a cave and spread
> Into a liquid plain, then stood unmoved
> Pure as the expanse of heaven; I thither went
> With unexperienced thought, and laid me down

>   On the green bank, to look into the clear
>   Smooth lake, that to me seemed another sky.
>
>   (IV, 453–59)

At line 458 "clear" is visually detached from "Smooth lake" and seems to take on a substantive form. The effect suggests a sense of clarity and space, which is confirmed by an OED usage from 1694: "Between nine and ten o'clock there was a fine clear, by which I saw the land very plainly." And it is interesting that the only other example of this substantive form given by the dictionary is also concerned with clarity of vision at sea.[2] To a contemporary reader any unwonted pause at "clear" would suggest a potential narrative contradiction. Why would Eve emphasize a word of such familiar nautical currency when she is supposed to have no acquaintance with expanses of water, and, more significantly, how can she have such a firm grasp of the phenomenon presented by the lake when, as the succeeding sequence reveals, it is the delusive, mirrorlike qualities of water that provide the keynote of the episode (ll. 460–63)?

Perhaps Eve is relating an earlier instance of her consciousness in contact with reality; it is a retrospective relation. Adam and Eve, when they appear in the poem, possess a vocabulary not dissimilar to that of mid-seventeenth-century English, and it is therefore plausible that her double usage of "clear" could be an example of language closing the gap between the event and the memory of the event. What was intractable is now "clear."

But the point is that such a psychological or intentionalist model of signification is available only to the reader of the printed poem and not to the listener within the poem. To return to Attridge's concept of the "fact of optionality," which will allow "both readings to register the inherent tension of the line," we find that to be fully understood by Adam, Eve must repeat herself, or assume him to be conversant with Sheridan's technique of silent reading—neither of which is possible.

The effects created by Eve's written text are peculiarly disturbing, since the silent reader of the poem seems to be locked into a private communicative circuit with her consciousness. And it is this element of Milton's silent poetics that explains the shared awareness of critics who are divided by time and circumstance. Ricks, Hollander, and Davie maintain an allegiance to the voice, or to be more accurate, the voices, of the poem as the source of their own ingenious disclosures, but one reason for their reluctance to acknowledge the silent printed texture of the verse as the source of slippages, hesitations, and intensifications of meaning could be that in doing so they would also have to regard every poetic "voice" of the poem as prey to the uncertainties of the written text. One wonders why, if they are so willing to seek out the disguised motivations of Adam and Eve and to celebrate the skillful linguistic sophistications of the Miltonic voice, they do not apply the same "interpretive strategies" to the following lines from God's statement of intent in Book III:

> for so
> I formed them free, and free they must remain,
> Till they enthrall themselves: I else must change
> Their nature
>
> (III, 123–26)

Hollander's recognition of a "lingering hedging" at Eve's line ending should be remembered here because God appears to be doing something similar. God's consideration of an alternative, "I else must change," is a reaffirmation of his power to do as he wishes with Adam and Eve. But the spatial gap might just allow a suspicion of self-doubt ("I else must change myself"). The syntax resolves the ambiguity, but the moment forces the reader to see that his comfortable contemplation of Eve's paratactic slips is made available not by his listening to Eve but by his intervention in the play of textual figures and relations. Because just as there is a gap between our reading of Eve and Adam's understanding of her, so at this point there must be a gap between our reading of God and the Son's understanding of Him. It might be argued that it is a condition of dramatic contexts in literature that a possibility exists for the reader to understand characters better than they do each other. But the disjunction between written text and dramatic, spoken context is so radical in *Paradise Lost* that the reader becomes the uneasy recipient of meanings that bypass any form of oral exchange. It is our own sense of uncertainty that emerges from our intervention in the oral discourses of God, Satan, Adam, Eve, Milton, or any of the other voices of the poem. We read into their nonphonetic moments the instability of our sense of, as Derrida puts it, "life . . . the breath, the spirit, and history as the spirits relationship with itself." This effect can be confirmed by an examination of the eighteenth-century critics' responses to the silent voices of the poem. The question of why Woodford chose to devisualize Eve's speech now becomes a little clearer, since his implicit awareness of the effects of Milton's visual format must have generated a recognition of hesitancy very similar to that disclosed by Hollander. But for Woodford, the seventeenth-century clergyman, the notion of being complicit in the deceptions of a Biblical character must have involved rather more than a literary experience. And we find this sense of unease more explicitly foregrounded in the work of Sheridan. Sheridan's critical encounters with the poem would seem, superficially, to be unaffected by context; he seems to take pleasure in the formal creation of localized meanings without consideration of their effect upon the broader texture of the narrative. However, a closer examination of his close-readings reveals that practically all of his celebrations of the pause of suspension concentrate upon Milton's own first-person sophistications and Satan's betrayals of uncertainty and despair. But when he came to examine Eve's Book IV speech he literally contradicted his own critical procedures. We should remember that this sequence includes her recollection of the voice that tells her to

> follow me
> And I will bring thee where no shadow stays
> Thy coming.
>
> (IV, 469–71)

It would be impossible for Sheridan to have recognized the textual possibilities of Milton's "but not to me returns / Day," whose visual format "strikes the imagination with the immensity of his loss" and to have allowed the more disturbing hesitation of "stays" to have passed unnoticed. And it is difficult to imagine that his finely tuned critical faculties could remain immune from the curious ambivalence of the

>   clear
> Smooth lake
>
> (IV, 458–59)

But instead of bringing his critical awareness to bear upon the same effects in Eve's speech that he had celebrated in the speeches of Milton, he closes them down. He dismisses the visual format completely and turns the speech into a safely prosaic paraphrase.

> Follow me, and I will bring thee, not to a shadow, such as you see in the water, but to a substance; to him whose image thou art, as that in

> the watery gleam is thine. Him as a substance you may enjoy; this as a shadow you cannot. (pp. 378–79)

It is almost as though this rewriting is the version of the speech he would like to have "heard": the original message delivered to Eve and cleansed of her own poetic betrayals to the silent reader. This procedure is unprecedented in Sheridan's work because although he reprinted the opening lines to illustrate the loss of the original printed resonances, here he changes not only the shape, but the words themselves. It is as though he felt the need to totally expunge the more disturbing elements of silent poetics by removing even the memory of them.

Eve's speech is in itself sufficient evidence of the ability of Milton's verse structure to generate similar responses in readers from very different "interpretive communities", but to consider the full significance of these effects we must consider the reasons for their somewhat different reactions. Sheridan, Woodford, Benson, Kenrick, and Fogg chose not to deal with the silent poetics of God or Eve because to have done so would have led them to a consideration of the balance between language and reality for which they were unprepared. It would be useful here to recall Sheridan's remarkable statement upon the power of the eye to consider the different elements of a verse and to discern harmony in them. Milton's disruption of the linear succession to recreate the emotional effects of his own blindness or to convey Satan's sense of despair is, in Sheridan's sense, harmonious, because the reader's interpretation of the silent poetics is consistent with the poet's intention to create a particular effect. But when confronted with the same strategies of disruption in all the "voices" and contexts of the poem, the silent reader finds himself contemplating not only what language can convey, but language itself as a material barrier capable of displacing the safe assumption of one person communicating with another. Sheridan himself pointed out that, "Harmony therefore, in this sense of the word, can never be applied to poetic numbers, of which there can be only one reciter," and the consequent requirement to reassemble the disparate "voices" of the poet is obviously part of his notion of the "Art of Reading." But to communicate in such a manner with the "voices" of God or Eve could well lead one to the conclusion that language itself is an arbitrary system of contingencies and conventions whose contradictions and paradoxes we have to repair to satisfy our own sense of stability: Sheridan would have to admit that he "understands" the narcissistic play of Eve's words better than Adam, for whom she is the "one reciter"; and more disturbingly, he would have to perform a similar act of communicative interruption between God and His Son.

Milton's silent poetics created for the eighteenth-century critics the double response of attraction and unease because they draw the reader into contradictory relationship with the poetry, and here again we should recall Sheridan's analogy with the visual arts. When we look at a traditional landscape painting we experience a double sense of isolation and communication: the dispositions of color and proportion are immediately familiar yet we know that they have been *made* familiar by the hand of the artist. The painter does not communicate directly with the perceiver since his medium is totally dependent upon images and perspectives that are part of the perceiver's daily experience of life in the world, but it is equally possible for the painter to subtly distort this balanced familiarity to his own communicative purposes. The writer who deploys written language is granted a very similar opportunity to subvert the conventions of fact and perception, because our spontaneous conception of how linguistic units relate with one another to disclose meaning is thrown into a state of unease when new and unexpected relationships emerge from the configurations of words on the page.

Before proceeding with an examination of the use and critical reception of silent poetics beyond *Paradise Lost,* one important question should be asked. Why, if Milton had dispensed with all other concessions to poetic form, did he maintain an allegiance to the pentameter? Sheridan regarded its identity as preserved by the visual format, and Rice and Walker regarded it as an accident of printing convention; and its preservation as a recognizable component of the oral poem is dependent both upon the skill of the oral performer and his willingness to disrupt the continuities of meaning and rhythm. The argument that to have varied the length of his visual lines would have led Milton too far into uncharted experimental territory can be dismissed because of the existence of *Samson Agonistes,* which traces out irregular, though generally iambic, patterns very similar to those disclosed from *Paradise Lost* by Rice and Walker.

To answer this question we must first recognize that *Samson Agonistes* is intended as a dramatic text. Dryden's conception of dramatic poetry as a genre in which rhythmic structure is but a polished form of prose with no necessary attention given to the structure of individual lines was never challenged. As late as

1783, Hugh Blair[3] felt that there was no need to revise this perception, and no further evidence of the sense of *Samson* as intentionally unpoetic is required than the fact that, despite its superficial relevance to the visual/oral debate, none of the critics involved even mentions its existence. But Milton's awareness of this distinction of genre and form has deeper implications.

Sections of *Samson Agonistes* vary in line length from six to fourteen syllables, and this pattern must be regarded as a visual record of the hesitations and varied intonational structures of speech: the visual format does not cut into and disrupt the sequential structure in the manner of *Paradise Lost*. No one but the oral performer would need to see the lines. The most intriguing comment upon the effect of this form comes from Samson himself, after a lengthy free verse disquisition from the Chorus.

> I hear the sound of words, their sense the air
> Dissolves unjointed ere it reach my ear
> (ll. 174–75)

Samson Agonistes was written only for the ear, and there is a tantalizing intertextual correspondence between Samson's limited condition of aural perception, and Milton's self-referential use of the visual line in *Paradise Lost* as a more tangible point of contact with the world. The printed pentameter might "sound" unjointed, but for the eye to the reader the "sense dissolved" can be silently reassembled.

The blank verse pentameter of *Paradise Lost* is not merely a concession to formal precedent; it is a token reminder of the control of oral form by the silent visual text. Milton intended us to ask the question of why what we see on the page can contrast so radically with what we hear, and his invocation of tradition in his use of the pentameter invites us to confront the contradiction of a rhythmic and acoustic structure whose identity can only be guaranteed by its silent, typographic status. He invoked the shadow of a convention only to challenge the expectations of the reader by exposing it as an elusive and deceptive phenomenon. And as Sheridan showed, it is a small step from this state of awareness to a contemplation of language itself as a medium sown with impersonal dependencies and betrayals. The poem is, after all, concerned with matters that we, trapped in our postlapsarian communicative circuit, can invoke, but never fully comprehend.

Milton's silent poetics and their deeper implications that our sense of identity is interwoven with our linguistic condition were uncomfortably evident for a considerable number of eighteenth-century readers, but for reasons that will become apparent, they did not find a new creative environment until they reemerged in the poetry of Wordsworth.

Wordsworth's Rewritings of the Eighteenth Century

Idiomatic and stylistic connections have been traced between Milton's and Wordsworth's blank verse,[4] but one important distinction originates from Wordsworth's maintainance of a single lyrical persona, or voice, in his most celebrated work. Consider the following lines from *Home at Grasmere*:

> Dreamlike the blending of the whole
> Harmonious landscape; all along the shore
> The boundary lost, the line invisible
> That parts the image from reality;
>
> (574–77)

The reader might reflect upon the pleasing ambiguity of "whole" which seems to shift between its substantive and adjectival categories. The "Dreamlike" feeling of infinity that attends the "blending of the whole" is gradually transformed into a more specific reference to the "whole harmonious landscape" in exactly the same way that Eve responds to the "clear / smooth lake, that to me seemed another sky." The fingerprint of influence seems conclusive, but with Wordsworth there is a sense of self-conscious control. Again we find the tenuous balance of meanings which can be threatened by a single oral reading, since it would be difficult simultaneously to pause after "whole" *and* draw together the intonational structure of "whole harmonious." It seems that Wordsworth makes an ironic reference to the silent, visual status of this nuance in his reference to "the line invisible / That parts the image from reality," because it is the *visible* line that enables him to merge the "image" with "reality."

A more celebrated instance of perceptual merger occurs at the beginning of "Tintern Abbey":

> Once again
> Do I behold these steep and lofty cliffs,

> Which on a wild secluded scene impress
> Thoughts of more deep seclusion; and connect
> The landscape with the quiet of the sky.
>
> (4–8)

Isobel Armstrong (1978) and Antony Easthope (1983) note that there are crucial ambiguities at the terminal words "impress" and "connect." "Connect" could refer to an unbroken unity of panorama, "the cliffs connect the landscape to the sky," and it could also refer to the process of mediation, "I connect the landscape with the quietness of the sky." Similarly with "impress" there is a momentary hesitation between the cliffs literally imposing upon the landscape (a typical eighteenth-century inversion), and the revelation that the cliffs impress "thoughts of deep seclusion" upon Wordsworth himself. Both commentators identify these ambiguities as syntactic, Armstrong proposing the text as an example of the tendency of Romantic syntax to effect "transformations in perception and relationship" (p. 263) and Easthope as an example of parataxis, "the juxtaposed syntax of speech" (p. 127). What both share is an implicit belief in the poem as speech act, whether reified into the protocols of romantic epistemology or mimetically enacting the slippages and hesitancies of the speaking voice. But again we are faced with the problem of how a self-sufficient oral performance of these lines could mirror the contrapuntal shifts of meaning and rhythm identified by criticism. The syntax of the lines is, as a single oral sequence, relatively unambiguous; the traps, invitations to premature conclusions, and textual gaps depend upon the kind of clinical comparisons between different pauses and simultaneously present intonational patterns that can only take place in the silent realm of analysis.

The idea of one of the founders of lyrical Romanticism deploying techniques that satisfy the assumptions of the cool critical anatomist is one that most people would only entertain with a good deal of scepticism, but there is circumstantial evidence to suggest that the effects I describe are conscious and deliberate.

In 1971 Christopher Ricks published an essay called "Wordsworth: 'A Pure Organic Pleasure from the Lines'." He did not acknowledge the connection, but his recognition of what he regards as the creative potential of the "white space" of Wordsworth's blank verse is clearly related to his own earlier and very similar readings of Milton. His examination of how the "white space" can intensify the movement of syntax is brilliantly productive, but again he is reluctant to recognize the function of writing and silence in his interpretive process. But there is evidence to suggest that Wordsworth was directly influenced both by Milton and by Sheridan's readings. Ricks makes a brief reference to how the visual shape of poetry can both distinguish it from prose and affect its meaning, and he suggests a tentative connection between Wordsworth's poetic practice and his familiarity with the appropriately titled essay "Is Verse Essential to Poetry?" (1796). What he does not note is that William Enfield, the author of this article, was influenced by his contemporary and friend, Thomas Sheridan.[5] Sheridan's work on blank verse might seem to us to lie in a sphere of interpretive pedantry from which the romantics wished to detach themselves, but Wordsworth and Coleridge debated the existence and effect of the typographic line with the German poet Friedrich Klopstock, and both felt that debate and the topic were significant enough to record—in Coleridge's case in a section appended to the 1817 edition of *Biographia Literaria,* and in Wordsworth's, in his manuscript journal: "[Klopstock] preferred the blank verse of Glover (each verse separately considered) to that of Milton—but agreed with me that the true harmony of blank verse consisted in the periods and not in a succession of musical lines."[6] This would seem to ally Wordsworth with the Rice-Walker party, which favoured interlineal movement over typographic pattern, but in his *Preface to Poems* (1815) he betrays an apparently contradictory allegiance to the poetics of silence and shape.

Wordsworth is examining the ever-present problem of how to distinguish fancy from imagination, and comes to the conclusion that the former is but a "faithful copy, existing in the mind, of absent external objects," yet imagination is "of higher import, denoting operations of the mind upon those objects, and processes of creation or of composition." His choice of examples to illustrate this imaginative participation of the reader in the process of creation is intriguing. First he quotes a piece of Shakespeare's blank verse,

>   —half way down
> *Hangs* one who gathers samphire (Wordsworth's italic)

and observes that the mind, with but a "slight exertion" of the imaginative faculty, can contemplate the samphire gatherer literally hanging from the cliffs. One should note here that the point at which the imagination is invited to begin its work is, as

Wordsworth put it, "in the use of one word," and when he moves on to a more complex example from *Paradise Lost* we come to realize that by "use" he also means "positioning."

> As when far off at sea a fleet descried
> *Hangs* in the clouds, by equinoctial winds
> Close sailing from Bengola.

> Here is the full strength of the imagination involved in the word *hangs*, and exerted upon the whole image: First, the fleet, an aggregate of many ships, is represented as one mighty person, whose track, we know and feel, is upon the waters; but, taking advantage of its senses, the Poet dares to represent it as *hanging in the clouds*, both for the gratification of the mind in contemplating the image itself, and in reference to the motion and appearance of the sublime object to which it is compared.[7]

This reading places Wordsworth at the center of a critical tradition. His double perspective on how the word "hangs" shifts meaning back to the "mighty person" of the fleet and forward to the broader vision of the sea linked with the sky preempts Hollander. "Whenever brilliantly framed and patterned lines occur, they are opened out at their closing to allow their apparent syntactic closure to flow forward." The whole passage echoes the close-readings of Sheridan and Benson—particularly Sheridan's reference to the "action of the mind in comparing the different members of the verse . . . with each other, and perceiving a due and beautiful proportion between them"—and one must wonder how his implicit awareness of this context of critical appreciation influenced Wordsworth's own deployment of the visual pattern of words. Ricks offers a clue by identifying a series of apparently simultaneous poetic uses of and references to the attraction of the eye to the silent materiality of language. There are, for example, six instances of the word "vacancy" at the line endings of his blank verse, and one must here recall Walker's rather uneasy contemplation of the effects of typography: "but have we not reason to suspect, that the eye puts a cheat on the ear, by making us imagine a pause to exist, where there is only a *vacancy* to the eye?" Wordsworth in the *Excursion* offers the same question in verse.

> What terror doth it strike into the mind
> To think of one, blind and alone, advancing
> Straight toward some precipice's airy brink!

> But, timely warned, He would have stayed his steps,
> Protected, say enlightened, by his ear;
> And on the very edge of vacancy
> Not more endangered than a man whose eye
> Beholds the gulf beneath.
>
> (VII, 491–98)

Compare this passage with Walker's equally anxious description of what happens to the silent reader when the poet leads him toward an unexpected visual break: "The . . . reader cannot at first prevail on himself to follow him, but finds himself stopped at the end of the line as if it terminated by a precipice" (*Rhetorical Grammar,* p. 333). And Sheridan reminds us that an earlier poet "blind and alone" had contemplated the "brink" of perception: "*Day,* stops you unexpectedly, and strikes the imagination with the immensity of his loss. He can no more see—what?—Day!—Day and all its glories rush into the mind." It would seem that Milton "enlightened by his ear" did indeed create a verse texture in which only the reader's,

>   eye
> Beholds the gulf beneath

To adjust the context slightly, we also find that the texture of Wordsworth's passage, with its shift back and forth from ear to eye, echoes Thomas Barnes's conception of verse "when *read with the eye only,* without the accompaniment of the voice, there is a fainter association of the sound, *the shadow of the music . . .* so that we can judge exactly of the composition as if it were audible to the ear." The connections between Wordsworth's verse and the eighteenth-century critics become almost a dialogue.

Wordsworth, after reminding the reader of "Tintern Abbey" of the "landscape to the blind man's eye," evokes,

>   an eye quiet by the power
> Of harmony, and the deep power of joy,
> We see into the life of things.
>
> (46–48)

Sheridan:

> Harmony therefore, in this sense of the word, can never be applied to poetic numbers, of which there can be only one reciter, and consequently the sounds can only be in succession . . . in this figurative

sense of the word, it has been introduced into arts where the ear has no concern.

Milton:

> Harmony
> So smooths their charming tones, that God's own ear
> Listens delighted.

Kenrick, on these lines and others:

> Might it not be said of the numbers of these, and many other passages in Milton, in the language of Comus,
>
>> How sweetly do they float upon the wings
>> Of silence!

And Wordsworth:

> when a lengthened pause
> Of silence came and baffled his best skill,
> Then sometimes, in that silence while he hung
> Listening
>
> (Prelude, V, 380–83)

One feels tempted here to follow Wordsworth's example in the *Preface of Poems* (1815) and italicize the word "hung," because in using it the poet reminds us of his perceptions as a reader. He, the figure in the poem, waits for the owls to answer his shout: he acts as a pivot between his experience of sound and silence in the world and the reader's experience of it in the poem. His literal state of suspension between communication and reply is reproduced by the silent poetics. What Sheridan called the "pause of suspension" becomes the "lengthened pause / Of silence," an effect, a process of recognition, which not only relies upon, but actually becomes, the visual structure of the words. Were we to attempt a Rice-Walker experiment in the devisualization of these lines we would, literally, deprive them of their meaning.

For Wordsworth silent poetics provides the perfect medium for the uneasy relationship between his poetic persona and the physical world. In *Paradise Lost* we find that Milton systematically disrupts the ability of language to provide access to a fully comprehensible system of meaning and reality, and one must assume that his deployment of this technique is part of a reminder that our chief communicative medium is as far removed from a condition of truth and understanding as are its postlapsarian users. The closest point of contact between the two poets is to be found in Eve's hesitant contemplation of her existential presence and its relation to the natural world and Wordsworth's more self-conscious mediation of the "world / Of eye and ear,—both what they half create / And half perceive."

If more proof of both poets' awareness and deployment of the visual format were required, we should compare their work with that of eighteenth-century practitioners who also found blank verse to be an appropriate medium for observations upon the natural world.

Consider this uncomplicated, picturesque passage from Akenside's *Pleasures of the Imagination*,

> Down the stream
> Look how the mountains with their double range
> Embrace the vale of Tempe.[8]

Akenside places the two verbs "Look" and "Embrace" at points in the lineal/syntactic sequence that cautiously avoids any complication of reference: the reader is asked to "look" at how the mountains "embrace" the vale. One is immediately prompted to compare this orderly demarcation of the perceiver from the perceived with Wordsworth's double-edged placing of "impress," which links the cliffs both with the "secluded scene" and with his own "thoughts of deep seclusion."

It is very likely that Wordsworth was familiar with Cowper's *Task*, and the formal landscape description in Book I reminds us again of the beginning of "Tintern Abbey."

> Here Ouse, slow winding through a level plain
> Of spacious meads with cattle sprinkled o'er,
> Conducts the eye along its sinuous course
> Delighted. There, fast rooted in the bank,
> Stand, never overlook'd, our fav'rite elms,
> That screen the herdsman's solitary hut;
>
> (ll. 163–68)

Cowper, like Akenside, maintains a firm distinction between the perceiver and the perceived. The eye is conducted sedately by the thread of the river to the contemplation of a wider landscape.

But consider the effect upon this distinction when the visual shape of the lines is changed.

> Here Ouse, slow winding
> Through a level plain of spacious meads
> With cattle sprinkled o'er, conducts
> The eye along its sinuous course, Delighted
> There, fast rooted in the bank, stand,
> Never overlook'd, our fav'rite elms,
> That screen the herdsman's solitary hut;

In the reprinted lines, the sense of continuity established by "winding / Through" leads the reader to expect the isolated "conducts" to reconnect with something like, "conducts / Its glassy thread" or "conducts / The solitary vessel," but the sudden return from the landscape to "the eye" of the perceiver reminds us of Wordsworth's subtle vacillation between the landscape and the self. Similarly, the isolation of "stand" delays its connection with the "elms" and must initially suggest that the reader is being asked to "stand," "Delighted, there fast rooted in the bank," a shifting chain of connections, which is echoed by Wordsworth's use of the "I" to both reflect upon the texture of the landscape and to actively "connect" it with a more subjective vision.

I have changed neither the words nor the punctuation of Cowper's poem, but the change in its visual shape causes what amounts to a form of grammatical parallax that destabilizes any fixed relationship between an objective vision and its subjective effects.

The correspondences between Akenside's and Cowper's lines and those from "Tintern Abbey" are so close that it would be plausible to claim that Wordsworth could have imposed his familiarity with Miltonic style upon their more linear and less disruptive format. The question of why a technique that drew so much attention from eighteenth-century critics should be systematically marginalized by the poets of that century draws us into another exploration of the effects and priorities of eighteenth-century criticism.

Randomly selected sequences from the work of Thomson, Akenside, Dyer, Cowper, and Young will reveal that each poet, in subtly distinct ways, neutralized the most challenging elements of Miltonic visual form in accordance with what could be called the prescriptive prosodic tradition, of which Johnson was but one representative.

Prescriptive Criticism and Visual Form

"Prescriptive" criticism carries this title because, unlike most of the elocutionists, its practitioners sought to deal with the interpretive problems offered by English verse by judging them against abstract criteria of correctness and incorrectness. The best elocutionists would adjust their own a priori conceptions of structure and form in accordance with what appeared to be happening in the poem, but the prescriptive critics valued the abstract categories of form and formlessness as a method of preserving discriminations of genre, and, more significantly, of preventing poetic language from challenging more fundamental beliefs in how language reflects, rather than distorts, reality.

The most intriguing prescriptive engagements with poetry occurred when they came to deal with the formal identity and effect of nondramatic blank verse. The standard was set by Dryden, and his early judgements on what is and what is not verse migrate through the work of a large number of eighteenth-century critics, and, as they do so, gather an astounding degree of complexity.

The crudest manifestation of prescriptive writing will be found in the popular guide to composition, Edward Bysshe's *Art of English Poetry* (1702). His "Rules for Making English Verse" opens with the following declaration:

> The Structure of our Verses, whether Blank, or in Rhyme, consists in a certain number of Syllables; and not in Feet compos'd of long and short Syllables as in the Verses of the Greeks and Romans. (I, p. 1)

A. Dwight Culler, in his valuable study of Bysshe, points out that "to follow his phrase 'a certain number of Syllables' as it recurs again and again in eighteenth and early nineteenth century metrical criticism is merely a task of multiplying instances."[9] Paul Fussell takes up this challenge and establishes what he calls "Syllabism" as the single most important principle of eighteenth-century prosody.[10] What both ignore is the fact that by merely stating that the pentameter is limited to ten syllables Bysshe cautiously avoids the more complex problem of how a line that does not end with rhyme or a pause can be regarded as a formal unit at all.

Without explicitly identifying this problem Bysshe attempts to solve it by, in effect, imposing syntactic limitations upon the structure of the line. He identifies the two most important components of English verse as "The Seat of the Accent" and "The Pause." The "Seat of the Accent" will always be either on the second, fourth, or sixth syllable of the verse (p. 4). This whole concept is rhetorical and syntactic rather than metrical, since it is the "Seat of the Accent" that determines the placement of the caesura. When the accent occurs at the second syllable the pause will follow at the third or fourth. When it occurs at the fourth the pause will fall at the fourth, fifth, or sixth, and when the accent is on the sixth the pause will fall at the sixth or seventh.

This rather tedious excursion into pedantry is in fact based upon an anxious desire to preserve the identity of the line. If the abstract model is adhered to in practice, the rhetorical weight of the sentence will move towards the center of the line, and Bysshe gives an example of the disharmony produced when his system is flouted:

> Bright Hesper *twinkles from afar—Away*
> *My kids . . . for you have had a Feast today.*
>
> (p. 6)

The Seat of the Accent and the caesural pause are thrown toward "afar" and "Away," and although in this case the rhyme preserves a discernible conflict between the line and the syntactic movement, a very serious problem of structural identity would occur with an unrhymed version of these lines. We would be able to see the line break, but in order to hear it we would have to intervene in, to interrupt, the dominant rhythmic and syntactic pattern.

Isaac Watts in his *Relquiae Juveniles* (1734) promotes a more subtle but theoretically consistent version of Bysshe's syntactic formula. He states that "a line should never end with a word, which is so closely connected in grammar with the word following that it requires a continued voice to unite them" (p. 221), and goes on to give a number of examples of this fault from Milton, including, "divine / Historian" (VIII, 5–6), "cold / Climate" (IX, 44–45) and "the Worst / Of Evils" (Vi, 462–63). Significantly, he also condemns the break at "must be / Worse," which both Sheridan and Hollander praised for the effect of leaving "be" hanging between predicative and existential states. Watts's objection is grounded upon the same analytical perspective as Sheridan's and Hollander's celebrations, but for him the effect is not legitimate because an oral performance could not reproduce both meanings at the same time. Watts also states that, "if the beginning and ending of every vese is not distinguished by the hearer it differs too little from a sort of poetical prose" (p. 223). Thus the kind of verse which, in Hollander's words, discharges "two impulses . . . the warp and weft of the verse fabric," causes for Watts a disjunction between what is seen on the page as "so closely connected in grammar" and "which ought to be distinguished by the hearer"— two mutually destructive patterns that emerge from the conflict between the visual materiality of language and the ideal of an oral sequence. He implicitly invokes, but dismisses, the technique of silent reading.

Here we should recall Johnson, who saw those spatial breaks that cut into the sequence of rhythm and sense as forcing components of language to "stand alone and with regard to music be superfluous." The prescriptive critics mirror the visualist readers in their awareness of the power of the silent printed text to disturb the unitary balance between form and meaning, and the most detailed and rigorous manifestation of this awareness is to be found in Lord Kames's *Elements of Criticism* (1762). Kames confirmed what Bysshe had implied: that the touchstone of formal regularity was to be found in the balanced, closed structure of the rhymed couplet. "In a word, the rules of melody in blank verse, are the same that obtain with respect to the first line of a couplet" (vol. II, p. 162). According to Kames, it is the distinction between caesural and terminal pauses, as much as meter, that creates the "melody" of blank verse. He imagines the poet disposing his pauses across the formless raw material of iambic prose and producing an evenly sliced *prose tranchée* of manageable, discete blocks (II, pp. 121–24). But more significantly, he acknowledges a distinction between the poetic, melodic, pause and the syntactic pause: the poetic pause, "ought to coincide, if possible, with a pause in the sense" (II, p. 124). Thus, like Watts, he invokes, but attempts to neutralize, the presence of a system of meaning that is outside, and potentially disruptive of, the sequential syntagmatic chain—and this tension emerges from the silent printed form of the poem. The full significance of Kames's rulings on this threat to linguistic balance will be examined in the following section, but for the moment it should be noted the prescriptive model of form and meaning represented the orthodoxy of eighteenth-century criticism. Watts's and Kames's judgments are echoed in the work of Joseph Priestley, Hugh Blair, and William Mitford,[11] and the premise of preserving a unitary balance between the visual format and the oral movement underlies Rice's and Walker's rewritings of blank verse. Until the emergence of Miltonic traces in the work of Wordsworth and, as chapter 5 will show, in Blake, eighteenth-century blank verse writers maintained a dutiful allegiance to the prescriptive ideals.

Consider the following lines from Watts's *Horae Lyricae* (1709):

> Read o'er the Covenant of Eternal Life
> Brought down to Men; sealed by the sacred Three
> In Heav'n, and seal'd on Earth with God's own Blood.[12]

The lines do not effect full grammatical closures, but their visual and oral identities are perfectly matched. Even the potentially daring stress reversal at "sealed by" is placed close enough to the center of the line to prevent the kind of disjunction that Watts found so disturbing in Milton's verse. The lines' shape and their internal rhythmic and grammatical structures act almost as a record of their oral performance, with the enjambment at "Life / Brought" perfectly reflecting the subordination of "Men" to the "Eternal."

These lines enact what became virtually the formal idiom of eighteenth-century blank verse, and if we consider the degree of caution with which poets handled the material of the physical line, it becomes evident that they, like their critical counterparts, were just as aware of its dangerous potential. The following is from Thomson's *Summer*:

> From these the Prospect varies. Plains immense
> Lie stretch's below, interminable Meads
> And vast Savannahs, where the wandering Eye,
> Unfixt, is in a verdant Ocean lost.
>
> (ll. 690–94)

The hesitation between "Eye" and "unfixt" is meticulously, almost anxiously, preempted by the references to the varied Prospect, "interminable Meads," and the careful establishment of "wandering" prior to its echo in "Unfixt." The disruptive effect of the visual pattern is thus neutralized by subtle warnings of the line breaks *before* they occur. Consider the following sequence from *Autumn*

> Thence expanding far,
> The huge Dusk, gradual, swallows up the Plain.

> Vanish the Woods. The dim-seen river seems
> Sullen, and slow, to rowl the misty Wave.
>
> (717–20)

The river could be nothing other than "Sullen," since the impression of vagueness, slowness, is already well established in the sequence prior to "seems"—a "dim seen" river could hardly appear to be lively or bright. Even the enjambed pattern of assonance and alliteration cannot entirely destroy the sense of there being a natural, yet carefully staged, hesitation between "seems" and "Sullen." These enjambments are not unlike Milton's,

> Season's return, but not to be returns
> Day
>
> (III, 41–42)

But they lack what Sheridan saw as the visual effect that "stops you unexpectedly, and forcibly strikes the imagination."

For the eighteenth-century blank verse poets, visual structure presented a challenge very similar to that which divided critics such as Sheridan from the prescriptive orthodoxy. But for the most part the poets chose to follow the spirit, if not the letter, of the prescriptive injunctions by using what amounted to syntactic patterns to diffuse the conflict between typography and sequence, silence and sound. Poems such as *Night Thoughts* came very close to being unrhymed couplets, and Young was lavishly praised for this by Johnson in, appropriately enough, the same *Rambler* essay in which he accused Milton of disrupting the rules of musical linearity.[13] But stylistic compromise could be more subtle than this, as Thomson demonstrates in the following sequence from *Summer*

> The dripping Rock, the Mountain's misty Top
> Swell on the Sight, and brighten with the Dawn
> Blue thro' the Dusk, the smoking Currents shine;
> And from the bladed Field the fearful Hare
> Limps, awkward: while along the Forest-glade
> The wild Deer trip, and often turning gaze
> At early Passenger. Musick awakes,
> The native voice of undissembled joy;
> And thick around the woodland hymns arise.
> Roused by the cock, the soon-clad shepherd leaves
> His mossy cottage, where with Peace he dwells;
> And from the crowded Fold, in Order drives
> His flock to taste the Verdure of the Morn.
>
> (54–66)

We should note that at line 59 a subtle but effective change in the textual and referential pattern takes place, and this is controlled by Thomson's use of the visual format. Up to that point the passage is hesitant, almost indecisive, with "misty Top / Swell," "the Dawn / Blue," and the "fearful Hare / Limps." Kames approves of this technique: "when in a sentence the substantive takes the lead, we know not that the action is to follow; and as rest must precede the commencement of motion, this interval is a proper opportunity for a pause" (II, p. 132). He approves because a visual space between rest and motion does not *disrupt* the sequential pattern of meaning—it merely controls the pace. Thomson, too, seems to be aware of the need to preserve sequence outside visual juxtaposition because to quicken the pace of this description of a landscape coming to life he reverses the pattern and places verbs before the line ending—"awakes / The native joy," "leaves / His mossy cottage," "drives / His flock." The whole texture of the verse is transformed from the passive to the active, but at each stage in this process the reader, both as silent peruser and listener, is carefully warned of changes about to take place. It is not surprising that the "*fearful* Hare / Limps," that the "*soon clad* shepherd leaves / His mossy cottage," or that from the "*crowded Fold*" he "drives / His flock": the syntax of the passage is carefully sown with preemptive clues to the eventual effect of the visual breaks. If we are to speak of the prosody of these lines we must accept that as much attention is given to synchronizing the syntactic sequence with the visual identity of the lines as is given to their internal rhythmic structure. Traditional prosodic studies of unrhymed, enjambed verse are obviously restricted by their emphasis only on *internal* metrical structure of the line, because it is the line itself as an extra grammatical component that exerts a crucial influence upon the complex texture of the verse.

Thomson's subtlety and caution are themselves evidence that an awareness of the power of the silent printed text reached beyond the uncreative anxieties of the prescriptive critics. But it is in the meticulous injunctions of Kames that we find the most vivid, if unintended, correspondences with the visualist ideas of Sheridan, and more significantly, with the poetic practices and strategies of reading of the twentieth century.

Silence, Criticism, and Literary History

Kames found that the Miltonic disturbances of formal balance constituted a threat to the transparency of language. He will, he says, "unfold some latent principles, that tend to regulate our taste even where we are scarce sensible of them" (II, p. 129), and he goes on to assimilate prosodic analysis to the methods of associative psychology.

The most intimate of grammatical components, he says, are the adjective and substantive. A "quality cannot exist independent of a subject; nor are they separable even in imagination, because they make parts of the same idea: and for that reason, with respect to melody as well as sense, it must be disagreeable to bestow upon the adjective a sort of independent existence by interjecting a pause between it and its substantive" (II, p. 129). Milton's "divine / Historian" would seem to be a prime example of this fault, and beneath the casuistic precision of Kames's rulings on practically every grammatical relationship there is a deeper implication. By "pause" he does not mean grammatical pause, since there clearly is not one between "divine / Historian" or "cold / Climate." The only reason to acknowledge the existence of a pause is in the recognition of the spatial, typographic separation of words as a kind of metagrammar that is unique to the printed poem; a system, moreover, that is capable of challenging the conventional relationship between individual units of meaning. The poetic line is implicitly acknowledged as a unit of evocative logic that stands outside the abstract notions of meter and syntax: "Colour, for example, cannot be conceived independent of the surface coloured" (II, p. 130). Kames's anxiety about language coming adrift from things could in this case be fueled by lines such as the following from *Paradise Lost:*

> Now in loose garlands thick thrown off the bright
> Pavement
>
> (III, 362–63)

Sheridan, as if in direct response to Kames, defended this construction:

> now here by finishing the verse with the adjective *bright*, it is separated from its substantive *pavement*, contrary to the genius of our tongue. And yet in the right manner of repeating it, there appears to be no defect, but rather the idea seems to acquire new force from this very circumstance. . . . But this separation in point of sound between the quality and its subject, gives time for the quality to make a stronger impression on us; and therefore should never be used, but when the poet means that the quality not the subject, should be the principal idea; which is the case in the above instance; where the

intention of the poet is, to fix our thoughts not on the pavement itself, but on the brightness of the pavement. (II, pp. 257–58)

Similar textual relations are disclosed from "cold / Climate," "sweet / Recess," and "pure / Intelligence."

Sheridan eventually abandoned the hope of transferring the effect of the visual configuration to oral performance, and Kames's discussion of the cognitive response to linguistic divisions also shifts the focus back again to the silent interpretive realm.

(It is) possible to take the action to pieces and to consider it first with relation to the agent, and next with relation to the patient. But after all, so intimately connected are the parts of the thought, that it requires an effort to make a separation even for a moment: the subtilising to such a degree is not agreeable, especially in works of the imagination. (II, p. 133)

Kames clearly regards Sheridan's technique of reading as dangerously subversive of the orderly, sequential structure of language, but it is equally clear that he is aware of the existence of this technique. The eighteenth-century critical agenda extends much further into considerations of formal ontology and the attendant cognitive processes than traditional histories of prosody would have us believe. Debates on whether this or that iambic sequence satisfies a priori expectations of metricality seemed to have receded into the background, and the more challenging questions of what happens when our eye makes contact with the juxtapositions of visible language had become the vital issue. In post-1800 prosody the emphasis has shifted to the internal composition of the line, and the ontological problems of whether it actually exists and, if it does, what effect it has upon meaning have been effectively marginalized by literary historians such as Fussell and Omond. But for a perfect demonstration that Sheridan's active participation in the spatial resonances of "bright / pavement" and Kames's anxious contemplation of linguistic disorder are neither personal eccentricities nor accidents of history, we should examine John Hollander's analysis of William Carlos Williams's "The Red Wheelbarrow."

> so much depends
> upon
>
> a red wheel
> barrow

Shape and Identity

> glazed with rain
> water
>
> beside the white
> chickens

Hollander:

> the line termini cut the words "wheelbarrow" and "rainwater" into their constituents, without the use of hyphenation to warn that the first noun is part of a compound, *with the implication that they are phenomenological constituents as well*. The wheel plus the barrow equals the wheelbarrow, and in the freshness of the light after the rain (it is the kind of light which the poem is about, although never mentioned directly), things seem to lose their compounded properties. (*Vision and Resonance*, p. 111)

Hollander has finally demolished his own conception of the visual format as "the mask through which the voice sounds," because his interaction with the spatial components of the poem tells us that it is "about" something that it never mentions. It is impossible to imagine how his reading of these lines could be based upon an oral performance, and it would seem that Milton's and Wordsworth's use of the visual perspective to disrupt and intensify the linear movement of the verse has become the single structural element of this verse: the notion of language as a temporal sequence of units whose grammatical interactions coordinate meaning has been replaced by the process of interaction itself. It is almost as though Isaac Watts's list of Miltonic offenses has been, literally, detached from its broader syntactic context and offered for the occular contemplation of the reader.

> render thee, divine
> Historian
>
> the grey
> Dawn
>
> or cold
> Climate.

These visual effects are from three different books of *Paradise Lost*, but the gaps between them, their absence from context, can easily be remedied by a readerly strategy very similar to that employed by Hollander and Sheridan. One might suggest that the "divine / Historian" has clearly been granted the power to render the phenomenological constituents of a "grey dawn" and a "cold climate."

With Milton and Wordsworth, the points at which the visual format interrupts the movement of syntax act as pivots for changes in context and rhythmic pattern. But with the modern format it is the "voice" of the reader that responds to the intensifications of meaning to *provide* the broader context. The eighteenth-century critics' responses to *Paradise Lost* establish the printed text as the entry point for the disclosure of textual depth and intensity, but the interaction between Williams's text and Hollander points us toward a poetic in which shape replaces sequence as a structural determinant.

The question to be asked is if there is a productive rather than merely coincidental relation between these two patterns of writing and reading. Traditional prosodic opinion would have us believe that the iambic pentameter is the principle structural component of poems such as *Paradise Lost* and *Tintern Abbey* and that to claim that there are close textual correspondences between Williams's sparse, disconnected fragments and the form that has maintained its identity as the backbone of prosodic tradition would be absurd. But consider what is the single, unifying factor in the readings of Woodford, Rice, Sheridan, Walker, Young . . . ? The eye of the reader is drawn not to a mathematical sequence of roughly iambic syllables, but to the way in which the visual isolation of these units establishes their metrical identity and, more significantly, invites the reader to contemplate the striking configurations of the visual text. These eighteenth-century critics agreed that the use of the pentameter in enjambed, unrhymed poetry was a concession to outdated convention: for Sheridan this form is preserved only by its visual status, and for Walker and Rice a similar recognition led them to dispense with such a restraint to true rhythmic movement. The common denominator is the effect of the visual text, and it is a short step from such awareness to the replacement of the traditional prosodic sequence by a form that explicitly centralizes the visual format as its key structural component. It would be a century and a half before poetry took such a step, but we should be aware that the conditions for doing so were in no sense the direct consequences of historical and aesthetic circumstances. Silent poetics transcends these, and as the final section on "The Modern Perspective" will show, the eighteenth-century visualist readers provide us with an illuminating point of comparison for the examination of twentieth-century verse.

These anticipations of poetic history also have serious implications for criticism. The techniques of "close reading" developed by the New Critics allow the critical reader to anatomize the poem, to treat its printed format as a map of its structural and thematic landscape. This process of clinical intervention allows the critic to describe, in technical terms, how form produces meaning while maintaining the assumption that these dissected nuances will be reassembled in an oral reading—an analogy might be drawn between a close-reader and a film critic who is able to stop the sequence in order to make a specific point about how the sequence influences the viewer's understanding. And this can effectively be regarded as the theoretical premise of Ricks, Davie, and Hollander. But Sheridan and others were drawn to a form of close reading that is in itself an aesthetic experience, with the implication that certain effects can only operate silently within the spaces of the printed text and in opposition to the oral, sequential movement of the poem. This sense of the verse, and the poet, preempting and displacing the protocols of critical reading also becomes evident in a number of modern poems, and this will be considered in Part Three.

PART TWO
Sound

5

The Voice of Form

It has already become clear that the work of critics such as John Rice and John Walker presents an alternative model of form and interpretation to that offered by silent readers such as Sheridan. Rice and Walker agreed that there was a poetic structure that transcended the outdated visual format of the pentameter, and as this chapter will show, their rewritings of *Paradise Lost* represent one element of a much broader network of investigative techniques and creative hypotheses. All of these were based upon the traditional notion of poetry as a spoken medium, but their conclusions often contrast very sharply with what we still understand to be the tradition of pre-twentieth-century poetic form.

John Dennis

The first English critic to promote unstructured expressionism as a determinant of verse structure was John Dennis. In the preface to *Britannia Triumphans* (1704) he engages with the contemporary debate on whether the unrhymed precedent, set by Milton, can be regarded as an appropriate verse form for the English heroic or epic poem. He points out that Dryden and Roscommon, though users of rhyme, had come to be as sceptical of its aesthetic value as were Milton and himself, and that he, Dennis, will furnish some "entirely new arguments why Rime must of Necessity debase the Majesty and weaken the Spirit of the greater Poetry."

> The sentiments in Poetry create the Spirit, or the Passion, which are but two Words for the same thing; and the Spirit or Passion produces the Expression, and begets the Harmony. Now 'tis the Expression which shews the Spirit, and 'tis the Harmony which causes it to make its utmost Impression. And when all these things are adjusted, when the Sentiments are adapted to the subject, the Spirit or Passion in a just Degree to the Sentiments, and the Harmony and the Expres-

sion to the particular kind and Degree of Spirit or Passion, when then the result of all this is what the Men of Art call Perfection or the Truth of Nature. (Hooker, I, p. 375)

There is, it seems, an innate sense of proportion in the poet that modulates and controls the relationship between the three stages of poetic creation: the passion; the expression, and the harmony. The first two terms represent the stage at which prelinguistic inspiration metamorphoses into language, and the result, according to Dennis, represents the poetic equivalent of the word-idea theory expressed in logical terms by Thomas Sprat and John Wilkins—a form of structural transparency.

The use of rhyme in this poetic process "destroys its Beauty, and the greater part of its Force; makes it less strong, less sounding, less significant, and weakens the Spirit, and sets the Sentiment in a false Light." This is a radically different conception of the function of poetic form from that proposed by the most respected theorist of the period, Dryden. The whole mechanism of the fancy and the judgment, balanced by rhyme, is abandoned in favor of a covenant of trust that rests upon the purity and intensity of the passion in determining its own formal linguistic expression—its harmony.

From the point of view of the reader, Dennis's model of creativity predicates a different set of expectations from those governing Dryden's and, perhaps more significantly, Woodford's theories. Dryden's promotion of rhyme as a restraint to the lawlessness of the imagination is closely related to his belief that without an aural signal the English line, and by implication, the formal identity of the poem, would be lost. Woodford elaborated upon this concept of aesthetic-structural order to construct a double axis of appreciation for the reader. According to Woodford, to read what is definable as a poem we must be able to discern a structural element that stands outside and organizes the rhythmic and syntactic movement of the verse: a function that should be performed by rhyme, but which can, in some circumstances, depend upon the visual identity of the line. Woodford called this relation between contingent rhythm and arbitrary form "artifice." Dennis sets out to attack the core of this argument.

In the structural equation of "Number, Measure, Cadence, and Rime," rhyme is the superfluous element since its arbitrary nature restricts and limits the more organic concept of harmony. "Rime consisting of Unisons can have no Harmony in itself, and being independent of Numbers, Cadence and Measure can never promote the Harmony which they produce" (Hooker I, p. 377). This notion of rhyme as a restrictive concession to form will be dealt with more fully in the following chapter, but for the moment let us consider the implications of Dennis's proposition. His idea of the relationship between unrhymed meter and language is that of a flexible and contingent coexistence, where the only criterion of order seems to be that the disposition of rhythm and pause should produce an aesthetic effect appropriate to the intensity of the passion. So the conventional belief in the aural identification of the line as a token of the poem's formal identity is abandoned. Dennis does not challenge Dryden's concept of accentual meter as in itself incapable of constructing discrete, lineal structures outside syntax; instead he suggests that these structures might be infinitely variable in length and composition.

We have only to compare De Quincey's, "the rhythmus is both a cause of impassioned feeling, an ally to such feeling, and a natural effect of it" with Dennis's "the spirit or Passion produces the Expression and begets the Harmony" to recognize the fingerprint of preromanticism, and we might even cite a correspondence between Dennis's expressionist model and Wordsworth's "spontaneous overflow of powerful feelings." But as I shall show, practice lagged far behind theory, and it would be two centuries before Dennis's recognition of the potential for the "natural slide" of harmony found its full creative manifestation.

There was a substantial number of eighteenth-century critics who drew out the implications of Dennis's expressionist model into, in some cases, a manifesto for free verse, and the thread of unity that runs through this tradition places it in direct opposition to the work of the critics dealt with in Part One on "Silence." For the latter, the printed poem functioned as a subtle, refractory medium in the communicative circuit between poet and reader: it drew in the silent reader as a participant in the interplay between form and meaning, but it is evident that Dennis's concept of composition and appreciation shifts the priority back to the classical ideal of poetic discourse as one person literally speaking to another.

Dennis's hypothetical conception of prosodic freedom lacked any precise critical illustration of how the new form of harmonized structure could be realized, and it was not until the mid-eighteenth century that the implications of his model were pursued in any detail. The delay was due to a reluctance among critics to contemplate accentual form as productive of structures which might finally demolish classical expectations of regularity in the English line.

Milton's unrhymed pentameter presented a challenge: the structural unity that it offered to the eye of the reader could easily be lost to the ear.

Some critics, such as William Coward (1709), Henry Pemberton (1738), John Mason (1749), and John Foster (1762)[1] attempted to cope with the tension between sight and sound by claiming that rhythmic, mostly iambic, structures traced out corresponding patterns of quantitative values. Such readings were patently absurd, but their existence reflected the degree of anxiety that attended the notion of rhythmic irregularity. In two of the most popular grammar books of the period, John Brightland's *A Grammar Book of the English tongue* (1711) and Thomas Dilworth's *A New Guide to the English Tongue* (1740),[2] the terms "long," "short," "quantity," and "accent" become confusingly interchangeable, not because of the interpretive incompetence of the authors, but because of their reluctance to separate the contingent movement of accentual meter from the idealized order of classical form. Brightland was honest enough to recognize the difficulty of constructing an abstract grammar of form based upon accent. It is "an Art of which we have little use, and know less, in the English Tongue; nor are we likely to improve our knowledge in this Particular, unless the Art of *Delivery* or *Utterance*, were a little more study'd" (p. 131). This is a remarkably perceptive comment because as the interpretive perspective began to shift away from expectations of formal coherence and toward the empirical evidence of spoken delivery, there was a correspondent change in the conception of what English verse form actually is.

Samuel Say

The first attempt to effectively rewrite the rules and expectations of English poetic form was made by Samuel Say.

Say's two essays on prosody were published with his *Poems on Several Occasions* in 1745 but might have been written some years earlier, since the volume was his only publication and is, in effect, his Collected Poetry and Prose. He was educated at one of the better dissenting academies, Thomas Rowe's in Newington Green, and three his two closest friends were John Hughes and

Isaac Watts.³ All three were to publish works on poetic form, and in the cases of Say and Watts, dissent seems to have played a significant part in their approaches to poetic structure. Watts became an endearingly eccentric member of the Prescriptive tendency, and Say's essay was later to be influential upon the more revolutionary propositions of Steele and Walker.

Say suggests, in the manner of Dennis, that rhyme is superfluous to English poetry. To drive this point home he claims that MIlton himself distinguishes between "rhime," which is derivative of "rhythmus" or the metrical organization of words, and "rime," which is derived from *runes,* and denotes the "*Jingling Sound of like Endings;* and so he spells it [rime] five times in the *later* Copies of the First Edition of *Paradise Lost,* added at the request of the Bookseller and again in the SECOND. But his own Immortal Poem is written properly in RHYME as it stands fairly printed in all Three First Editions of PARADISE LOST, B.i. Ver 16" (p. 117). Say contends that "RHYME" in this latter sense means the "variety of Power of Numbers" without, of course, "rime."⁴

His prosodic thesis seems, superficially, to depend upon the conflationist notion of quantity equalling accentual pattern, but he introduces a subtle adjustment to the equation: Each line "rhymes, that is, *corresponds* and answers to the others in Times that are Proportional and nearly Equal, tho' the Movements are otherwise entirely different" (p. 121). He is clearly reluctant to dismiss the notion of an English line that has a metrical identity beyond its reliance upon syntactic and aural signals, but he is also aware that the structural effect of syntax must be taken into account.

> Pleasēd thŏu / shălt hēar / aňd lĕarn / the Sē/crēet Pōwer
> Of Hár/moňy / iň Tōnes / aňd Núm / bĕrs hít
> Bў Vōice / ŏr Hānd—

In the First of these Movements the Voice dwells with pleasure on the First Syllable, and runs off hastily from the Second . . . the Four Syllables which begin the Next Line are ALL Naturally short; but the Voice rises on the Second and Distinguishes it by a Sharper Accent. (p. 102)

His scansion symbols reflect his perceptive yet ambivalent acknowledgment of English as a melting pot of quantity and lexical and rhetorical stress: is a short, but not always unstressed syllable;   is a long and usually stressed syllable; / is a syllable either long or short, but distinguished from the others by the degree of emphasis given to it as a central part of a syntactic movement.

It would require a mathematician to justify this notation as indicative of a kind of isochronous balance between blank verse lines, and Say's inaccuracies are widespread, but it is in his faults that we find the key to his later influence. Consider the following lines from Milton:

> Wing'd with red Lightning and impetuous Rage
> Perhaps has spent his shafts, and ceases Now
> To bellow thro' the Vast and Boundless Deep.
>
> (p. 129)

His use of the / mark clearly acknowledges the points at which the rhythmic movement overshadows quantitative balance, but we should ask why he refrains from applying the mark to "Now" when that word could be argued to have as much rhetorical emphasis as "shafts" and "Vast"? Had he done so he would have destroyed the vestigial ideal of the line as an autonomous structure outside the broader rhythmic movement of syntax, and we should note that he consistently deafens himself to such imbalances and contrives rarely to place the major rhetorical stress close to what Wordsworth saw as the precipice of the typographic line ending. But he could never remain entirely immune from the interlineal effects of Miltonic verse, and at one point he is obliged to acknowledge the disappearance of the pentameter.

> [W]here not STRENGTH, but SWEETNESS OF SOUND is requir'd, and Numbers that lull and enchant the Mind, the Same Strong or Pure *Iambics* are industriously avoided, and exchang'd for such other Movements, as Steal along more Soft and Silent, as far as the Law of *Iambic* Measures will admit, and which may seem to resemble the Music of the Spheres, the Music rather of Heav'n itself, where
>
> > Harmony
> > So Smoothes her Charming Tones, that God's own Ear
> > Listens delighted
>
> (p. 126)

It is at this point that we become aware of Say's work as a point of departure for two traditions of eighteenth-century criticism. It is clear that Kenrick borrowed both the quotation and Say's critical language to illustrate his own perception of silent poetics, but it is by no means certain that Say's reference to measures that "Steal along more Soft and Silent" is intended to predicate the notion of occular balance between typography and movement. Indeed, his placing of the most emphatic scansion marks at "Harmony" and "Listens" seems to diminish the identity of the intervening typography of the line. It may be that in this one instance he recognizes that it is the "Law of Iambic Measures" that is silenced. It is in the work of Joshua Steele that we find the most complex extension of Say's system of notation—to the extent that the conventions of the foot and the pentameter become formal irrelevances.

Joshua Steele

Steele's *Prosodia Rationalis: or an Essay Towards Establishing the Melody and Measure of Speech, to be Expressed and Perpetuated by Peculiar Symbols* was first published in 1775,[5] the same year as Sheridan's *Lectures on the Art of Reading*. This is a peculiar coincidence because each work epitomizes the two divergent traditions of formal analysis.

Sheridan's system of accentual/quantitative notation is an extended version of Say's, with more emphasis given to the fact that stress movements must supersede quantitative values, but the most crucial element of his technique is his concept of the pause of suspension. This enabled him to concentrate upon metrical tensions within the typographic line, while also allowing him to disclose how the visual format can throw subtle elements of textual meaning into sharper focus. Sheridan represented a virtual surrender to the power of the written text, but Steele, as we shall see, attempted to bring about its elimination as anything other than a purely transparent medium.

Prosodia Rationalis is structured almost as a debate between Steele and his friend Lord Monboddo, with the former using extracts from Monboddo's published work and letters as starting points for his own more extended propositions. To a certain degree, Monboddo's presence as the representative of the traditional expectations of lineal closure and the bland relativity of unstress/stress values is exploited by Steele as a point of contrast with the more revolutionary aspects of his own method. The effect is rather like an invitation to compare the innovative linguistics of the 1956 *Kenyon Review* symposium with the technique of George Saintsbury.

The following is Steele's own explanation of his apparatus of Peculiar Symbols:

1st ACCENT. ACUTE ∕ grave ∖ , or both combined ⌒ , in avariety of circumflexes.

2nd QUANTITY. Longest ⎤ , long ⌉ , short ⊤ , shortest | .

3rdly PAUSE or *silence*. Semibrief rest | , minim rest — , crochet rest ⌐ , quaver rest ⌐⎤ .

4thly EMPHASIS or *Cadence*. Heavy △ , light ˙ ˙ , lightest ˙ ˙ ,

5thly Force or *quality of sound*. Loud ℮ , louder ℮℮, soft ℈ , softer ℈℈. Swelling or increasing in loudness ⋀⋀⋀ , decreasing in loudness or dying away ⋀⋀⋀ , Loudness uniformly continued ⋀⋀⋀ . (p24)

In Steele's application of this apparatus to the opening three lines of *Paradise Lost* we find the conventional printed poem transformed into a diagram of its aural identity.

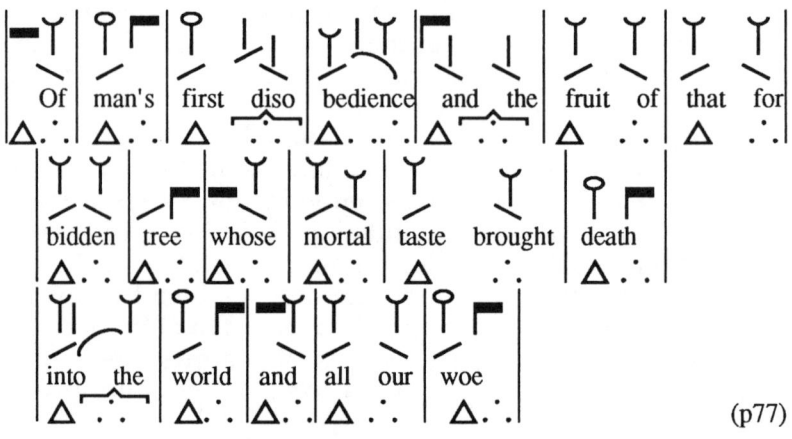

(p77)

Whatever our opinion upon the accuracy of Steele's interpretive technique, we must accept that he succeeds in exposing a number of tacit assumptions about the poem on the page that we, in the later twentieth century, still often take for granted. It is difficult to determine precisely how the cognitive function of recognizing a poem as a printed format influences the complex procedure of understanding its effects and reading it aloud, but if we are to accept the traditional precept of verse as an aural medium, with its printed form as a record or a guide to performance, then we must also accept that the logical outcome of such beliefs is Steele's rejection of the poem in lines in favor of a quasi-musical format, where written language and symbols are predicates of its ideal aural presence. But the implications of such a procedure for the related acceptance of the intrinsic complexity of poetic writing are somewhat disturbing.

With Sheridan it became clear that the interpreter of printed poetry maintained an active role in the disclosure and resolution of divergent and often conflicting patterns of form and meaning. In Steele's model the reader is effectively removed from this position and becomes the recipient of structures and patterns that are only temporarily frozen at their printed form. It became clear in Part One that instances of formal complexity and counterpoint arose from the capacity of the printed text to contain and discharge different voices, and a comparison of the interpretations of these opening lines by Walker, Sheridan, and Hollander was sufficient evidence of this multiple presence, but the precision and sophistication of Steele's method effectively reduces the same lines to one movement and one meaning.

Such a concept of interpretation might seem to us to be a dogmatic manifestation of intentionalism, and Steele finds himself facing this unendearing possibility after comparing his "score" of Hamlet's "To be or not to be" soliloquy with a slightly different performance of this by Garrick. Garrick asks him:

> Supposing a speech was noted according to these rules, in the manner he spoke it, whether any other person, by the help of these notes, could pronounce his words in the same tone and manner exactly as he did. (p. 54)

Garrick the professional interpreter is clearly dismayed by the possibility that poetic variation could be effectively limited by the precise imperatives of musical symbols. Steele's answer is subtle, evasive, but oddly informative.

Suppose a first rate musician had written down a piece of music, which he had played exquisitely well on an exceeding fine tuned violin; another performer with an ordinary fiddle might undoubtedly play every note the same as the great master, though perhaps with less ease and elegance of expression; but not withstanding his correctness in the same tone and manner, nothing could prevent the audience from perceiving that the natural tone of his instrument was execrable. (p. 54)

To fully understand Steele's conception of poetic interpretation we must decode his analogy: the musician/composer with the finely tuned violin represents the perfect interplay of poet and reader, but the "other performer" with the "ordinary fiddle" represents what could happen to the poem when it is detached from its moment of composition and becomes prey to misinterpretation and poor performance. Clearly the poem cannot be preserved forever in its original oral form, and the dangers of misinterpretation are intensified by its existence as a silent printed text. Steele's objective with his complex system of "peculiar symbols" was to minimize the potential for interpretive variation when the reader's first experience of the poem is as words on the page. He regarded the traditional printed form of the unrhymed pentameter as an arbitrary point of intervention between the true "rhythmus" of the verse and the interpretive faculty of the reader. "If it were not for the rhymes in modern poetry, the ear would never discover the ends of verses, when properly pronounced . . . the rhythmus is continued to the end of the piece; and by that continuance every *pause* is measured" (p. 162).

Steele has succeeded in disclosing a peculiar contradiction between what are usually regarded as parallel coordinates in the interpretation of poetry, because if we regard the discharge of multiple patterns of form and meaning as a uniquely, and some would say definitively, poetic effect, are we compromising both the autonomy and the individuality of the poet's intention? Did the poet intend to mean two things at the same time? Steele claims that multiple patterns and effects are evidence of misreading, and his belief in the single oral pattern as providing direct access to the poet's original moment of composition leads him into a discourse on poetic language as the most perfect realization of prelinguistic feeling. At the beginning of the *Prosodia* he examines what he believes to be the origins of the formal sturcture of poetry: "Our breathing, the beating of our pulse, and our movement in walking, make the division of time by pointed and regular *cadences*, familiar and natural to us" (p. 20). He goes on to extend this natural analogy to include the notion of counterpoint between the movement of a man and that of his horse, and the concept of rhythmic irregularity as the equivalent of the pacing of a lame man or progress over rough ground. His explanation of how the rhythmic and synchronic pulsations of the natural world can be accommodated within a medium based upon the arbitrary balance of individual integers and grammatical structures involves a practice that might seem to belong to the ethos of poststructuralism. The following is his explanation of why his scansion of the opening of *Paradise Lost* must effectively demolish the iambic, linear pattern in favor of a system that follows the spontaneities of sound and sense.

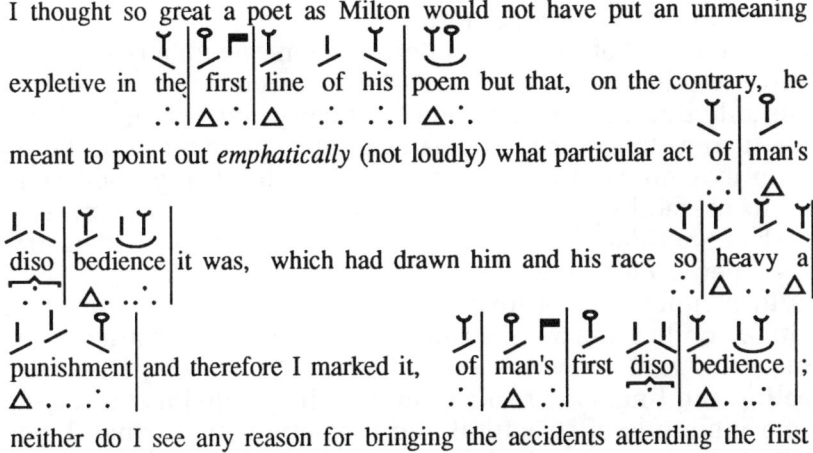

neither do I see any reason for bringing the accidents attending the first line of a distich to tally numerically with those of the second. (p167)

Steele's habit of scanning his own writing occurs almost at random and without warning throughout the book. He does not excuse or explain the practice, but we must assume that it is intended as a continual reminder that the rhythmus and the poetic cadence are naturally part of our expressive faculty, and that it is the intensification of such random movements that constitutes the structure of poetry—he states that "I consider our sense of *rhythmus* to be more *instinctive* than *rational*" (p. 78). At one point he considers the potential for a form of tension between the artifice or structure of language and the natural music of poetic form and offers the analogy of a meeting between a brilliant but illiterate musician and a sophisticated practitioner of the established conventions.

> This then is the state of the art between the two men: we will suppose the ignorant player to be the best performer, but that he conceives not the possibility of reducing his musical ideas to rules of art, or of communicating them to others by words or writing; while the other by setting down all the wild notes of the unlettered man, convinces even him that the rules existed although he knew them not. (p158)

Thus the rules of poetic form are not abstract criteria, but self-defining patterns and structures that are both produced and coordinated by the natural rhythms of the spoken utterance. Writing is an unfortunate necessity, which should record, rather than impose upon, the original form.

This concept of form and interpretation sets up a radical alternative to what might be regarded as a number of complicit and mutually limiting developments in poetry and criticism. Categories such as traditional foot patterns and the identity of the line as an extragrammatical component are, in an important sense, points of stability for the reader, and we have only to examine the work of Sheridan, Ricks, and Hollander to see how written structure operates as a framework upon which the critic/reader can build complexities of texture and meaning. Thus we are faced with a conflict: the aural structure can transcend abstract formal categories and convey the original symbiosis of prelinguistic feeling and linguistic realization, but the printed text can generate a plenitude of structural and thematic patterns that depend upon the silent reader's ability to impose coherence.

During his lengthy attack on Sheridan's visualist concept of the pause of suspension, John Walker states the case for the poet.

> If the author has so united to preceding and following lines in verse as to make them real prose, why is a reader to do that which his author has neglected to do, and indeed seems to have forbidden by the very nature of the composition. (*Elements of Elocution* II, p. 207)

And this echoes John Rice's declarations that unrhymed verse depends "very little, in any Case, on its mechanical division into lines, consisting of a certain Number of Syllables . . . the Melody of the Verse, [depends] on the Facility with which such Syllables succeed each other" (p. 181).

Comparisons

These statements effectively invalidate traditional notions of meter and lineation and move the structural priority away from what Fish was to eventually regard as the reader's "appropriation of the line ending" and toward what Steele regarded as the poet's "instinctive" sense of "rhythmus."

It might be useful, at this point, to consider if the work of these critics represents anything more significant than a rather eccentric backwater of literary history. To make such a judgment it is necessary to compare their observations with some of the more recent developments in linguistic metrics. Central to Trager's and Smith's work was their "discovery" that intonational patterns in English involve a relative scale of values, in which abstract distinctions between what is and what is not stressed virtually disappear.[6] An iambic pattern thus becomes a series of syllables whose metrical identity is defined by their contiguous relations and not by an abstract binary distinction. It would, for instance, be possible for a syllable that was in traditional terms unstressed because it falls between two syllables of higher accentual value, to be of greater rhetorical weight than a syllable that occupies a stressed position in another part of the line. Some of the most influential developments of this model have emerged in Morris Halle's and Samuel Keyser's *English Stress: Its Form Its Growth and Its Role in Verse* (1971) and in two important essays by Paul Kiparsky, "Stress, Syntax and Metre" (1975) and "The Rhythmic Structure of English Verse" (1977). Halle and Keyser established "correspondence rules" for comparing the abstract pattern of an iambic pentameter with the more varied relations that emerge from the confluence of lexical structure, syntactic movement, and rhetorical positioning, and Kiparsky elaborated upon this system to locate what he calls "matches" and "mismatches" as a guide to points at which the iambic sequence is actually disrupted.

Their replacement of abstract metrical formulae with a more sensitive methodology was clearly preempted by Say and Steele. But there the resemblance ends, because the modern critics at no point explore the implications of their discoveries for the identity of the traditional poetic line. Indeed, their method of analysis is predicated upon the existence of the line as a linguistic fact.

For instance, in Kiparsky's 1975 essay he considers individual lines from Wyatt, Shakespeare, Pope, and Wordsworth and compares and contrasts their internal rhythmic variations, but he does not state whether these lines rhyme or whether their internal composition is affected by the broader interlineal pattern. For an eighteenth-century critic, such an approach would have to be qualified by an engagement with the metrical function of rhyme and closure, and a statement of how and why English metrical patterns should be restricted to, as Rice put it, the "mechanical division of lines, consisting of a certain number of Syllables." At one point in the essay, Kiparsky briefly considers a number of line breaks of the adjective/noun type from *Paradise Lost* and states: "Milton allows lines to end in the middle of a phrase." But if we recall Walker's question of "why is a reader to do that which his author has neglected to do, and indeed seems to have forbidden by the very nature of the composition?" we find ourselves rewriting the modern critic, as "*Kiparsky* allows lines to end in the middle of a phrase."

For the modern critics, the intriguing questions of whether the line itself is compromised by broader metrical patterns and of whether its existence depends upon a complex process of visualist reading have ceased to be asked. There are several reasons for this. First, the hypothesis of free verse, toward which Steele, Rice, and Walker found that their readings led them, did not achieve full creative realization until the twentieth century. Thus the debate on what the poetic line actually is and how our a priori conceptions of form might cloud our appreciation of its poetic function was revived, but only in relation to verse that was explicitly and radically nontraditional.

The importance of the eighteenth-century critics rests in their offer to us of a new perspective on the distinction between modernist and premodernist verse. Kiparsky might regard Shakespeare, Milton, and Pope as united in their allegiance to the tradition of the pentameter, but for the eighteenth-century critics they raised the vision of radically distinct forms of poetic writing. Kiparsky did not consider the full implications of whether the Miltonic pentameter destroys its own identity, because precedents for such manifestations of formal irregularity had already been set by the modernists. The eighteenth-century critics establish patterns of writing and reading that preempt modernism and are inscribed within certain already very radical diversities that the conceptions and terminology of the traditional line can only obscure.

At the end of his 1977 essay, Kiparsky considers some of the questions raised by the new linguistics of meter, including: "What esthetic ends are served by the formal patterns that I have tried to uncover here?" He did not, of course, mean that it might be possible to discover the origins of a new form of writing in Milton; this already existed in free verse and was fully documented. But in the eighteenth century such "esthetic ends" were still intriguing possibilities.

Walker, Rice, and Saussurean Prosody

John Walker says in the preface to *Element of Elocution* that "while I was engaged in the present undertaking, I met with a work called *Prosodia Rationalis*. This ingenious treatise undertakes to reduce speaking sounds to such rules as shall enable a person to imitate the notes of a speaker, as closely as he can follow him in singing" (I, p. xi). It has already been shown how Steele's conception of stress patterns led him to suggest that poems should be printed not in lines, but as a kind of musical score. Walker adjusted Steele's complex system of notation to his own definition of a cadence as the smallest divisible syntactic group in which there is one major or emphatic stress. The result of Walker's concept can be seen in his rewriting of a relatively regular couplet from Pope.

> Such plays alone, should please a British ear,
> As Cato's self had not disdain'd to hear

Here we shall find the word *plays* is pronounced like an unaccented syllable of the word *such; should* of *please; a* and *ear* of *British; As* of *Cato's; had* of *not;* and *to,* of *hear.* If, therefore, we were to arrange the unaccented words with the accented ones as if they were one word, we should present to the eye the same union which is actually made by the ear.

> Suchplays / alone / shouldplease / abritishear
> AsCato's / self / hadnot / disdain'd / tohear
> (*The Melody of Speaking,* pp. 12–13)

Walker's technique is based upon conceptions of form very similar to those of the modern linguistic prosodists. Kiparsky erected diagrams of the complex architectonics of weak-strong patterns, but Walker deals with the same realization of lexical-syntactic tension by visually isolating cadence groups that are defined by the dominance of what Halle and Keyser call the "stress maximum," or the moment at which one point of emphasis effectively organizes its surrounding movements. The difference between Walker's and the modern prosodists' methods is that the latter maintain a belief in the tension or "correspondence" between the surface structure and the traditional unstress/stress pattern of the iambic line, but Walker completely abandons any concession to traditional, classically based concepts of foot and line composition. The structural damage done to the closed couplet by such analysis is slight since there is always the natural sense of completion engendered by rhyme to establish the line as a discrete unit. But for unrhymed verse, where isolated cadences often cross line boundaries, the implications are more serious. Walker, and Rice, found a solution to this problem by reprinting unrhymed cadences in accordance with their assumed "union made by the ear."

Some of the results of these typographic enterprises are even more striking to us, in our postmodernist ethos, than they were to Walker's contemporaries. Consider the following extract from his rewritings of Milton:

> I thence invoke thy aid to my adven'trous song,
> That with no middle flight intends to soar
> Above the Aonian mount,
> While it pursues
> Things
> Unattempted yet in prose or rhyme
> (*Rhetorical Grammar*, p. 344)

In his closing conjectures Kiparsky claims that, "Just the linguistics that we already can show to be implicit in the process of composing a line of blank verse would fill volumes if made explicit." Walker exposes a rather disturbing flaw in this approach, because his notion of units defined by their "union by the ear" reveal the linguistics of a "line of blank verse" to be a rather fragile concept preserved only by the analytical perspective of the eye. Walker sees, or rather hears, behind the artificial convention of the printed pentameter and discloses not a form of tension between surface and abstract patterns, but what was at the time a completely new conception of English verse form. One might dismiss this merger of interpretive ingenuity with creative possibility as an eccentricity, a footnote in the history of poetry and analysis, since it is clear that its influence upon criticism and poetic writing had by the beginning of the nineteenth century become insignificant. But, just as Sheridan's visualist disclosures eventually found correspondent patterns in the work of William Carlos Williams, Walker's notion of the poetic line as a flexible realization of vocal/aural units has also found its way into the modern canon. Compare Walker's Milton with this lyrical section from Eliot's *Burnt Norton.*

> Will the sunflower turn to us, will the clematis
> Stray down, bend to us; tendril and spray
> Clutch and cling?
> Chill
> Fingers of yew be curled
> Down on us?

It would not be too extravagant to claim that the gradual tightening and intensification of the syntactic and rhythmic texture, which Walker found to be best represented "by having the lines arranged out of the usual order" (p. 333), is mirrored by Eliot's method of composition. Milton's expansive invocation of the Muse, his references to the song that soars above the Aonian mount, becomes suddenly immediate in the,

> Things
> Unattempted

And in a similar way Eliot's lyrical realization of natural images becomes more strikingly personal with the,

> Chill
> Fingers of yew

Walker's rewritings were extensive and many of the results produce moments of recognition that could only be available to the reader of free verse. The following is a section from his rewriting of Othello's apology

> True, I have married her;
> The very head and front of my offending
> Hath this extent;
> No more.
> Rude I am in speech,
> And little bless'd with the set phrase of peace.
> (*Rhetorical Grammar,* p. 345)

Again, Walker's structural alterations isolate those syntactical/rhythmic groupings which, in terms of the texture of the passage, make not only the existence of unstress/stress patterns, but also the existence of the pentameter line, a misleading irrelevance compared with the balance between form and meaning offered by the new shape.

In attempting to clear the communicative circuit between poet and reader of those gratuitous elements of form that seem to encumber the shifting contours of feeling and intensity, Walker has come across what was to be a central axiom in the ex *cathedra* defenses of free verse—that an adherence to the convention of abstract form is a restriction to the poet. The extension of these eighteenth-century perceptions into the poetics of modernism will be explored more fully in the final part, but for the moment we should consider the precept that underpins these critical exercises. Walker's objective to "present to the eye the same union which is actually made by the ear" could serve as the common manifesto for the analysts of the voice. Within the context of modern linguistics, it places these critics in alliance with Saussure's belief that it is the vocal utterance that provides the point of unity for language and meaning.

Saussure was aware that the relationship between the materiality of language and its purchase upon the continuum of reality was arbitrary, but he also argued that for an understanding of the conventions and limits of this relationship we must give priority to a study of spoken language, a medium for which writing should be regarded only as a temporary record. It has already been shown that the visualist critics preempted Jacques Derrida in their recognition of writing as, in itself, the source of signification, and if we examine the following statements by John Rice we will find that the Saussurean linguistics of speech also existed long before the birth of their creator.

This is Rice on the relationship between words and meaning.

> That a fertile imagination may find some faint Traces of such a Connection, among the radical [by which he means onomatopoeic] words of most Languages, I will not dispute; it is sufficient, however, for the present Purpose, to suppose the Meaning annexed to particular Words altogether arbitrary; or rather that the Sounds adopted to express our Ideas, are purely conventional, and bear no natural Relation, Resemblance or Affinity whatever to such Ideas, or to the objects they express. (p. 193)

It has now become almost obligatory for any work that engages with modern critical theory to include a reference to Saussure's allegedly seminal statement that "in language there are only differences without positive terms," but Rice is fully aware of the arbitrary and conventional relationship between words and things/concepts, and his treatment of the distinction between speech and writing is equally prescient.

> In the same Manner, I suppose the Types or Marks of written Language to be equally arbitrary, and to have little natural Relation, Resemblance or Affinity to the ideas or objects they serve to represent.
>
> Now the Art of Reading, being in fact the Art of converting *Writing* into *Speech*, the relation which the *living Voice* bears to the *dead Letter*, becomes a very peculiar Object of the Readers Attention. (p. 194)

So it is the duty of the reader or, in literary terms the critic, to recreate the intention of the *"living Voice"* from the *"dead Letter,"* but Rice is also aware that the relation between the two media can be sown with diversions and betrayals of meaning.

> There is another Advantage also, which Writing hath over Speaking; and that is Precision. What is spoken may be more nervous and affecting, but it is never so exact and intelligible as what is written. It is the Province of the *Reader* to unite both these Advantages, and give the Energy of the living Voice to the Precision of the dead Letter. This is principally effected by a due observation of Emphasis. (p. 195)

We are back again to the problem raised in part one of how distinct, but simultaneously present, patterns of rhythm and meaning can be united in a single oral reading. Unlike his visualist contemporaries, Rice came to the conclusion that the convention of the pentameter lent too much weight to the "dead Letter," and that in order to free the Energy of the "living Voice" it must either be ignored or, for the benefit of silent readers, be typographically removed.

Rice's recognition of the difficulty of preserving the "nervous and affecting" immediacy of the "living Voice" within the organized precision of print neatly encapsulates the sense of unease with which, from Dennis onwards, these critics contemplated the mechanics, the terminology, and the apparently arbitrary nature of traditional poetic form. It has already become clear that the questions generated by these critics reach far beyond the accepted parameters of prosody. It is in Rice's insistence upon the parallel coordinates of vocal spontaneity and interpretive immediacy that we can recognize a thread that runs through what have come to be known as primitivist theories of language; and this correspondence also emerges in the work of the one poet where the theory and the poetic practice of the Voice of Form are tentatively united.

Primitivist Theory and Blake's Practice

In *Remarks on the Beauty of Poetry* (1762) Daniel Webb suggests that in rhymed poetry there is a "balance" between the conspicuous terminal signal and the medial pause, and that it is upon this, "that the monotony of the verse depends." But in blank verse, when "the second pause is sunk" there emerges a powerful system of rhythmic movements that cut across the printed pentameter (p. 9–10). In his later *Observations on the Correspondences between Poetry and Music* (1769) he preempts Steele and develops these empirical observations into a rationale on the origins of poetic form.

> Let us imagine ourselves in a state not far removed from the origin of things. Let our voice follow freely the impulse of sentiment, and run uncontrolled into the natural variations of emphasis and accent. We have traced in these variations the origin of measure. (p. 84)

M. H. Abrams has traced the origins of primitivst theories of language and poetry to such contemporaries of Webb as Hugh Blair, William Duff, and William Jones, and echoes of Duff's 1767 *Essay on Original Genius* will be found in Webb's *Observations*. Duff, without going into much detail on the geneology of modern prosody, suggests that the first poetic utterances were produced without the awareness or acknowledgment of abstract form: "excepting its own spontaneous impulse, which it obeys without control." Eighteenth-century primitivist poetics were an aesthetic byproduct of that century's elaborate and sometimes rather bizarre speculations on the origins of language. Thomas Blackwell in the *Enquiry into the Life and Writings of Homer* (1735) imagined that our ancestors, the "naked company of scrambling Mortals," emitted sounds "by Chance" in response to the "Passion, Fear, Wonder or Pain," which were no doubt part of their quotidien experience. He also argued that in their exposure to what we might regard as the extremities of life, they would "put several of these vocal Marks together, they would then seem *to* sing. . . . And hence came the ancient opinion, which appears to strange to us that 'Poetry was before Prose'."[7]

These linguistic historians share with the elocutionists a rather generalized ideal of poetic form as determined and structured by, in Dennis's term, the "Passion" behind the act of creation. What both lack is a productive model of established poetic practice upon which to build a provisional structure of the new poetic. Rice, Walker, Steele, and Webb were contemporaries of those poets that have come to be known as preromantic, but the work of Gray, Collins, and Goldsmith strayed no further toward formal experiment than in their use of the rhymed ode; and, as the following chapter will show, rhyme, even irregular rhyme, was consistently regarded as an arbitrary concession to artifice. At the other end of the prosodic spectrum there emerged such formal eccentricities as Macpherson's *Ossian*, but these were largely ignored as contributions to the new hypothetical canon. William Belsham in his essay "On English Versification" attacks the prescriptive rulings of Kames and praises the sense of "liberty" offered by blank verse, but he dismisses "such performances as Selemaque and Fingal" as veering too far towards the prosaic.[8]

Blank verse came closest to being the established form that offered the most fruitful possibilities for experiment, but we find the attention of critics returning again and again to Milton because the verse of such contemporaries as Thomson had subtly fallen into line with the rules of the prescriptive critics. And even with Miltonic structure, the early free versifiers found themselves fighting a rearguard action against critics such as Sheridan, who had succeeded in establishing the printed line as a productive instrument of meaning.

This sense of theory operating in a vacuum, of an uncertainty as to what exactly is the difference between natural, spontaneous structure, and form as an arbitrary restriction, becomes evident when we compare the statements of Webb, the theorist, and Blake, the practitioner. This is Webb on how the "constant and even tenor" of the "balanced" iambic line had become a concession to form for its own sake:

> Strong passions, the warm effusions of the soul, were never destin'd to creep through monotonous parallels; they call for a more liberal rhythmus; for movements, not balanced by rule, but measured by sentiment, and flowing in ever new yet musical proportions. (p. 113)

This is Blake considering the same problem in the introduction to *Jerusalem:*

> When this Verse was first dictated to me, I considered a Monotonous Cadence, like that used by Milton and Shakespeare and all writers of English Blank Verse, derived from the Modern bondage of rhyming, to be a necessary and indispensible part of Verse. But I soon found that in the mouth of a true Orator such monotony was not only awkward, but as much a bondage as rhyme itself. I therefore have produced a variety in every line both of cadences and of number of syllables. Every word and every letter is studied and put into its fit place; the terrific numbers are reserved for the terrific parts, the mild and gentle for the mild and gentle parts, and the prosaic for the inferior parts; all are necessary to each other. Poetry Fetter'd Fetters the Human Race.[9]

Blake's juxtaposition of "monotony," "bondage," and "Fetters" with "variety" and "cadence" echoes the elocutionists. He sees the conventions of meter and form, even in the work of Shakespeare and Milton, as inherent restrictions to the shifting contours of feeling and imagination, and we should note that he equates this point of origin with the spoken medium. His evocation of a state of tension, almost of conflict, between the conventional structures of poetry, which are stabilized and operate most excessively in print, and the unified moment of form and meaning in the vocal utterance is reflected in the development of his own prosodic practice.

Poetical Sketches (1783) contains a number of short blank verse lyrics written in the 1770s, and the relation between the pentameter and syntax in this work suggests a direct Miltonic influence. At the beginning of "To Winter" there is a particularly impressive moment.

> Oh Winter! bar thine adamantine doors:
> The north is thine; there hast thou built thy dark
> Deep founded habitation.

The feeling, as the eye pauses at the break, is of "dark" in its substantive form, a vision of "dark" as a place in itself. The effect depends upon a tension between the broader syntactic movement, which relocates dark in an adjectival position, and the visual isolation of a very different rhythmic and syntactic development, in which "dark" seems to be something "built" by Winter. We might be reminded here of Eve's hesitant recollection of the "clear / Smooth lake," and with line breaks such as the following, from "To the Evening Star" we find that typography cuts into the syntactic/rhythmic continuum in exactly the way that the prescriptive critics had ruled against.

>   Let the west wind sleep on
> The lake

"Sleep on" forever, or "Sleep on the lake"? A more orthodox version of this movement can be found in Thomson's *Winter*

> There, warm together pressed, the trooping deer
> Sleep on the new fallen snows;
> (ll. 816–17)

In the blank verse pieces in the *Poetical Sketches*, the foregrounded tension between the material identity of the line and the syntactic sequence emerges as their most striking formal component, with adjective/noun and verb/object breaks such as "bleak / Hills" and "light / Thy bright torch" offered continuously, almost as a challenge to what had become the orthodoxy of blank verse writing. Blake's experiments with this form occurred at the same time that Sheridan's visualist interpretations of Milton were generating what amounted to a public debate, but it is significant that after the 1770s, Blake never again used blank verse. It is possible that by the time he came to write his longer poems he had found that the physical existence of the line had become, as he put in the introduction to *Jerusalem*, "as much a bondage as rhyme itself." The "lines" of such later works as *Vala*, *Milton*, and *Jerusalem* are only distinguished visually from a prose format by the uncertain typesetting of their right-hand side. Their identity as formal components seem determined only by the width of the page—or, in Blake's original, by the shape of his surrounding illustrations. But there was a transitional period, in the 1790s, when he produced forms for which the only immediate precedent could be found in Walker's and Rice's reprintings. Consider, for example, this irregular sequence from "The Argument" to *The Marriage of Heaven and Hell*.

> To walk in perilous paths and drive
> The just man into barren climes.
>
> Now the sneaking serpent walks
> In mild humility,

> And the just man rages in the wilds
> Where lions roam.
>
> (15–20)

This is, in effect, the form of free verse predicated by the theorists of "The Voice." But it is almost as though the ghost of the solid pentameter lurks behind the apparently unpredictable surface.

> To walk in perilous paths, and drive the just
> Man into barren climes. Now the sneaking
> Serpent walks in mild humility, and
> The just man rages in the wilds where lions roam.

Sheridan or Hollander might comment upon how, in this form, the visual line reduces the "just / Man" to the same disturbing existential condition as the "sneaking / Serpent," and then creates a more vivid representation of his state of rage in the rhythmic continuity of the last line. It is almost as though the visual line intensifies and complements the process of uncertainty turning into clarity that is traced out by the syntax.

It is difficult to dismiss this new format and its attendant effects as coincidental, because practically all of "The Argument" masks a system of regular pentameters that betray visual intrications of meaning very similar to those found in the *Poetical Sketches*. Consider the following,

> The just man kept his course along
> The vale of death
>
> (original, 4–5)

> The just man kept his course along the vale
> Of death
>
> (hidden pentameter)

The sense of shock discharged by the visual arrangement of the second format is effectively neutralized in the original. Such correspondences exist throughout "The Argument," and it would not be too improbable to imagine that in its composition Blake first created and then destroyed the pattern with which, as the *Poetical Sketches* show, he was very familiar.

In *The First Book of Urizen*, *The Book of Ahania*, and *The Song of Los* we find a similar though more irregular deployment of unrhymed irregular iambics, usually varying in length between six and fourteen syllables, whose only principle of composition seems to be, as Walker put it, "to present to the eye the same union which is actually made by the ear." There is no sense of tension between the material existence of each line and the progress of the irregular rhythmic and syntactic groups. And it was a short step from these works of the early 1790s to his unequivocal rejection of the poetic line itself as "awkward" and a "bondage" to the "mouth of the true Orator."

Blake represents the one contemporary correspondence between the findings and hypotheses of the theorists of the voice and the development of English poetry. The only other premodernist rejection of the traditional line occurred in Whitman's preface to *Leaves of Grass* in 1855.

> The rhyme and uniformity of perfect poems show the free growth of metrical laws and bud from them as unerringly and loosely as lilacs or roses on a bush, and take shapes as compact as the shapes of chestnuts and oranges and lemons and pears and shed the perfume impalpable to form.[10]

Whitman like the later Blake abandons the line as a point of interaction between two different textual levels, but both poets represent only slight interruptions in the otherwise regular process of what, until the end of the nineteenth century, was the established formal tradition of English poetry.

Romantic Conservatism

Wordsworth and Coleridge, when compared with the writings of their immediate theoretical precursors, reveal themselves allied to the more conservative elements of eighteenth-century poetics. The one exception is in Wordsworth's enactment of an ingenious and productive compromise between the lineal techniques of Miltonic blank verse and an awareness of a Sheridanesque notion of the silent reader.

There is a certain irony in the fact that his now almost mythical definition of verse as "the spontaneous overflow of powerful feelings" is qualified by "the tendency of metre [is] to divest language in a certain degree of its reality ... an indistinct perception perpetually renewed of language closely resembling that of real life, and yet, in the circumstance of metre, differing from it so widely."[11] The second statement represents an outright dismissal of the thread of argument, running from Dennis to Walker, that metrical form should, especially in moments of "Passion," assume a shape and structure that are determined by the irregularities of the "language of real life."

In his most intense evocations of subjective experience Wordsworth drew his formal shapes from the already established repertoire of regular blank verse, rhymed odes, stanzas, and the ballad. We do not find, amidst his profusion of otherwise fractured conventions, the form of unfettered rhythmic structure upon which the theorists of the voice had based their new hypotheses of English versification.

With Coleridge, a similar compromise with formal convention seems to prevail. His most intense, visionary poetic moment is self consciously frozen in the preface to "Kubla Khan": "if that indeed can be called composition in which all the images rose up before him as *things*, with a parallel of the correspondent expressions, without any sensation or consciousness of effort." It would be difficult to find a more unequivocal echo of the expressionist ideal of transparency, but the result is almost a monument to the devices of artifice—the obsessive synthesis of shifting rhyme scheme, alliteration, assonance, and rhythmic intensity was not what Webb had imagined as "a more liberal rhythmus . . . not balanced by rule, but measured by sentiment."

His other *ex cathedra* engagement with expressionist form occurs in the Preface to *Christabel*, with the "occasional variation in number of syllables . . . in correspondence with some transition in the nature of the imagery or passion." His words, yet again, echo the earlier theorists, but his poem with its use of rhyme and its idiomatic concessions to the ballad, in no sense realizes their vision of the poetic future.

His most specific reference, in the *Biographia*, to the structure of unrhymed verse betrays an almost dutiful allegiance to the formal conservatism of Johnson and Kames.

> It will happen, as I have indeed before observed, that the metre itself, the sole acknowledged difference [between verse and prose] will occasionally become metre to the eye only . . . a number of successive lines can be rendered, even to the most delicate ear, unrecognisable as verse, or as having even been intended for verse, by simply transcribing them as prose: when if the poem be in blank verse, this can be effected without any alteration, or at most by merely restoring one or two words to their proper places from which they had been transplanted.[12]

This is a straightforward restatement of Johnson's "verse only to the eye": and Coleridge's rather dogmatic reiteration of the attendant beliefs in poetry as defined by its audible acknowledgment of regular formal units could in many ways stand as a manifesto for the vast majority of romantic writing. True, the romantics did break the metrical stranglehold of the couplet and disrupt the idiomatic conventions of conversational and nature poetry, but they also maintained an allegiance to formal tradition. The revolutionary freshness of romantic style has been extensively celebrated, but we tend to forget that there is a peculiar contrast between their visionary, existential message and the relative familiarity of the forms through which these effects are realized.

Oddly, the experimentalist theories of form continued beyond the period of Steele and Walker, but their influence upon poetic practice would seem to have been negligible.

John Thelwall was an associate of both Wordsworth and Coleridge and an active literary as well as political figure in the early nineteenth century. He was also a devotee of Walker and a self-acknowledged practitioner to the techniques of Steele. In his single publication on poetic form (1812) he adopts the method and terminology of Steele and virtually abandons the concept of the traditional foot and line in favor of the more contingent form of the unrhymed "cadence."

> Verse is constituted of a regular succession of like cadences, or of a limited variety of cadences, divided by grammatical pauses, emphases, and caesurae, into obviously proportional clauses; so as to present sensible responses, at proportional intervals, to the ear.[13]

Again there is the implication that the audible structure of verse should be unlimited by formal convention and determined by the more contingent contours of feeling and emotion—a concept diametrically opposed to Coleridge's statement in the *Biographia*.

J. Odell in *An Essay on the Elements, Accents and Prosody of the English Language* (1806) acknowledges a debt both to Steele and Walker. He objects to the a priori designation of limits on syntax and meter, but states that the rules governing the broader organization of rhythmical cadences form "a system which has never yet been fully investigated." And here he indicates the key to an understanding of this separation of theory from practice. These had been partially investigated within the critical framework generated by *Paradise Lost*, but the attendant conceptions of blank verse as a stage in the further development of an unrhymed, loosely structured English form remained unrealized in poetry. It is significant that the last known attempt to disclose the hidden patterns of *Paradise Lost* occurred in 1831, in William Forde's appropriately titled *The True Spirit of Milton's Versification*. Forde extended Walker's experiment and reprinted the whole of Book I according to its "true" acoustic rhythmus, but by then every established poet wrote either within the relatively stable conventions of blank verse or drew variations upon regularity from the traditional repertoire to stanzaic and rhymed forms. And this state of conventional eclecticism continued, uninterrupted by the unpublished work of Hopkins, until the emergence of modernism.

The contrast between the theoretical hypothesis offered by the likes of Webb and the compromise with traditional meters in poetic practice is economically, if rather coyly, summarized in Alexander Smith's essay on "The Philosophy of Poetry," published in the *Blackwood Magazine* in 1835.

> It is well known that emotions express themselves in different *tones* and *inflections* of voice from those that are used to communicate mere processes of thought, properly so called; and also that, in the former case, the words of the speaker fall into more smooth and rhythmical combinations than the latter. Our feelings are conveyed in a melodious succession of tones, and in a measured flow of words; our thoughts (and in a greater degree the less they are accompanied by feeling) are conveyed in irregular periods and at harsh intervals of tone. Blank verse and rhyme are *but more artificial dispositions of the natural expressions of feeling* i.e. suitable for poetry—but not necessary to it.[14]

The concluding sentence is conveniently ambivalent, because although blank verse and rhyme may be arbitrary conventions, there were no recognized alternatives upon which an equation of "emotions" with "mere processes" of thought might be based.

Prosodic and formal studies that explored the potential for experiment in English effectively died out inthe 1830s, because the notion of blank verse as a crucial stage in the emergency of a formal practice based entirely upon the irregular accentual movement of postclassical language was no longer a real critical issue. *Paradise Lost* had lost its status as a formal experiment, and blank verse had been admitted to the realtively stable context of formal tradition. Consequently the study of prosody began to adhere to standards set by such works as Edwin Guest's *History of English Rhythms* (1838), in which questions of whether a line really existed were replaced by conjectures upon metrical form within the line—an agenda that has remained consistent even since the merger of traditional prosodic study with modern linguistics.

Conjectures

The value of the eighteenth-century theorists of the voice is that they establish an intriguing correspondence between the aesthetic of free verse and a period of writing and critical speculation that it is all too easy to regard as traditional. Two significant points emerge from this. First, it becomes clear that a poetics of spontaneity transcends particular historical and cultural circumstances: Dennis's conception of structural transparency, Steele's notion of rhythmic form as causally related to natural patterns of human experience, and Blake's ideal of form as "dictated" to him—all of these were closely echoed in the early justifications of free verse technique. The principal point of conflict between these ideals and the other ahistorical conception of form, the silent, visual perspective, was in the problems offered by blank verse, particularly Milton's blank verse. Did this form signal, yet subtly disguise, a poetic future based upon irregular vocal patterns, or did it foreground an equally unprecedented poetic strategy in its apparent use of the visual format? In the eighteenth century this question could only be addressed with reference to poetry that appeared to strike a tantalizingly fragile balance between both perspectives. But as part Three will show, free verse, in its varied manifestations, provided exaggerated instances of both conceptions of form, and it will become clear that although the eighteenth-century conflict was generated by a single poem, its degree of precision and subtlety can also provide us with a framework for the consideration of a perplexing question: what is free verse?

The second point concerns criticism. The ideal of the poem as a spoken form and its implications for prosodic structure impose serious limitations upon certain strategies of reading which, as Part One showed, were widely practiced as early as the eighteenth century. The belief that reading with the eye is merely a stage, a contributory element, in the ultimate objective of oral performance still produces a sense almost of guilt when the reader finds patterns and effects that are generated only by the written text. I have already found evidence of this anxiety in the work of critics such as Hollander and Ricks, who are reluctant to acknowledge the origin of their interpretive procedures. As part Three will demonstrate, modern poets have written themselves into this critical debate and have produced forms that can only be fully appreciated if we acknowledge silent reading as an experience separate from, if not entirely independent of, oral performance.

6
Rhyme

The most important determinant in the eighteenth-century critic's conception of poetic form is his attitude to how the printed text is to be realized in oral performance. Rhyme offers him a perplexing series of problems because on the one hand it can act as a structural substitute for quantity, defining each line as a unit separate from the flexible movement of accent and syntax, but on the other it creates a sense of tension between a coincidence of sound and a quite distinct progression of meaning. Dryden's notion of rhyme as the only audible record of the existence of the English line is subtly elaborated in his admission that this new technique of measure includes effects entirely absent from its classical predecessors: "in the help it brings to memory, which rhyme so knits up, by the affinity of sounds, that, by remembering the last word in one line, we often call to mind both verses" (Ker, I, p. 7). The intriguing implication is that a crucial component of English verse form is capable of producing an extrasyntactic pattern of meaning. But Dryden did not fully explore the creative and interpretive possibilities of this tension, and for the modern reader the most influential and penetrating discussion of the eighteenth-century rhymed couplet is to be found in W. K. Wimsatt's "One Relation of Rhyme to Reason" (1944). In this essay Wimsatt seeks to codify some of the effects produced when a regular coincidence of sound is combined with the tight syntactic and rhetorical framework of the closed heroic line. It is an important piece of work because it vividly represents the way in which twentieth-century critical techniques can broaden and enrich our understanding of how poetry works, but at the same time it shows how easy it is for such persuasive readings to allow us to forget that any critical interpretation is, as much as the poem on which it focuses, the product of historically variable circumstances.

Wimsatt's most significant point concerns the capacity of Pope's rhymes to deepen the texture and expand the meaning of the verse. Rhyme momentarily detains the reader so that the straightforward sequential progression of the language is interrupted, and since this interruption can occur at words in a close or extended semantic range or at parallel or dissimilar parts of speech, the poet has at his disposal an instrument for varying and refocusing the rather predictable alternatives offered by the closed, balanced couplet.

Wimsatt's theoretical assumption is that one of the defining characteristics of all poetic language is its tendency to exhibit various kinds of tension; and in this case the tension arises from the simultaneous presence of the logical structure of syntax and the disruptive illogic of rhyme:

> In literary art only the wedding of the alogical with the logical gives the former an aesthetic value. The words of a rhyme, with their curious harmony of sound and distinction of sense, are an amalgam of the sensory and the logical, or an arrest and precipitation of the logical in sensory form; they are the ikon in which the idea is caught. (p. 163)

The following is an example of how he applies this theoretical merger of logic and illogic, meaning and sound, to a reading of Pope.

> It maybe said, broadly, that difference in meaning of rhyme words can be recognised in difference of parts of speech, and that both of these differences will be qualified by the degree of parallel or of obliquity appearing between the two whole lines of a rhyming pair.
>
> > One speaks the glory of the British Queen,
> > And one describes a charming Indian screen
> >
> > Do thou, Crispissa tend her fav'rite Lock;
> > Ariel himself shall be the guard of Shock
>
> From "British Queen" to "Indian screen" from Lock" to "Shock," here is the same bathos he more often puts into one line—"when husbands, or when lap dogs breath their last." (p. 162)

In certain ways, Wimsatt's readings of Pope bear a close resemblance to Hollander's, Rick's, and Davie's readings of Miltonic blank verse. All disclose two separate patterns of meaning, and their interpretive conclusions emerge from the point of interaction. The blank verse readers base their procedure upon the tension between the line and syntax, and Wimsatt identifies a related sense of tension between syntactic progression and the extrasyntactic echo of the rhyme words. More significantly, both techniques also depend upon the merger of separate levels of interpretive awareness. It has already been shown how the blank verse readers reconciled the processes of seeing and hearing the verse, but with Wimsatt the double perspective is even more complex. His recognition of a semantic relation between "Queen" and "Screen," "Lock" and "Shock" involves him "hearing" two distinct syntactic complexes: the acoustic echo supports and intensifies the conventional meaning of the syntax, but the semantic interplay between them results from a coincidence, an accident, of sound—illogic and logic become disturbingly interchangeable.

Thus the issue of whether or not our visual recognition of the line affects meaning is deepened because, having both seen *and* heard the extra syntactic signal, we have to decide how to balance this potentially disruptive relation of form to meaning. We have seen how certain eighteenth-century critics became aware of the influence of the visual format upon meaning, but as will be shown, the correspondences between visualist readers of the eighteenth and twentieth centuries were not reproduced in the case of rhyme, and this absence provides one more dimension to our understanding of how sound and print can interact in the interpretation of poetry.

After Dryden

As Thomas Blount's barometric survey of 1694 revealed, the theorists of the Restoration found themselves either supporting or attacking two basic formal structures as pointers to the future of English poetry; blank verse and the rhymed couplet. Much of this early work lacked any close interpretive detail, but it is significant that Blount regarded Dryden's conception of rhyme as a prosodic keystone as the conventional wisdom.[1]

Dryden and John Dennis represented a fundamental difference of opinion of rhyme's contribution to orderly poetic expression, but what they, and most of the other commentators, share is a reluctance to examine the possibility that rhyme could generate a multilayered poetic texture beyond the generally predictable mechanisms of syntax and meter. When the more lengthy and systematic analyses of English poetry began to appear in the mid-eighteenth century this emphasis remained unchanged. There is overwhelming evidence that the major commentators on verse form of the century, irrespective of whether or not they actually liked or approved of rhymed poetry, accepted that rhyme was a formal counterweight to the loose and contingent nature of English accent. Even Thomas Sheridan, the great defender of Miltonic blank verse, admitted that his elocutionist concept of the pause of suspension to mark the line ending was in one sense a formal replacement for the function of rhyme.

Sheridan, Kames, Priestley, Blair, Young, Johnson, Mitford, Walker, and a fair number of less notable critics all assumed that to use rhyme was, except in the lyric, to engage attendant syntactic patterns peculiar to the closed couplet.[2] Their treatment of rhyme's structural function in the stanza or the ode was perfunctory and brief. For instance, in the *Lectures on the Art of Reading*, Sheridan devoted an entire lecture to the study of the couplet, but gave practically no space to the stanza, and regarded his favorite lyric, Dryden's *Ode on St. Cecilia's Day*, as "sufficient to shew what advantage our lyric poetry might receive if our writers would follow the example of Dryden, in observing the decorum of numbers, and varying their metre suitably to their subject." In other words, metrical and lineal variation in the ode was an acceptable convention and undeserving of lengthy analysis. Similarly, the stanza represented a closed, predictable formula. But the couplet was the most popular form of the period, deployed in every category and genre of poetic writing, and, more significantly, it represented the closest point of contact between the backbone of traditional English prosody, the rhymed pentameter, and the one major challenge to convention and expectation, blank verse. Thus the vast majority of eighteenth-century discussions of form focused upon the distinction between the two.

Kames represents what was probably the most extreme and dogmatic form of prescriptive prosody, and his whole conception of the structure and identity of the pentameter was based upon the effects produced by the closed, balanced form of the rhymed couplet. The couplet offered the prescriptive critics the perfect model of coherence and order from which they might safely legislate upon the allowable syntactic and rhythmic patterns of unrhymed poetry. The premise from which Johnson launched his attack on *Paradise Lost* as "verse only to the eye" was that the "musick" of the English heroic line can only be secured by "the preservation of every verse unmingled with another . . . and this distinctness is obtained and preserved by the artifice of rhyme."

What is remarkable about the prescriptive critics is their reluctance to examine the distinction between effects discharged by lines that are preserved by a pause and those closed by rhyme. Kames goes part of the way towards such an analysis, but his cautious omissions are as significant as his positive statements. He claims that each couplet "makes a complete musical period," and so confident is he of being able to describe the operation of this form that he actually enumerates four "orders" of couplet line, whose combinations produce predictable effects upon the reader such as elevation, depression, and joy (II, pp. 149–60). These depend upon the relationship between the movement of the caesura and the stability of the final pause, but not once does Kames mention the influence of rhyme upon these patterns. He acknowledges that in blank verse these relationships are less predictable and that the poet "is at liberty to attend the imagination in its boldest flights" (II, p. 160), but he does not state how rhyme might produce effects far more complex than its function as a closure of syntax might suggest. The omission is made more remarkable if we recall the amount of detail and ingenuity that went into his examination of the typographic line as a component of meaning—to grant a similar status to rhyme would seem to fracture some unstated rule.

Hugh Blair's *Lectures on Rhetoric and Belles Lettres* (1783) came into being long before its date of publication, and the acknowledged influence of Kames is most evident in Blair's treatment of the couplet. He considers it possible to predict the expressive limits of four basic types of couplet line that vary their caesurae between the fourth and seventh syllables: a pause after the fourth syllable produces "a most spirited air"; after the fifth it is "smooth gentle and flowing"; after the sixth it is "more solemn and grave"; and after the seventh it produces "a slow Alexandrian air" (II, pp. 320–30). The permutations of this scheme are increased when lines of different sorts are combined into couplets, but the overall effects are, apparently, still predictable. This tendency towards boiling down poetic language into manageable chunks could, with some justification, be dismissed as simplistic and inaccurate. Pope's "Majesty of Spades," "Puts forth one manly leg," which is at the sixth syllable, "to sight revealed" (*The Rape of the Lock* III, 57). This mock heroic moment in the card game can hardly be regarded as a "solemn" or "grave" act of exposure.

Leaving aside the dogmatic crudity of their application, Kames's and Blair's systems bear a close resemblance to Wimsatt's modern conception of the couplet as a tight rhetorical framework. The difference emerges in the eighteenth-century critics' complete refusal to acknowledge rhyme as a point of intensification in these rhetorical mechanisms.

Rhyme, it seems, has a strangely paradoxical function in the prescriptive model of poetic structure: its role in the mechanism of the couplet clearly produces effects that are not so evident in blank verse, but no critic is willing or able to acknowledge its status as anything more than a preservative of order. To have recognized that there is an interplay between the sequential movement of grammar and a secondary audible pattern, a pattern moreover that draws attention to language as an arbitrary system of coincidences, they would then have been faced with a problem even more perplexing than the one that they sought to rectify in the structure of unrhymed verse.

Sheridan

The intention of these critics was legislative, to codify poetic effects that did not run against their attendant rules for composition. But what of those critics whose work shifted the balance away from the putative poet and toward the flexible interpretive faculties of the reader? Thomas Sheridan was, particularly in his treatment of blank verse, one of the most ingenious and imaginative of the elocutionist critics, but in his examinations of the rhymed couplet he exhibits a curious degree of consistency with the prescriptive writers.

Kames's and Blair's conception of line divisions as productive of particular emotional effects is adapted by Sheridan in the *Lectures on the Art of Reading* (1775) to a more technical description of what almost amounts to the geometry of the closed couplet: "The first and lowest perception of harmony, arises from comparing two members of the same line with each other . . . because the beauty of proportion in the members, accorded to each of these divisions is founded in nature." He illustrates this vision of *concordia discors* with, not surprisingly, the opening lines of Pope's *Windsor Forest*,

> Thy forests Windsor // and thy green retreats
> At once the monarchs // and the muses seats,
> Invite my lays. // Be present Sylvan maids,
> Unlock your springs // and open all your shades.

[Here] we find that the caesura is in the middle of the verse in each line at the first couplet, and at the end of the second foot, in each line of the last: this produces a similarity in each couplet, distinctly considered; a diversity when one is compared with the other; which has a pleasing effect. (II, p. 173)

Sheridan implies that Pope's ordered representation of the landscape is accurately realized in the couplet's representation of formal perfection with its slight, but permissible variations. And to this extent he preempts the post-1930s' revival of interest in the poetic qualities of Augustan writing. Works such as E. R. Wasserman's *The Subtler Language* (1959) and W. B. Piper's *The Heroic Couplet* (1969) contain analyses of couplet poetry as a particular rhetorical idiom, capable of merging tight syntactic form with an, albeit idealized and artificial, conception of order and disorder in the world. But there is a crucial difference.

Wimsatt's close-readings represented one element of this New Critical interest in Augustan technique, and the function of rhyme in these readings is economically put in his essay: "They [rhyme words] impose upon the logical pattern of expressed argument a kind of fixative counterpattern of alogical implication" (p. 153). The difference is that Sheridan similarly admires the "logic" of the couplet form while systematically excluding any reference to the "alogic" of rhyme.

In Lecture II, which is almost entirely given to analyses of the couplet, Sheridan offers an analogy to explain how the couplet can discharge the "lowest perception of harmony." The analogy is of a "spectator" enjoying the sight of "four troops of horse drawn up in a field." Sheridan considers the pleasure derived from perceptions of symmetry and balance when the troops divide into two, and eventually four, separate units.

the diversity of comparison is thereby introduced; for a spectator properly placed, not only perceives that the proportion of the middle space, is double that of either of the other, and equal to them both; but one has the opportunity also of comparing, at one look, the two bodies divided by the larger space, with the opposite two bodies; and each with each divided by the smaller spaces. (II, p. 145)

This leads him into a discussion of how the caesura and demi-caesura operate as similar points of division in the heroic line. He considers the almost chiasmic correspondences in a line from Pope's *Essay on Criticism*.

140 SOUND

> Glows "while he reads" "but trembles" as he writes . . . the opposition in the thought, naturally obliges the mind to a comparison of those portions of the verse which are more directly opposed to each other—as,
>
> > Glows | but trembles |
> > While he reads || as he writes ||
>
> Here then is another perception of diversity and uniformity; of diversity in comparing the first and third member; . . . of uniformity in comparing the second and last, . . . which answer precisely to each other, both in syllables and accent. (II, pp. 147–48)

We should note here that there are peculiar connections between Sheridan's interpretive approach to the couplet and his more striking analyses of Miltonic blank verse. Both are dependent upon analogies drawn from the visual arts: with blank verse the eye establishes a point of interaction between the spatial typography of the verse and its sequential progression, but with the couplet Sheridan regards the spatial divisions, the proportions and diversities, as an exact representation of the process of comparison as it is felt by the ear. Sheridan's method was eventually to be extended by Peter Walkden Fogg into his system of black marks as representations of sequential groups and cadences. As has been shown, Fogg found himself unable to represent unrhymed enjambments in this way because it would have been impossible to produce a black line that simultaneously opened and closed itself. This multiple pattern of meaning and form can, as Sheridan put it, "never be applied to numbers of which there can be only one reciter," and the implication is that with the rhymed couplet, the "lowest perception of harmony" can be appreciated with a single recital. But what about the function of rhyme itself, an echo of phonemic similarity that is not dependent upon the typographic form, but that cuts deeply into the rhythmic sound pattern and establishes an alternative formal sequence? Why, in his lengthy analysis of the structure of the rhymed couplet, did he not actually engage with the potential for a double pattern? If he was capable of recognizing the extrasyntactic effect of

                                                        bright
Pavement

why did he not come to consider the effect upon meaning of the phonemic-semantic interplay between "retreats/seats," "maids/

shades," "dull/full"? One explanation of this case of apparent self-contradiction can be found in his essay, a "Dissertation on Rhime," first published in 1756, but clearly thought important enough to be attached, almost as an appendix, to the *Lectures on the Art of Reading* (1775). The opening sentences make his position clear enough.

> Nothing has contributed so much to destroy all true taste for poetry as the establishment of rhime. A foolish admiration of this trifling and artificial ornament, has turned people's thoughts from the contemplation of the real and natural beauty of numbers. (p. 323)

He proceeds with a short historical survey of postclassical languages and attendant developments in poetry. English poetry had been built upon "the same Gothic model as other European tongues," with rhyme emerging as a desperate contingency, a replacement for quantity. These developments had eventually produced the "simplicity of modulation" of the couplet measure but with an attendant ignorance of the "peculiar graces and force" of unrhymed numbers. To Sheridan, the pernicious influence of rhyme had created in certain readers—and here he clearly refers to the likes of Kames—an expectation of parallelism and uniformity in the rhythm and syntax of *all* poetry.

> To such [readers], the introduction of different feet into the same measure, and their judicious combinations, appear only to create disorder and confusion; and the want of rhime is with them the want of measure, which used to be their unerring guide in making the close. (p. 364)

Rhymed poetry had become for Sheridan not merely a separate prosodic category, but a separate genre of poetic writing particularly suited both to the generation of a sense of balance, an improvement of unkempt reality, and to the rhetorical, comparative techniques of satire. For him to have examined rhyme itself as a productive intrication of meaning would have involved an imputation of textual depth to a form that he regarded as of secondary status to Miltonic blank verse. It is almost as though Arnold's demotion of Dryden and Pope to "classics of our prose" had taken place a century earlier.

So we find the rather ambivalent attitude toward rhyme, which lingered in the margins of prescriptive criticism, more vividly realized in the work of Sheridan: rhyme is an indisputable component of one genre of poetic writing, but to grant it the status of a productive poetic effect would be to reduce poetic appreciation to "the foolish admiration of this trifling and artificial ornament." It might seem rather odd to us that such an opinion could exist in the century that has contributed the most familiar uses of rhyme to literary history, but as the following section will show Sheridan was by no means alone in his beliefs.

Rhyme and Uncertainty

Wimsatt is an archetypal New Critic in the sense that his ingenious readings of Pope's technique are unencumbered by contemporary evidence of Pope's intention to create the disclosed effects or of his readers' inclination to appreciate them. But in "Rhetoric and Poems: Alexander Pope" (1949) he considers the relationship between his own interpretations and the general mood of the early eighteenth-century critical environment.

> [We] are confronted by an extremely curious and challenging situation in the heroic couplet of Pope: where a verse basically ordered by the rational rules of parallel and antithesis and showing at least a certain characteristic restraint of imagination, as contrasted say with metaphysical verse, at the same time is found to rely so heavily for "support" or "stiffening"—to use again the terms of Pope—on so barbarous and Gothic a device as rhyme. (pp. 182–83)

Wimsatt is, in one sense, correct in his association of rhyme with the "Gothic," since, from Milton's "Note" to Sheridan's "Dissertation," critics agreed that rhyme, along with accentual meter, was the product of postclassical linguistic developments. John Rice sums this up:

> Thus from the Gothic Source we deduce the Rules laid down for an equal Number of Syllables; the alternative Movement of *loud* and *soft*; the mechanical Regularity of Pause, and Cadence, and Rhime.
> From the classical Source, we deduce the Mode of Scanning by long and short Syllables; of the Modulation of Feet and Measure; and the true Method of forming harmonious Periods in general. (pp. 168–69)

I suspect that Wimsatt's use of Gothic differs radically from Rice's straightforward historical reference. It is likely that Wimsatt's notion of Gothic effects is consistent with his own conception of rhyme as productive of illogic and disorder, the sort of spontaneous unpredictability that the modern critic might well impute to all poetic effects. This is precisely what the eighteenth-century critics of rhyme sought to exclude both from its use and appreciation.

In his famous *Spectator* sequence on wit, Addison states that "True Wit consists in the Resemblance of Ideas, and *false Wit* in the Resemblance of Words." (*Spectator* 58, 1711). By implication Addison places rhyme in the same category of false wit as the celebrations of linguistic material in the seventeenth-century pattern poems. And Shaftsbury, writing at around the same time, clarifies his own reference to poets "taken up in seeking out that monstrous ornament which we call rhyme" with the following footnote.

> And perhaps Nature wants opposites too, and wants to make harmony out of them, not out of similars; as for instance, she brings the male to the female and not each of these to one of his or her own sex; and she made the first concord by means of opposites, not similars.[3]

Shaftsbury here reminds us of Wimsatt's distinction between the semantic depth and the superficial coincidences of language. But, unlike Wimsatt, Shaftsbury argues that the ideal of "harmony" in art and nature is in some way threatened by a technique that draws upon the relation of "similars." This sense of superficial pattern as disruptive of ordered meaning also emerges in William Mason's 1749 attack on the rhymed couplet. It,

> lays [poetry] under the most miserable Restraint, hampers it with the most unreasonable Fetters, cramps a true poetic Fancy, and whilst it keeps the Attention fixt to the structure and sound of the Words, takes it off from that which is the very Life and Spirit of all true poetical Composition, *viz* sublime thought and strong Language, it pleases the ear at the expence of our Understanding, and puts us off with Sound instead of Sense. (*Essay on the Power and Harmony of Prosaic Numbers*, p. 47)

Mason objects to rhyme for precisely the same reason that Wimsatt praised it. It draws the reader into a pattern of effects based upon the "sound of words," pleasing "the ear at the expence of our Understanding." The simultaneous presence of the logical with the alogical upon which Wimsatt's readings are based, is just as central to Mason's objection.

In his *Course of Lectures on Oratory and Criticism* (1777) Joseph Priestley launches an extended attack on the appreciation of poetic effects for their own sake, and he goes on to elaborate a scale of correspondences between style and meaning which, although superficially consistent with the celebrated Augustan tenet of *ut pictura poesis*, is clearly critical of the creation of linguistic effects as correlatives to their extralinguistic objects.

> It cannot be supposed, therefore, that any person describing such a scene [which wholly engrosses the mind], and properly impressed with it, should at the same time attend to, and introduce into his description, any other ornaments than those which necessarily belong to it. . . . The appearance of *verse* of any kind, which shews a *double attention*, could not be borne. (p. 268)

"Double attention" perfectly encapsulates the notion of separate levels of interpretive awareness upon which Wimsatt's critical technique depends. And where would this effect of "double attention" be most intense?

> the more manifest signs there are of *art* in any composition, the more the mind is drawn off from an attention to the subject of it . . . there are more of those marks of artful composition in blank verse than in prose, and more of them in rhyme than in blank verse. (p. 268)

Later in the same section Priestley admits that the couplet could be appreciated as a token of the greater technical difficulties it offers to the poet, but the criterion of skill in such an enterprise depends upon the poet's ability to subdue the conspicuous illogic of rhyme, "for nothing is more universally disgusting than rhyme, when it is not the effect of art and design." This interpretive opinion is perfectly consistent with the prescriptive critics rulings on closure and balance in the couplet; any deviation from this would expose rhyme as artifice. William Cockin in his *The Art of Delivering Written Language; or, an Essay on Reading* (1775) considers the responsibility of the oral reader in the preservation of this sense of subdued artifice.

> [It is] absurd to attempt to smother rhymes by feeble pronunciation and running one line into another as is often affected by many of our modern readers and speakers. By this method they not only destroy one source of pleasure intended by the composer (which though not great is nevertheless genuine) but even often supply its place with what is really disagreeable, by making the rhymes, as they are interruptedly perceived, appear accidental blemishes of a different Style, arising from an unmeaning recurrence of similar sounds. (pp. 138–39)

The significant phrases here are "accidental blemishes of a different style" and "unmeaning recurrence of similar sounds," because Cockin evokes a notion of the reader desperately attempting to preserve sequential, ordered meaning to the exclusion of "the double attention" which might disrupt it.

Wimsatt's readings of Pope's stylistic subtleties exceed those of the eighteenth century because he foregrounded the illogic of aural coincidence while his predecessors attempted to subdue it. A more extravagant, but not inconsistent, statement of the twentieth-century attitude to rhyme can be found in Edward Stankiewicz's 1961 essay on "Poetic and Non-Poetic Language."

> Successful rhyme is illogical and canny, striking and familiar, prominent and subsumed; it provides the condensed formula of poetic language: identity and variation, obligatariness and freedom, sound and meaning, unity and plurality, texture and structure. (p. 16)

Stankiewicz emphasizes what for the eighteenth-century reader was rhyme's least attractive potential, its randomness, its tendency to detain the reader at points in a sequence of meanings where such attention is unintended or obliquely disruptive of the orderly progression of sense.

In the *Rhetorical Grammar* (1785) John Walker displays the same anxious unease with the signifying potential of rhyme that had attended his treatment of the materiality of written language. Just as he rewrote Miltonic blank verse to prevent the intervention of the silent printed text in the ideal circuit of oral communication, so he similarly rewrote sequences from Pope's couplet poetry in order to remove the double attention offered by rhyme.

> Which, without passing through the judgment, gains
> The heart, and all its end at once obtains
> (original)

> Which, without passing through the judgment,
> Gains the heart,
> And all its end at once obtains
> (Walker's reprinting, p. 333)

> Music resembles poetry: in each
> Are nameless graces which no methods teach
> (original)

> Music resembles poetry:
> In each are nameless graces which no methods teach
> (Walker's reprinting, p. 335)

> And to their proper operation still
> Ascribe all good to their improper ill
>
> (original)
>
> And to their proper operation
> Still ascribe all good
> To their improper,
> Ill
>
> (Walker's reprinting, p. 334)

Walker admits that with most of Pope's verse such changes would be unnecessary, but in certain cases, "[although] this common boundary of sense and sound is often broken down by the poet for the noblest of purposes of composition, the young reader cannot at first prevail on himself to follow him, but finds himself stopped at the end of the line" (p. 333). It is precisely this effect of the broken boundary of sound and sense, of the invitation to "double attention," that Wimsatt and Stankiewicz regard as crucial to the signifying potential of the rhymed couplet.

It should be noted that Walker's policy of rewriting is principally directed at those couplets where the sense of almost geometric rhetorical balance, so meticulously described by Sheridan, is disrupted; where the rhyme word intersects with the syntactic sequence to an extent that its presence as a threat to sequential order becomes more conspicuous. The implication is that the closed, balanced couplet, the archetype of Augustan poetic technique, is at least capable of subduing the sense of rhyme as artifice. The enjambed couplet was a rare phenomenon in the eighteenth century, and even when poets such as Pope allowed themselves such small eccentricities they usually limited the effect of disruption by only allowing lineal overruns within the couplet itself. One of the more extravagant practitioners was Charles Churchill.

> Let War, will all his needy, Ruffian band,
> In pomp of horror stalk through Gotham's land
> Knee deep in blood, let all her stately towers
> Sink in the dust; that Court which now is our's
> Become a den, where beasts may, if they can,
> A lodging find, nor fear rebuke from Man.
>
> (*Gotham*, 1754, II, l. 277–82)

Even in these freer couplet movements the second line enjambments are softened, making them depend upon inversion, or allowing the enjambed phrase to become a kind of afterthought, a qualification of the thought of the couplet itself, in a very similar fashion to the *allowable* types of blank verse enjambment. H. A. Beers wrote that "the blank verse of *The Seasons* . . . has been passed through the strainer of the heroic couplet,"[4] and it might, from another perspective, be added that the enjambed couplets of the period were at least as observant of the prescriptive rules as blank verse was supposed to be. This reluctance to create the effect of linear disruption that we find in Donne's *Satyres* is further evidence of the sense of apprehension that the double attention of rhyme created in the eighteenth century. Even Churchill's rather innocuous experiments were capable of prompting the *Monthly Review* commentator to write of his couplet verse that, "This is certainly not poetry, but measured prose."[5] This comment echoes many early reactions to Milton's blank verse and both responses emerge from a belief that when a recognized formal arrangement is violated, the reader will be in some doubt as to the appropriate response. A more extensive, though lighthearted, attack on Churchill takes us closer to the fundamental reasons for such objections.

> O Thou sonorous Churchill, teach my line
> To flow exuberantly wild like thine,
> Teach me to twist a thought a thousand ways,
> And string with idle particles my lays,
> That one poor sentiment exhausted, when
> The weary reader hopes a respite, then
> I may spring on with force redoubled, till
> I break him panting breathless to my will,
> And make him, tired of periods of a mile,
> Gape in deep wonder at my rapid style.[6]

The satirist's reference to "twisted thoughts" and "idle particles" is echoed in John Rice's remark that English is a language circumstantially "addicted to Rhime; the numerous Similarity of Sounds frequently causing us to fall into it in common Conversation" (p. 170). Again there is a sense of threat, of rhyme as a reminder of the unstructured accidents of linguistic surface imposing upon the ideal of poetic order and stability.

Watts Contemplates Chaos

The most intriguing example of the eighteenth century's ambivalent, almost contradictory, relationship with rhyme emerges in the case of Isaac Watts. I have already shown that the keystone of the couplet's manifestation of order and transparency was provided by a device that was, paradoxically, regarded as a disturbing token of linguistic disorder. It was Milton's refractory deployment of unrhymed form that drew critics into their most adventurous explorations of the relationship between poetry, language, and the prelinguistic world, but in Watts's attitude to the couplet we find a perfect encapsulation of the century's shifting condition of caution and experiment. This is Watts's preface to *Horae Lyricae* (1709)

> In the *Poems of Heroic Measure* I have attempted in Rhime the same Variety of Cadence, Comma and Period, which Blank Verse glories in as its peculiar Elegance and Ornament. It degrades the Excellency of the best Versification when the Lines run on by Couplets, twenty together, just in the same Pace and with the same Pauses. It spoils the noblest Pleasure of the Sound: the Reader is tir'd with the tedious Uniformity or charm'd to sleep with the unmanly Softness of the Numbers, and the perpetual Chime of even Cadences. (p. xx)

This is a quite remarkable dismissal of the effects of the closed couplet in the period of its preeminence. But when we examine Watts's practice we find the same degree of cautious compromise that influences his use of blank verse. The most notable couplet poem in *Horae Lyricae* is *A Funeral Poem on the Death of Thomas Gunston*. Its closest thematic relative would be *Lycidas*, and it is clear that Watts attempted to marry the fluid structure of Milton's poem with the currently fashionable solidity of the couplet. His working maxim seems to have been that the balanced symmetry of the couplet could be made to submit to the shifting expressionistic contours of lyricism and tragic loss.

> But Night, eternal Night hangs black around
> The dismal Chambers of the hollow Ground,
> And solid Shades unmingled round his Bed
> Stand Hideous: Earthy fogs embrace his Head,
> And noisom Vapours glide along his Face
> Rising perpetual.
>
> (p. 317)

The two delayed phrases "Stand Hideous" and "Rising Perpetual" are reminiscent of the safely institutionalized mannerisms of post-Miltonic blank verse: each preceeding line is, to a degree, closed, and the enjambed phrase neither intricates the movement of syntax nor significantly distorts the already established sense. This section is typical of Watts's oddly nerveless practice, as if he has one eye on the violent enjambments of Donne but cannot quite bring himself to compromise the revered structural identity of the line. As Kames later put it, both lines of the couplet "should accompany a pause in the sense" (p. 138).

Rhyme came to represent an even more serious threat to the balance between form and meaning than the unrhymed line, because the syntactic/typographic tensions of blank verse could at least be closed down in a single oral delivery. But as Walker's rewritings unwittingly demonstrate, it was felt necessary to attempt to "hide" phonemic patterns within the sequential movement of syntax.

One other instance of the century's attempt to disguise the self-consciousness of rhyme as artifice occurs in the attitude to "off" or pararhymes. Dennis in the "Preface to the *Passion of Byblis*" (1692) condemns "imperfect" rhyme as "jarring" and "harsh" (Hooker, I, p. 4) and similar condemnations will be found in Coward's *Licentia Poetica discuss'd* (1709, p. 74) and in Atterbury's "Preface to . . . *Waller's Poems*" (1690, sig A6v). Priestley's objection to the disruption of "a chain of ideas strongly connected" was particularly strong in the case of phonemic dissonance: "Let any person but recollect when a musician stops before he has finished his tune; when a bad rhyme, or no rhyme at all, occurs in a poem composed in generally good rhyme" (p. 272). The chief distinction between Bysshe's dictionary of rhymes (1702) and Poole's (1657), which the former replaced as the most popular handbook, was in the systematic exclusion of words that Bysshe felt to be insufficiently alike in pronunciation to satisfy his "stricter standard."

Bysshe also excluded, "Words that ought not to end a verse; as the Particles *An, And, As Of, The* etc," and it is significant that "thy," "but," "or," "your," "my," "nor," and "than" are present in Poole's dictionary but are removed from Bysshe's. Bysshe seems to have paid unwonted attention to this matter since "our" is included in the 1702 first edition but removed in the 1708 revisions. Unlike verbs and adjectives, none of these connectives is capable of inversion, and would thus cause violent and phonemically intensified enjambments.[7]

Both of these developments reflect the widespread desire to neutralize rhyme as a point at which the arbitrary, superficial structure of language interferes with the ideal of transparency—and we may return again to Watts for evidence that this awareness of language as a tenuous point of stability between order and chaos lingers uneasily beneath the surface of eighteenth-century theory and practice. Watts's *Horae Lyricae* abounds with vowel-based off-rhymes such as "Deceit / Estate" (p. 43), and so regular is his use of these in comparison with their very rare occurrences in the poetry of his contemporaries that we must assume that they exercise an attraction for him similar to that of the enjambed couplet. And just as he exhibited a sense of conformity in his use of enjambment, so with off-rhymes he never departed from a relatively unprovocative variation within a closely related phonemic range. His technique never comes close to the more recent, archetypal, use of off-rhymes in Wilfred Owen's "Strange Meeting," where such instances as "grained / ground" and "bestirred / stared" create dissonant echoes of the poem's surreal vision. But Watts's own copy of Poole's *English Parnassus*, now in the Bodleian Library, Oxford, contains a large number of autograph emendations to the dictionary of rhymes that reveal a tantalizing degree of awareness of rhyme's ability to draw us into the illogic of linguistic surface. For instance, next to Poole's phonetic category, "OAD, ODE," Watts adds "OOD," "OUD," "OD," "UD," "UDE," and, more adventurously, he experiments with consonant distinctions such as "OWN" and "OUND"—a correspondence that seems almost to reach forward to Owen's tortured "grained" and "ground."[8]

The point is that Watts never went so far as to use these in his poetry, and it would not be a too adventurous interpretation of circumstances to suggest that his decision to curb these extravagant tendencies is symptomatic of the widespread eighteenth-century attitude toward rhyme as an even more disruptive departure into the realm of linguistic materiality than that presented by the typographic line.

Rhyme and the Visionary Experience

Hugh Kenner in an essay called "Pope's Reasonable Rhymes" takes Wimsatt's work a stage further and attempts to establish a contemporary context for his readings of Pope. In an impressive virtuoso discussion of *The Rape of the Lock*, Kenner traces the way in which Pope moves between sequences of predictable semantic rhyming patterns, such as "detains/Chains," "betray/Prey," "insnare/Hair," and less decorous couplings such as "Mankind/behind." He argues that such transitions are generally appropriate to the broader tone of the poem, a system "which would zone out the poem's orders and disorders according to a sense of linguistic fitness his readers might intuit but need not articulate" (p. 74). The question of why Kenner is able to "articulate" rather than merely "intuit" these patterns becomes less perplexing when one examines the final and perhaps most interesting section of his essay. Here Kenner finds a tentative affinity between the canniness of Pope's rhymes and the contemporary interest in the idea of universal language, specifically Bishop Wilkins's attempt in his *Essay Toward a Real Character and a Philosophical Language* (1668) to recreate what he imagined was the pre-Babel taxonomy of sounds and signs, untouched by the arbitrariness of contemporary linguistic practice. Kenner calls Wilkins's enterprise a "fantasy of linguistic order" in which a word's phonetic identity, in post-Saussurean terms the signifier, would immediately and naturally suggest the place in the universal taxonomy of the thing it denoted, the signified: if the system of the world is closed and available for inventory, argues Wilkins, then it must be possible to recreate a system of signs that originates from and directly articulates this system of things. Kenner suggests that there is some connection between Wilkins's "fantasy" and Pope's poetics.

> In the light of such fantasies of linguistic order as Wilkins' project illustrates, every real language, every language accessible to poets, affirms a hint of shattered perfection. Order, congruence, universal truths, these a poet might hint at by careful exploitation of such few congruous rhymes as his tongue placed at his disposal. They are what we have been calling the normal rhymes, and the sense of propriety they denote can seem to come from beyond the world. How this sense of things, never clearly articulated, could validate the prevalence of the rhymed couplet itself we may easily guess, and why such tame criteria as "correctness" seemed of self-evident pertinence, conveying as they did hints of comprehensive wisdom, glinting from behind the aberrances of speech. (p. 79)

It is clear that the primitivist theoreticians of language and poetry allied themselves with the poetic ideals explored in the preceding chapter on "The Voice of Form." These critics, from Dennis onwards, consistently regarded rhyme as a restraint to the unfettered movements of form and rhythm. Daniel Webb in the *Remarks on the Beauties of Poetry* (1762) attacked the "monotony of the couplet . . . the repetition of the rhymes . . . the sameness in movement of the verse" (p. 12). And we might compare Kenner's notion of rhyme as providing access to "a hint of shattered perfection . . . from beyond the world" with Webb's judgment upon Pope's use of the rhymed couplet in *Windsor Forest* to present an image of nature.

> Here you cannot but be sensible, how the enthusiasm is tamed by the precision of the couplet, and the consequent littleness of the scenery. (p. 19)

For Webb, Kenner's "hints of comprehensive wisdom, glinting from behind the aberrances of speech" came not from the use of rhyme, but required a freer, unrhymed prosody—"these sudden breaks or transitions in the verse, which so strongly characterise the passions; and dart as it were a sentiment into the utmost soul of the reader" (pp. 20–21).

The interpretive distinction between Kenner and Webb perfectly illustrates the degree of contrast between modern conceptions of rhyme and those of the eighteenth century. I have already examined Priestley's dismissive attitude toward how the double attention produced for the reader by the rhymed couplet is in conflict with Wimsatt's assumption that a form of double attention was what Pope intended. Kenner takes the conflict a stage further by imputing to Pope a creative and formal complicity with the primitivist theories of poetic structure, and in doing so he not only takes critical speculation a step too far, but further clouds our awareness of the radically polarized condition of eighteenth-century theories of interpretation. Not a single critic of the period regarded the couplet as an appropriate vehicle for the quasi-visionary enterprises that Kenner associates with the primitivists. The critics who did foresee the development of poetic form as connected in some way with an existential vision, based their hypotheses on the study of unrhymed, varied verse. The reason for this was that rhyme was seen as securing the existence of the traditional poetic line, and such conventions were regarded by the experimentalists as a concession to an outdated classical ideal. Even Kames, the archetypal conservative, regarded rhyme as a necessary condition of form, but one that was not conducive to what he calls the "Sublime" vision.

> In the chapter of Grandeur and Sublimity it is established, that a grand or sublime object, inspires a warm enthusiastic emotion disdaining strict regularity and order; which emotion is very different

from that inspired by the moderately enlivening music of rhyme. Supposing then an elevated subject to be expressed in rhyme, what must be the effect? The intimate union of the music with the subject, produces an intimate union of their emotions; one inspired by the subject, which tends to elevate and expand the mind; and one inspired by the music, which, confining the mind within the narrow limits of regular cadence and similar sound, tends to prevent all elevation above its own pitch. Emotions so little concordant, cannot in union have a happy effect. (*Elements of Criticism*, p. 172)

Kames offers what is an almost precise anticipation of Wimsatt's "challenging situation" of the "rational rules of parallel and antithesis" juxtaposed with "the barbarous and Gothic device" of rhyme. The difference is that Wimsatt and Kenner take up the challenge by regarding rhyme as, in itself, a device that opens up a plenitude of tensions and formal/thematic diversities, whereas Kames and his contemporaries are united in the belief that "emotions so little concordant, cannot in union have a happy effect."

Rhyme and Intention

The question of whether it is the eighteenth century or the modern critics who are closer to the correct interpretation of rhyme is less intriguing than the question of why such a fervent disagreement exists. Priestley provides us with a clue in his Lecture on "The Resemblance Between Sound and Sense." Rhyme,

> shows us how naturally we transfer the properties of *ideas* upon the *words* which express them. Hence it is easy to *imagine* a resemblance of the sound to the sense in almost everything. But since this is wholly the work of the readers imagination a writer doth not need to give himself trouble about it. Those who understand the language will imagine the correspondence. (*A Course of Lectures on Oratory and Criticism*, 1777, p. 292)

Priestley postulates two systems of meaning; that of the poem, which structures and formalizes sound patterns, and that of language, from which these patterns are drawn. But he insists that it is "wholly the work of the reader" to disclose connections between the two, connections that were not, it seems, intended by the poet. He could be offering a theoretical pretext for modern criticism because Wimsatt's analyses of how rhyme is "an amalgam of the sensory and the logical" involves a process of seeing the poem not as a fully autonomous statement but as part of a broader, impersonal system of linguistic relations. It is the critic who acts as casuist in this potentially chaotic conflict of system and instance; and thus we find Kenner extending Wimsatt's practice into the much wider thesis of how the conventions of linguistic structure might provide access to an independent system of relations—in eighteenth-century terms, a universal language.

It has become clear that some eighteenth-century critics were willing to assume the role of casuist in other circumstances, so why did they take exception to doing so with rhyme? Here we should seek the assistance of one of the most influential practitioners of literary linguistics, Roman Jakobson: "The poetic function projects the principle of equivalence from the axis of selection to the axis of combination."[9] A rough explanation of this formula would be that the combinative mode is metonymic, it is dependent primarily upon the contiguous grammatical relation of words; while the selective mode is metaphoric, in the sense that it depends upon choices made from the repertory of words available to be fitted into each point in the combinative, grammatical chain. In poetic structures, according to Jakobson, we become aware of a greater emphasis upon the selective mode because the words chosen exhibit a tendency to intensify or even disrupt the calm progress of the combinative sequence. Jakobson again: "The principle of similarity underlies poetry; the metrical parallelism of lines, or the phonic equivalence of rhyming words prompts the question of semantic similarity or contrast."[10] Here he provides the unstated premise for the readings of Wimsatt and Kenner. Rhyme acts as a prompter to their disclosure of its metaphoric effects of intensity and resonance. But there is a problem with this formula because it does not state whether the reader should also try to distinguish between this prompt as a signal from the poet or merely as the opportunity to practice a comparative analysis of the poem with the system of communication upon which it depends.

Consider the following diagram, which is very often used to illustrate Jakobson's model of poetic language.

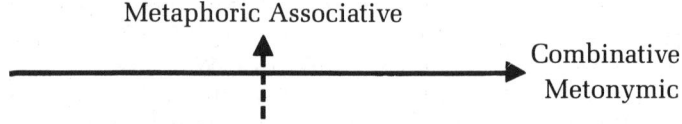

By a peculiar coincidence this visual representation bears a close physical resemblance to a number of concrete poetic effects, because the horizontal axis could well be the poetic line, and its point of intersection with the vertical axis could possibly occur either with its physical termination or with the aural signal that marks it. For instance,

> Now in loose garlands thick thrown off the bright
> Pavement

causes Sheridan to observe that the "separation . . . between the quality and its subject, gives time for the quality to make a stronger impression on us." Sheridan would seem to have been, in Jakobson's words, "prompted" to recognize an almost metaphoric intensification of an otherwise straightforward combinative chain, and to conclude that "the intention of the poet is to fix our thoughts not on the pavement itself, but on the brightness of the pavement." His assertion that this effect is created by the poet is crucial to our understanding of why neither he nor any of his contemporaries could recognize a similar metaphoric projection in lines such as,

> Thy forests Windsor and thy green retreats
> At once the monarchs and the muses seats.

For Sheridan to recognize an interplay of meaning between "retreats/seats" would be to acknowledge the fact that he, the reader, was interpreting a series of effects which, by contemporary standards, could not have been intended by the poet. Wimsatt or Kenner might be prompted to consider the sense in which these two words signal one element of the poem's more complex metaphoric theme—military "retreats," monarchial "seats"? But in doing so they would draw upon their own awareness of a separate impersonal system of linguistic relations. For Sheridan his readings of Milton's visual poetics were justified by his certainty that they were created by the author, but the widespread reluctance to "read" correspondences between rhyme patterns existed because of their status as a mysterious coincidence, as providing access to a system of correspondences over which neither poet nor reader has full control. The written text could be manipulated as a point of silent correspondence between poet and reader, but with an arbitrary coincidence of sound both would seem to be at the mercy of a more perplexing and unpredictable system of relations.

Neither Wimsatt nor Kenner states whether the poet's use of rhyme is always productive of extralogical effects or whether these occur only when the semantic interaction of the words connects thematically with some broader textual meaning. They do not really need to make such a distinction, because the competent reader will always be able to trace semantic connections between any two words drawn at random from the same phonemic category and state how this relation either supports or disrupts the broader chain of meanings to which they are attached. All rhyme words offer the possibility of a fruitful semantic interplay, because no absolute semantic discrimination can operate between any two words in the same language. But the critic's controlling perspective over the working of two linguistic systems places the poet in a less secure position within the communicative circuit. Compare the choices offered to the rhyming poet with those offered to the practitioner of the unrhymed line. The latter can manipulate his syntax to the degree that the typographic line can close a syntactic unit or break into it and throw emphasis either upon the units of sense that precede or those that follow the spatial break. The poet has far more control over the system of relations and integers and the reader responds accordingly. But with rhyme the reader must assume the role of the casuist, the ultimate judicial voice in the conflict between two autonomous systems of meaning.

The modern critic's lack of anxiety in assuming this role can best be explained with reference to Wimsatt's (and Monroe Beardsley's) seminal article on "The Intentional Fallacy" (1946). A central precept of the essay is that whatever the critic is able to disclose from the poem must necessarily have been put there by the poet: "If the poet succeeded in doing it, then the poem itself shows what he was trying to do" (p. 4). Quite so, but with rhyme this claim faces a number of challenges. Elsewhere Wimsatt and Beardsley state that "A poem does not come into existence by accident. The words of a poem . . . come out of a head, not out of a hat" (p. 4). But for the eighteenth-century critics, rhyme did indeed "come out of a hat" in the sense that the poet's degree of control was compromised by his use of an arbitrary system of relations, and Cockin provides a very dissonant echo of the modern critics' phrase with his references to "*accidental blemishes of a different style*" and "*unmeaning recurrences of similar sounds.*" It would be absurd to claim that the rhyming poet is completely at the mercy of a random system, but to assume, as the modern critics do, that it is the poet, and not themselves, who successfully rectifies the balance between illogic and logic is to push their claims to intentionalist justification a little too far. There is a degree of consistency in the modern critics' attitudes toward rhyme and typography. Wimsatt and Kenner on rhyme are united with Culler and Fish on typography in the precedence given to the system of conventions from which the poem emerges at the expense of the poet's status as the ultimate source of a complex plenitude of effects. But Sheridan, as a representative of the eighteenth century, interprets Milton's typographic effects *because* of his belief in the poet's control over convention, and he refuses to perform similar analyses of Pope's use of rhyme for exactly the same reason—that to do so would move the source of meaning away from Pope and toward the signifying power of an impersonal system. And although the critics covered in the "Voice of Form" were in conflict with many of their contemporaries, their desire to give precedence to the certainty and authority of the poet's voice over such conventions as the line, the foot, and rhyme is based upon a very similar faith in the poet as the single source of meaning.

A curious relationship exists between the eighteenth-century critical attitudes toward rhyme and a number of modern poetic techniques. I shall explore this in chapter 7, but I shall close this chapter with a sequence of eighteenth- to twentieth-century correspondences that both confirms the already established pattern of conflicts and, with the help of Pope, introduces an element of humor into these rather dry exchanges. Kenner, when arguing that the phonemic coincidence of rhyme provides the reader with access to the power of language as a mysterious impersonal system, uses an interesting example.

> From the very first pun we used to learn as children—"When is a door not a door? When it's ajar"—we may recall learning nothing at all about doors, not even the answer to the question, and if we do learn a fact about language we may reject it as an annoying fact . . . So with rhyme we may feel. (p. 64)

Dryden's brother-in-law, Robert Howard, was eventually to assume the role of Crites in the *Essay of Dramatic Poesy*, but when speaking as himself in the Preface to *Four New Plays* (1664) he did indeed feel that such a use of rhyme was both annoying and not entirely informative as to the linguistic and epistemological status of a door.

> Nor is great thoughts more adorned by Verse than Verse unbeautified by mean ones so that Verse seems not only unfit in the best use of it,

but more in the worse, when a servant is called or a Door bid to be shut in Rhime.[11]

It would not stretch circumstantial plausibility too far to suggest that Pope had one eye on this when he began his most self-consciously poetic exploration of poetry.

> Shut, shut the door, good John! fagigued I said,
> Tye up the knocker, say I'm sick, I'm dead.
> *(Epistle to Dr. Arbuthnot* ll 1–2)

John was slamming the door against those enthusiastic young apprentices, who might want to engage with Pope in a critical discussion of their work. Perhaps in this case Pope foresaw the critical procedures of Wimsatt and Kenner, because in the evasive illogic of something "said" while "dead," we find the late poet in admirable control of the impersonal system.

PART THREE
Silence and Sound: The Modern Perspective

Introduction

The two preceding parts of this book have dealt with the varied and very often conflicting opinions of eighteenth-century critics upon how the silent printed text and the spoken poem interact in the reader's appreciation of poetic form. I move from the eighteenth to the twentieth century, because the critical issues that made the work of men such as Sheridan and Steele so penetrative and intriguing had in the postromantic period become marginal considerations. Questions of whether the unrhymed pentameter is a recognizable component of poetic form and, if recognized, of what effect it has upon the reader, had been gradually displaced by more powerful developments in literary history. The fact that the majority of romantic poets drew their formal models from varied but well-established precedents was of minor importance compared with the much more complex questions of aesthetics and existence offered to contemporary commentators upon romanticism. The threat that Milton's experiment posed to the incipient formal protocols of Augustan prosody created an agenda for the epistemologists of form that would not be so enthusiastically returned to until the emergence of free verse at the beginning of the twentieth century.

The purpose of this part will be to explore the ways in which the eighteenth-century conceptions of poetic form and their influence upon meaning can assist in our understanding of how free verse operates in the variable equation of structure and effect.

In order to address this issue we must also consider the question of what free verse is. The question is circular because, unlike forms such as the sonnet or the couplet, free verse is capable of shifting in definition with every specific context or manifestation. The key is to be found in the one structural component from which free verse can never free itself—the line.

The disagreements over Milton's blank verse show that the poetic line can operate as a linguistic unit in two distinct ways. If it establishes a balanced and unproblematic relationship with the movements of syntax and rhythm, the reader's understanding of its poetic effects is based upon its symbiotic function within a relatively predictable formal structure. But if it establishes its own independent status outside the movement and structure of other linguistic elements, then the reader is obliged to deal with two patterns of form and meaning—a distinction that is generated by the line as a visual phenomenon. This notion of the line as an autonomous source of poetic effects was first considered by the eighteenth-century critics, but with the formal experiments of this century the complex relationship between what we hear and what we see has virtually replaced traditional conceptions of prosody. The questions of whether the line is a visual or an oral unit, of how this affects meaning, and of whether a priori considerations of form should influence composition—all of these have returned after two centuries to become central to the identity and effect of free verse.

This part of the book is divided into two chapters: the first will consider the tension between the potential for the line as an independent visual structure and the tenacious and widespread belief that such a phenomenon would subvert the ideal of poetry as an oral medium; the second will examine how a number of modern poets have diffused this conflict by deploying silent poetics as a productive and individual component of form.

7
Fenollosa and the Silence-Sound Conflict

Fenollosa

Ernest Fenollosa's *The Chinese Written Character as a Medium for Poetry* was edited by Ezra Pound and published in 1919.[1] It has since come to be regarded as one of the monuments to change in literary history. Hugh Kenner, in his study of modernist poetics *The Pound Era*, called it "the *Ars Poetica* of our time" and Donald Davie has compared it with Sidney's *Apologie*, Wordsworth's Preface to *Lyrical Ballads*, and Shelley's *Defence of Poetry*.

Connections have been suggested between Fenollosa's propositions and the theories of imagism—disparate and often conflicting as the latter tend to be—and his concentration upon the Chinese ideogram has provided the name for an entire tradition of, mostly American, poetry—the work of Pound, Williams, Olson, Duncan, and Creeley being regarded as the archetypes of ideogrammic technique.

The essay's connections with the eighteenth century would thus appear to be exceedingly tenuous, but as I shall show, Fenollosa created what is, in effect, a program for the creative application of the critical discoveries of the eighteenth-century silent readers. He, and Pound, were completely unaware of the latter's existence, and the sources for the essay are, as its title suggests, far outside the Western tradition of language and poetry, but the correspondences are striking enough to suggest that silent poetics is a creative and interpretive attraction strong enough to transcend cultural and historical categories.

Fenollosa argued that the Chinese written sign, the ideogram, was capable of representing images, metaphors, and natural processes in a way that bypassed the systematic, logical protocols of Western langauge.

If, using Western language, we wish to convey the relationship between two objects, the movement, or even the attitude of one thing in relation to another, our link point is provided by the grammatical structures in which verbs, adjectives, and connectives enact a representation of reality. Fenollosa regarded this form of expression and representation as limited and confined by its own methodology, and he argued that the rules and conventions of grammar imposed an artificial and arbitary medium upon our perceptions of the world.

He illustrated his point by inviting the reader to contrast Gray's line, "The curfew tolls the knell of parting day" with the Chinese line

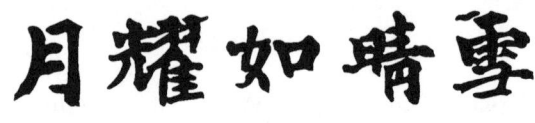

Moon rays like pure snow

(p. 139)

The essential difference between the two is that in Gray's line individual words become units of meaning only because of their role in the grammatical sequence of verbs, nouns, and connectives, but in the Chinese line the individual units are in themselves complex representations of movement and image—linguistic pictures. Fenollosa clarifies this by comparing another Chinese line with its translation into English.

Man Sees Horse

First stands the man on two legs. Second, his eye moves through space: a bold figure represented by running legs under an eye, a modified picture of an eye, a modified picture of running legs but unforgettable once you have seen it. Third stands the horse on his four legs.

The thought picture is not only called up by these signs as well as by words but far more vividly and concretely. Legs belong to all three characters: they are *alive*. The group holds something of the quality of a continuous moving picture. (p. 140)

It would seem that the pictorial representations of the ideogram grant the visual reader a level of perception that is systematically denied by the grammatical structure of English. As Fenollosa unwittingly demonstrates, it would require at least two paragraphs of sequential, grammatical language to describe the multidimensional effect of three Chinese units, and in English the perceptual sequence becomes the victim of what Fenollosa later calls "the inveterate logic of classification," whereas the Chinese medium grants us the transparency of the "moving picture."

The scholarly accuracy of Fenollosa's conception of Chinese as a nonphonetic, written medium has been the subject of subsequent debate, but leaving this aside, his thesis and its attraction for Pound is clear. Western language, and more specifically poetic language, can only provide access to the complex interrelationships of the prelinguistic world if it can in some way subvert and cut through its own logic of composition and create syntheses, concentrations of object, movement, and perspective similar to those of the visible language of the ideogram.

Three statements by early imagist poets on their intentions would appear to echo Fenollosa's thesis:

Williams (1908), "To paint the thing as I see it."
F. S. Flint (1913), "Direct treatment of the 'thing' whether subjective or objective."
Pound (1913), "An 'Image' is that which presents an intellectual and emotional complex in an instance of time."

But what is lacking, both from contemporary manifestoes and from later retrospective analyses of modernism and its origins, is a real attempt to specify how the signifying procedures of a visual medium could be adapted to the methodology and conventions of a language whose visual format is regarded as no more than a record of the grammar of its oral, sequential form.[2] And it is here that we find that the silent readings of the eighteenth century begin to resonate beyond their immediate cultural and historical circumstances and to clarify a number of critical and literary issues that we tend to associate only with modernism.

First of all, we should recall Kenrick, who identified "two distinct types of langauge," the "vocal," "which speaks to the ears" and the "written," and more significantly the "literary," which "speaks to the eyes." By "literary" he means poetic, and we should remind ourselves of the proliferation of critical emphases on the initial recognition of a poem as dependent upon its division into lines of words outside the continuities of grammar—two patterns which, according to Kenrick, "though arbitrarily connected by use, have no natural or physical dependence on each other." I have already referred to the active participation of the reader in signifying process of silent poetics, and it is to Sheridan whom we turn for the kind of productive participation that reconciles the sequential structure of English with Fenollosa's ideal of ideogrammic juxtaposition. Sheridan comments that the line ending,

>   hardening in his strength
> Glories

makes the word *glories* . . . project from the rest, the insolent vanity, and obstinate pride of Satan, are more strongly painted, than could have been done by the longest description. And yet no poet but Milton would have placed the word in its present situation. (II pp. 254–55)

Fenollosa explicates each Chinese ideogram as productive of a complexity of meanings through its juxtaposition of visual images, and compares a succession of these with a "vivid shorthand picture of the operations of nature," and we find Sheridan identifying almost exactly the same effect from the visual isolation of "glories," which makes it react with the phrase "his strength" in a way that is closer to the visual juxtaposition of the ideogram than it is to the linear continuities of grammar. And most importantly we find that Fenollosa's analogy of the "shorthand picture" is perfectly matched by Sheridan's description of an effect "more strongly painted, that could have been done by the longest description."

Sheridan's readings of Milton point to the only possible technique by which the grammatical medium of English can be adapted to the more concentrated visual mode of the ideogram, and this technique requires the active participation of the silent reader.

Later in his essay Fenollosa goes on to illustrate how the structure of English is built upon a series of discrete concepts of classification: "European logical thought is a kind of brick yard. It is baked into little hard units or concepts. These are piled in rows according to size and then labeled with words for future use" (p. 150). It is the grammatical relationships between these units that constitute linguistic meaning, and the possibility of creating extragrammatical relationships between units by visually juxtaposing them was a departure from the "logic" of grammar that certainly worried Kames: "a quality cannot exist independent of a subject; nor are they separable even in the imagination, because they make parts of the same idea." But as Sheridan and Hollander demonstrate, the reader is capable of intervening at this point of visual separation to propose a rather different idea. In Fenollosa's view: "We [in English] take a concept of lower attenuation, such as 'cherry'; we see that it is contained under one higher, such as 'redness.' Then we are permitted to say in sentence form 'Cherryness is contained under redness'" (p. 151). But what if the sentence form is broken in the manner of,

                                      bright
        Pavement

As Sheridan says, "the idea seems to acquire new force from this very circumstance . . . to fix our thought not on the pavement itself, but on the brightness of the pavement." It is the spatial gap between the two words that grants Sheridan an extra dimension of signification, displacing the compressed isolation of the "same idea"—to adapt Fenollosa's example, "[the] pavement is bright"—and allowing the two juxtaposed units of meaning to interrelate in a manner that is beyond the internal rules of sequential grammar. But it has become clear that in Sheridan's, Hollander's, and Ricks's readings of blank verse the reader, or, to be more accurate, the critic, must actually become part of the communicative circuit through which the poet and the poem produce meanings. The traditional notion of a poetic voice tracing a linear continuity of meaning is intensified and transformed into distinct voices, and it becomes the role of the silent reader to interact with the written poem and identify the points at which such intensifications and dispersals of meaning take place. It is here that Fenollosa's ideal of "the written Character" as a "Medium" for Western poetry becomes problematic, because neither he nor any of the later commentators on his essay has explained how the ideogram might maintain its multidimensional texture in an oral form. Sheridan claimed that the effects he identifies cannot be found in "poetic numbers, of which there can be only one reciter," in which "the sounds can only be in succession," But even if there were two or more "reciters" of the ideogram and the "succession" of its phonemic integers were varied, it is impossible to imagine how the "thought picture" of a "figure represented by running legs under an eye" could maintain its visual effect in an oral form.

In a footnote to his edition, Pound told of how the sculptor Gaudier-Brzeska was able to read the ideograms without translation. There could be no other reason for his inclusion of this anecdote than as token reassurance that the ideal of concrete transparency is at least a possibility. But Pound failed to pursue the implication that if the effect of these images upon Gaudier-Brzeska were to become a poetic objective, then all of the grammatical structures of language would have to be abandoned in favor of a form of spatial onomatopoeia. Pound the poet could not and did not attempt to do this, but instead relied upon a form of compromise between the ideal of ideogrammic synthesis and the inescapable conventions of English.

The term "juxtaposition" is often applied to Pound's poetry, especially the *Cantos;* it implies that the static, spatial relationships of the ideogram can be reproduced by in some way compromising the temporal, sequential nature of the sentence. Indeed there is an analogy to be drawn between Fenollosa's explication of the ideogram and the way in which we may be said to understand the juxtaposed or ideogrammic method in English. Fenollosa renders Chinese characters intelligible to the non-Chinese reader by breaking them up, literally "explaining" them in terms of the linguistic system to which they are opposed. He tacitly acknowledges the fact that a form of balance must be achieved between the sequential grammar of Western language and the visual juxtapositions of the ideogram. The problem is evident in his title: to make an essentially visual form of communication the medium for poetic writing in a system whose conventions and techniques are based upon an ideal of oral communication will inevitably involve a degree of compromise for one or the other. Compromise is probably something of a euphemism, because to accept that visual structures can, in themselves, represent a component of poetic meaning is to pose a threat to the belief, deeply ingrained both in the *ex cathedra* statements of poets and in the protocols of criticism, that poetry is an aural medium. Conflict would be a more accurate description of the way in which the visible text is seen by most writers to compromise the ideal of the vocal poem. Consider, for instance, the following critical encounter with a poem by Pound. The title of Harvey Gross's *Sound and Form in Modern Poetry* (1964) portends what his technique confirms; that spatial form should be regarded as a subcategory, almost an eccentricity, of free verse technique. The problems raised by this traditional, yet prejudicial, approach become vividly evident in his treatment of Pound's imagist prototype for the *Cantos,* "In A Station of the Metro." He prefaces his criticism with the claim that ideogrammatic technique is not capable of transference to Western language.

> In itself the ideogram is soundless. . . . A direct visual correspondence once existed between the ideogram and thing, thought or action. . . . English has no such correspondences. No English word "looks like" the thing it signifies. . . . The actual *thing* a word is, is sound; as physical objects words possess only phonetic reality. (p. 162)

Gross is correct to state that words do not physically resemble items or images, but what he does not recognize is the fact that the degree of interaction between phonetic integers can be radically changed when they are transferred to the visual format of the page—a process of interaction that depends entirely upon their identity as visible "things." In fact, Gross subverts his own premise in his treatment of Pound's poem.

> The apparation of these faces in the crowd;
> Petals on a wet black bough

> Here "ideogrammatic method" means poetry without complete sentences. The absence of verb and preposition enhances both rhythm and significance; a certain mystery evaporates if we supply the implied copula and relational word:

>> The apparation of these faces in the crowd
>> (Are like) Petals on a wet black bough

> No harm comes if we want to see this as vaguely *analagous* to Chinese writing; the two images have spatial and emotional relationships. Grammar, however, is not missing; it is automatically supplied by the reader. (p. 162)

Gross "supplies" the meaning of the poem—in the sense that it is concerned with the profundity of superficial impressions—but to do so he is obliged to neutralize its visual effect and effectively rewrite it in accordance with an idealized sense of continuity conveyed by the sequential pattern of grammar: he imposes an oral reading upon a visual effect. The inserted words could just as plausibly be "are unlike" or, to be more elaborate, "lack the beauty of." The poetic effect created by Pound is deliberately uncertain and evasive, and it is achieved by a visual juxtaposition of two syntactic units that disrupts the certainties of grammatical continuity. For Gross to reestablish such a continuity is to deprive the poem of its essential quality of instability. The visual juxtaposition invites the reader to participate in the plenitude of meanings. It is this sense of plenitude, or language detached from its own limiting conventions of form, that has established these lines as a point of attraction for two generations of critics, and as the following chapter will show, modern poets have consistently deployed the silent, printed text as a means of dispersing the single authoritative pattern of oral, sequential language. To understand why Gross's reading is so deeply rooted in a form of phonocentric idealism we have only to examine the statements of many of the earliest practitioners of free verse.

Conflict

In the eighteenth century the tension between writing and speech was foregrounded in the disagreements between the Sheridan group, who acknowledged the influence of print, and the writers covered under the "Voice of Form." In the twentieth century it is in the *ex cathedra* statements of poets that we find the most wholehearted defence of the spoken poem. In a letter to Harriet Monroe, Pound reveals a near obsessive preoccupation with the need to break away from the complicit structures of abstract form, tradition, and in effect, writing.

> rhythm MUST have meaning. It can't be merely a careless dash off, with no grip and no real hold on the words and sense, a tumty tum, tumty tum, tum ta. . . . Every literaryism, every book word, fritters away a scrap of the reader's patience, a scrap of his sense of your sincerity. When one really feels and thinks, one stammers with simple speech; it is only in the flurry, the shallow frothy excitement of writing, or the inebriety of a metre, that one falls into the easy—oh, how easy!—speech of books and poems that one has read.[3]

The "easy speech" of books and poems is the tainted and codified written text, the recorded tradition, threatening the purity and immediacy of the poet's voice. The printed poem seems to be in token allegiance with the stultifying practices of tradition, and we should note a resemblance between this plea and Blake's very similar evocation of the poet's voice as "fettered" by the arbitrary conventions of the line and rhyme. Blake eventually abandoned the poetic line, but the modernists, except with brief excursions into the prose poem, maintained an allegiance to it as a central component of structure. Consequently the problem to which Pound and the Imagists continually return is of how to maintain an effect of immediacy and spontaniety when the poem must also function in the absence of the poet's voice, its printed anonymity displacing the moment of origin and allowing in aberrant readings based upon the interaction between the reader and the silent printed text.

Amy Lowell acknowledged the status of the line as the basic formal unit of the poem and defined it as a "cadence," a "rhythmic curve . . . corresponding roughly to the necessity of breathing." She might have been paraphrasing Joshua Steele: "Our breathing, the beating of our pulse, and our movement in walking, make the division of time by pointed and regular *cadences* familiar and natural to us." Lowell continues this natural analogy and relates the organic structure of the poem to the prelinguistic rhythm of the body by claiming that the formal conventions of poetry, the foot, the line, and the strophe, are determined not by abstract formulae but by their more instinctive relation with the movement of walking, and concludes that the "poem must be rounded and recurring as the circular swing of the balanced pendulum."[4] Steele stated that he had based his methodology of analysis "neither on hypothesis nor on antient authorities," but "by actual experiment—by a pendulum or by my steps."

Both share a preference for the "cadence" over the more abstract and limiting categories of feet and lines, and believe that these rhythmic movements result from such instinctive rhythmic experiences as breathing and walking. The point to be made about these natural metaphors is that they are predicated upon the ideal of the vocal utterance as the source of intention and meaning: the rhythms of speech are determined by our instinctive sense of natural movement and pattern. But the ever-present problem is of how to preserve this sense of immediacy when the reader's first experience of the utterance is likely to be with its silent printed form. Lowell again:

> But one thing must be borne in mind; a cadenced poem is written to be read aloud, in this way only will its rhythm be felt. Poetry is a spoken and not a written art. . . . It is not a question of rules and forms. Poetry is the vision in a man's soul which he translates as best he can with the means at his disposal.[5]

Pound, echoing Lowell, identifies the written text as transparent: "All typographic disposition, placing of words on the page, is intended to facilitate the reader's intonation, whether he be reading silently or aloud to friends."[6] The most concise summary of these poets' attitudes toward the relation between speech and writing is Rice's order to the reader to resurrect the "living Voice" of the poet from the "dead Letter" of print. The early free verse poets would have been reluctant to acknowledge the influence of the silent printed medium upon their verse form, because to have done so would have been to play into the hands of their conservative critical opponents. This is Amy Lowell's response to John Livingstone Lowe's experiment with the visual format:

> Recently a writer in *The Nation* took some of Meredith's prose and made it into vers libre poems which any poet would have been glad to write. Then he took some of my poems and turned them into prose, with a result which he was kind enough to call beautiful. He then pertinently asked what was the difference. Typography is not relevant to the discussion. Whether a thing is written as prose or as verse is immaterial.[7]

Lowell contradicts herself, since in most of her other writing on free verse, she is concerned with validating the existence of lineal form. Her claim that "Poetry is a spoken and not a written art" holds the key to this, because unless some method of preserving the oral poem were developed, the reader would always find patterns, gaps, discontinuities that seem to be the product of writing.

This problem was also faced by the eighteenth-century "Voice of Form" theorists. Consider John Rice's rearrangement of *Paradise Lost* (V, 283–85).

> The third his feet shadow'd from either Heel with feather'd Mail,
> Sky tinctured Grain.
>
> (p. 179)

The visual space after "Mail" operates outside the conventions of syntax; the diffuse linguistic sequence of the first line seems to gather itself into a sharper, more concrete image, and the same use of the visual line as an extragrammatical instrument of focus, of perceptual concentration, is central to the opening sequence of Lowell's "An Aquarium."

Fenollosa and the Silence-Sound Conflict

> Streaks of green and yellow iridescence,
> Silver shiftings,
> Rings veering out of rings,
> Silver—gold—

Whatever Lowell might claim, the essential stylistic quality of these lines would be lost if they were printed as prose, and more significantly, if they were only conveyed orally.

The use of the visual format seems to be something of a guilty secret both for the Imagists and the eighteenth-century theorists. We might recall that Walker reprinted the opening sequence of *Paradise Lost* in accordance with his vocal ideal, but he found himself forced to abandon the conventions of punctuation when the impact of the single isolated word would have a far more striking effect:

> While it pursues
> Things
> Unattempted yet in prose or rhyme.

Walker, like his Imagist successors, never consciously explored the influence of typographic layout upon understanding, but in his reprinting of prose sequences as a guide to the intonational performance of the reader, he betrays an awareness of how the visual materiality of language can actually create meaning. Even when we take into account the idiomatic differences, the following sequence from his *Rhetorical Grammar* (1785) comes very close to being a case of eighteenth-century Imagism.

> What innumerable multitudes of people
> Lie confused together under the pavement of
> An ancient cathedral!
> How men and women;
> Friends and enemies;
> Priests and soldiers;
> Monks and prebendaries are crumbled amongst one
> Another, and blended together in the same common
> Mass.
>
> (p. 246)

This is from the *Spectator,* no. 26, but the way in which the visual structure traces a formula of reflective observation, catalogued precision, and thematic denouement could have inspired the following sequence from John Gould Fletcher's "Green Symphony."

> The trees are like a sea;
> Tossing,
> Trembling,
> Roaring,
> Wallowing,
> Darting their long green flickering fronds up at the sky,
> Spotted with white blossom-spray.

There is a curious consistency in the work of these two groups of writers, separated by one hundred and fifty years and an undocumentable amount of aesthetic circumstances: for both, the visual and the oral exist in a very uneasy communicative equation. It is possible to find resonances, intensities, ambiguities that cannot be directly translated from one medium to the other.

The only positive acknowledgement by an early modernist of this state of imbalance is to be found in T. E. Hulme's "Lecture on Modern Poetry."[8] Hulme makes a direct statement on the effect of traditional metrical form, restating Dryden's notion of "rhyme and metre as aids to the memory" and apparently plagiarizing Coleridge's vague diagnosis of meter as a narcotic: "the effect of rhythm, like that of music, is to produce a kind of hypnotic state, during which suggestions of grief or ecstasy are easily and powerfully effective." But instead of suggesting how the conventions of this oral medium might be adapted to the new aesthetic, he abandons them altogether: "the procedure of the new visual art is quite the contrary. It depends for its effect not on a kind of half sleep produced, but on arresting the attention, so much that the succession of visual images should exhaust one." This is a revolutionary proposition because Hulme implies that it is sound itself that erects an arbitrary barrier to transparency and that the visual materiality of language is the least refractory element of the medium: "This material, the ὑλη of Aristotle is image and not sound. It builds up a plastic image which it hands over to the reader, whereas the old art endeavoured to influence him physically by the hypnotic effect of rhythm" (pp. 267–70). This is as close as any of the early modernists came to acknowledging the visual structure as an independent source of meaning—not entirely in opposition to the sequential, grammatical pattern, but capable of creating resonances and intensities that are part of the silent realm of communication. The majority of writers, poets, and critics, maintained a belief in a unitary relation within the speech—writing hierarchy. They did so because to follow Hulme would have involved a form of submission to forces and structures that seem to be outside the control of the poet. Lowes forced Lowell to contradict herself because his critical exercise was an early example of Culler's and Fish's illustrations of reader-response technique. Lowes, Culler, and Fish all assume that the visual format allows the reader to become an active participant in the poetic medium. They compromise the individuality of the poet by classifying the visual format as part of a shared continuum of awareness, something that can be drawn upon almost at random and offered to the reader as a pattern upon which meanings can be imposed.

A resultant fear of betrayal, of a reluctance to fully contemplate the signifying potential of silent, printed language, emerges as a kind of nervous ambivalence in the writings of Pound. We should recall that his identification of the visual text as a brief stage in the process of oral communication is mysteriously qualified by the phrase "whether he be reading silently or aloud to friends." Oral and silent reading are by no means parallel coordinates of the same process, and one suspects that this possibility caused Pound to insert his rather anxious addendum. He came closest to exposing his own awareness of the uneasy relationship between speech and writing in the "Rhythm and Rhyme" section of "A Few Don'ts By An Imagist" (1913).[9]

> Don't chop your stuff into separate *iambs*. Don't make each line stop dead at the end, and then begin every next line with a heave. Let the beginning of the next line catch the rise of the rhythm wave unless you want a definite longish pause. (p. 133)

This rejection of the limiting expectations of classical foot structure evokes the revolutionary hypotheses of the "Voice of Form," but it also raises the attendant question of how such unlimited rhythmic movements could constitute poetic lines at all. Sheridan might have asked him how the line could be counterpointed with the "rhythm wave" unless you could actually see it? Such a dialogue becomes a little less fantastic when we find Pound challenging the notion of poetic "harmony."

> The term harmony is misapplied in poetry; it refers to simultaneous sounds of different pitch. There is, however, in the best verse a sort of

> residue of sound which remains in the ear of the hearer and acts more or less as an organ base. (p. 133)

Sheridan addressed exactly the same problem of how to convey distinct patterns of sound and meaning simultaneously in an oral sequence, and his conjectures led him to a conception of poetic "harmony" as something that could only be appreciated in silent visualist readings. Pound does not take his argument quite so far, but in a number of his early poems in the Imagist anthologies we find him using the line both as the visual record of aural patterns, and as an instrument of form whose signifying potential *emerges from* its visual condition. Consider the opening sequence of "The Return":

> See, they return; ah see the tentative
> Movements, and the slow feet,
> The trouble in the pace and the uncertain
> Wavering!

The enjambed phrases operate in two ways: first they imitate the "tentative" and "uncertain" condition of the poetic voice, but they also trace out the equally hesitant pattern of "they" who "return, one, and by one, / With fear, as half awakened." The perceiver seems to be united with the perceived, and Pound has, to a degree, succeeded in breaking through the conventions and rules of Western language that Fenollosa condemned as an arbitrary barrier between experience and communication. He has done so by using the physical identity of the line as a point of interaction between the visual and the aural.

But for Pound to explicitly acknowledge his use of the visual format would also involve an acknowledgment of the reader's role as a participant in the communicative circuit. Derrida has provided a sinister echo of Lowell's ideal of oral form as granting access to "the vision in a man's soul": "What writing itself in its non-phonetic moment betrays, is life. It menaces at once, the breath, the spirit, and history as the spirits relationship with itself" (*Grammatology*, p. 25).

Ironically, Derrida's diagnosis of a "necessary decentring" of this phonocentric ideal in the new poetic of Fenollosa and Pound actually resulted in an almost obsessive rejection of the printed poem as anything other than a temporary record or an oral event. And nowhere are these beliefs more tenaciously preserved than in the extended tradition of ideogrammic writing.

The Open Poem

There has hardly been a more vigorous attempt to distance speech from writing than in Charles Olson's essay "Projective Verse,"[10] a work that revived Poundian modernism in the midst of the New Critical atmosphere of 1950. Olson's crucial distinction is between "closed" and "open" poetry. "Closed" poetry is "print bred," frozen in the abstract formulae of meter and rhyme—in other words the greater part of poetry written before the twentieth century. Olson's attitude to closed poetry is an extension of Fenollosa's perception of the infelicitous tendencies of Western language; that the conventions of the medium itself absorb and restructure the relationship between the individual and reality. According to Olson, the formal protocols of the "closed" poem reify and delimit any genuine attempt at communication between poet and reader, so that the original subject and object, the poet and the world, are transformed into grammatical, stylistic categories. Olson's escape route leads directly away from an arbitrary relationship between poetic form and the "real" world:

> every element in an open poem (the syllable, the line, as well as the image, the sound, the sense) must be taken up as participants in the kinetic of the poem just as solidly as we are accustomed to take what we call the objects of reality; and these elements are to be seen as creating the tensions of a poem just as totally as do those whose objects create what we know as the world. (p. 20)

The most tangible constituent of the poem's identity, the line, is less a prosodic category or a link with tradition and more a function of the poet's interaction with his environment. "And the line comes (I swear it) from the breath, from the breathing of the man who writes, at the moment that he writes, and thus is, it is here that the daily, the WORK, gets in, for only he, the man who writes, can declare, at every moment, the line its metric and its ending—where its breathing shall come to, termination." Steele, Blake, and Lowell are recalled, and Olson goes on to deal with the problems of the "printers measure." The manuscript and printing press have, according to Olson, removed verse "from its place of origin *and* its destination"; he believes that the traditional metrical line was petrified by print into a barrier between poet and reader. His solution is provided by more recent technology, the typewriter, which

> due to its rigidity and its space precisions, it can, for a poet indicate exactly the breath, the pauses, the suspensions even of syllables, the juxtapostitions even of parts of phrases, which he intends. For the first time the poet has the stave and the bar a musician has had. For the first time he can, without the convention of rime and meter, record the listening he has done to his own speech and by that one act indicate how he would want any reader, silently or otherwise, to voice his own work. (p. 26)

Olson's desire to record the "listening he has done to his own speech" corresponds to the effect identified by Derrida, with the French verb *"s'entendre parler,* ('hearing/understanding—oneself speak') through the phonic substance—which *presents itself* as a non-exterior, non-mundane therefore non-empirical or non-contingent signifier."[11] But it is the evanescence of the signifier in speech that creates the impression of immediate access to a signified, the suppression of what Derrida calls difference. Once the typing stops, what Olson calls the "kinetic" of the poem becomes stasis, and the poem presents itself as the spaces, gaps, and formal units of the text to be thematized or naturalized by the process of interpretation—a menacing of "the breath."

Olson proposed a model of the creative process by which the poet must respond to the dynamics of phenomena, rather than impose upon them the falsifying strictures of closed form:

> Let me put it baldly. The two halves are:
>   The HEAD, by way of the EAR, to the SYLLABLE
>   The HEART, by way of the BREATH, to the LINE. (p. 19)

And Cid Corman in the section of his *Word for Word*[12] entitled "The Structure of Poetic Rhythms in relation to Oral Poetry," restates the Olson manifesto.

> The voice, as the articulator of expression, is the shaper of poetic style or personality, but always in conjunction with the ear, i.e. the voice and the ear (which supposes inevitably the mental faculty) modulate the breath . . . the breath is the unit of poetic energy. (p. 67–68)

His enthusiastic promotion of the "rhythmic cadence" and the "breath pause" takes us back yet again through the vocalist tradition, and at one point he recalls the Walker/Rice rewritings of Milton by breaking up four lines of Keats's *Endymion* into "breath pauses."

> Its loneliness' 'increases' 'it will never
> Pass' 'into nothingness;' 'but still will keep
> A Bower' 'quiet for us' 'and a sleep
> Full of sweet dreams' 'and health' and quiet breathing'.
>
> (p. 69)

We can be certain that Corman's intention in this exercise is essentially the same as that of his aesthetic precursors—to uncover the form of cadence or rhythmic pattern that is closest to the moment of creation. But the impression of continuity is deceptive, because the earlier theorists were, as Odell put it, uncovering "a system which has never been fully investigated." The "system" is now known as free verse and has been investigated to the extent that it has been admitted to the vocabulary of exegesis.

Consider how Corman's rewritings would look if reprinted in the form that had practically become an idiom for the post-Poundian poets.

> Its loneliness
> Increases
> It will never pass
>   Into nothingness;
> But still will keep a bower
> Quiet for us
> And a sleep
> Full of sweet dreams
>   and health
> And quiet breathing

The words are still Keats's, but the interpretive context has changed. Elements such as "Increases" and "Into nothingness" have been released from what Olson would regard as their closed condition within the sequential pattern of syntax and the pentameter. But they have also passed into a communicative realm where the ideal of oral immediacy is equally compromised. The so-called "breath pauses" resonate and intensify in meaning because of their visual isolation—they have escaped from the restrictions of traditional syntactic and metrical continuity, but they establish another system of conventions that the reader will recognize as part of an intertextual framework.

When Jonathan Culler reprinted the opening sentence of Quine's *From A Logical Point of View* he assumed two separate identities: the modernist poet, who arranges his words to create a particular spatial pattern; and the poet's readerly doppelganger, who is fully conversant with the techniques and intentions of modernist poetics. What he did not state is that this two-dimensional condition of awareness is always present in critical analysis. The reader will assume that the textual resonances of the printed page have been created by the poet for his appreciation. The problem arises when we attempt to distinguish between effects generated exclusively by the silent printed configurations and the original vocal patterns that these shapes are supposed only to record. Culler conveniently sidestepped this issue by claiming that it is the interplay between reader and text that creates meaning, but it is clearly not as simple as that. The printed format is a refractory medium: it draws the reader into a participatory role in the communicative circuit, but it also preserves elements of the original intention. Consider for instance the beginning of one of Olson's *Maximus* letters.

> I have this sense
> that I am one
> with my skin
>   Plus this—plus this:
> that forever the geography
> which leans in
> on me I compell
> backwards I compell Gloucester
> to yield, to
> change
>   Polis
> is this[13]

We could, as informed readers, assume that the irregular line breaks represent a printed record of "the listening he has done to his own speech," but then we begin to wonder if in the opening line the positioning of the "I" directly above the more grammatically subordinate "I" and "my" of the second and third lines is a subtle introduction to the major theme of how a sense of identity operates in the vast spatial continuum of "geography" and "Gloucester." And we then have to ask how this mere record of an oral event can begin to discharge textual intensities that are primarily dependent upon its silent visual pattern? Thus we have a tension, a conflict between the reader's silent engagement with the printed text and the poet's assumption that this text is but one stage in a largely transparent process of communication.

Olson's causal chain of "HEAD/HEART," "EAR/BREATH," AND

"SYLLABLE/LINE," through which "Form" becomes a natural "EXTENSION OF CONTENT," is the perfect model of oral transparency. But when the process is reversed by the reader/critic, the point of contact will almost certainly be the silent, printed text, and it has become clear that the resistances and diversions of writing cannot be relied upon to lead us back directly to the author's intention. From Dennis to Olson, formal experiment has upheld a sequence of ideals: the rejection of regular rhyme and lineal closure; the displacement of traditional and abstract prosodic categories by the "cadence" and the "breath pause"; the almost fanatical emphasis on the oral text as an assurance of transparency—all of these are attempts to break down the arbitrary barriers of poetic form between poet and reader. But writing cannot be abolished, and the question is how to reconcile the threat to the poet's individuality, the compromising of the "breath," the "life" of the vocal utterance, with the reader's awareness of how the silent visual format can itself produce intriguing intensities and subtleties of meaning.

The following chapter will shift the emphasis away from the critical debate and toward the poems themselves. Must the intersection of sound and silence inevitably produce interpretive conflict, or can this relation operate as a genuinely productive component of poetic form that effectively *unites* the poet with the reader?

8
The Spoken Word Unheard: Silence and Sound in Modern Poems

It will not be the purpose of this concluding chapter to document every instance of how the visual format functions as a poetic effect—phenomena such as enjambment are easy enough to recognize. Its purpose will be to examine a number of poems that seem to me to vividly encapsulate and to productively synthesize the disparate and often conflicting notions of writing and speech, sound and silence, which have divided critical perspectives in the eighteenth and the twentieth centuries. The last word in this debate will be given to the poem.

e. e. cummings and the Sliding Scale

Much of e. e. cummings's poetry represents an explicit and self-conscious tendency in modernist technique, and one that is quite inimical to its phonocatric bias; to make the visual materiality of language the theme as well as the functional condition of the poem. Most of cummings's best known and widely anthologized poems cannot be read aloud, nor can they be converted into an interpretive paraphrase that supersedes their visual identity. This is "57" from the collection of *73 Poems*.

```
57
mi (dreamlike) st

makes big each dim
inuti
ve turns obv

ious t
os
trange
```

               un

               til o
               urselve
               s are

               will be wor

               (magi
               c
               ally)

               Ids

The poem is about the effect of mist upon the perception and the imagination, but its repertoire of effects can hardly be mirrored in sequential interpretive language. It would be very difficult to describe the order in which things happen in the poem because the referential function and material identity of the language are so closely meshed. It is a complete departure from the continuities of oral language, but to regard "mi (dreamlike) st" and "turns / obv / ious/ t / os / trange" as meaningful at all we are placing them in the same formal context as Wordsworth's "impress / Thoughts." The difference is that with Wordsworth, and Milton, the silent visual text works against and subtly displaces the single strand of oral continuity, but with cummings the visual format literally replaces and silences the performative dimension of spoken language.

I use this comparison between cummings and Wordsworth because they exist at opposite ends of a sliding scale, along which we can establish an interactive relation between the visual and the oral in individual poems. Beyond Wordsworth's and Milton's end of the scale we would find the work of the more traditional eighteenth-century blank verse writers such as Thomson and Young, where the visual format is synchronized with the rhythmic and syntactic movement of the oral sequence—the visual text becomes the recording instrument for the single pattern of the spoken medium. To broaden this category even further we could include all forms of verse that create no essential point of disruption between what is seen on the page and what is heard.

Beyond cummings's end of the scale there exists a whole subgenre of writing that is generally categorized as concrete poetry.

The catalogue of the ICA exhibition "Between Poetry and

Painting" (1965) includes statements by the contributors on how they regard concretism as a genre that transcends the traditional distinctions between poetry and the visual arts, and the following is from Edwin Morgan.

> In all poetry which is written down or printed, a part of the effect is bound to be visual. Line-length, open or close texture, long or short words, light or heavy punctuation, use of capitals, exclamation marks, rhyme—all these produce characteristic variations of effect and induce different reactions in the viewer even before the viewer becomes in the strict sense a reader. A page of Milton's blank verse with its bristling and serried paragraphs looks quite different from a page of Wordsworth's, clear, open light, loose untormented. . . . The delicate cat-paw placing of words in poems by William Carlos Williams, Zukofsky, Creeley, and Ronald Johnson is halfway between being a guide to the ear and a pleasure to the eye. A more commitedly visual poetry like concrete is only emphasising and developing an already existing visual component of aesthetic effect. Concrete poems are therefore not in opposition to the spirit of poetry unless we demand that poetry should be able to be read aloud, or unless they move so far into the purely graphic or the mathematical that they are no longer making their appeal through language as such. (pp. 69–70)

Morgan claims that concrete poetry exaggerates and makes explicit a form of poetic appreciation that has existed, but has rarely been acknowledged, in readings of such traditional forms as blank verse, and we can identify the key to this reluctance in his reference to the "demand that poetry should be read aloud." What most concrete poems attempt to do is to separate the two dimensions of sight and sound. With concrete poetry we might be able to see a completely different series of effects from those that we hear, given that we can hear these poems at all, but in verse that preserves what Thomas Barnes called the "shadow of the music," each interpretive dimension is never quite immune from the influence of the other—we could "demand" that such verse should be read aloud, but we would consequently diffuse the tension between sight and sound.

In my opinion concrete poetry deserves attention because it operates as a commentary upon the more complex interplay of sight and sound in what, in comparison, would be regarded as traditional forms. One of the most fascinating inclusions in the ICA anthology is a piece by Man Ray later to be given the title "Lautgedicht" (1924).

Man Ray: Lautgedicht. 1924

(p. 22)

The "sound poem" joke has serious implications because we immediately recognize the shape and format of traditional stanzaic verse without ever being able to hear or understand it. We might recall that Peter Walkden Fogg also savoured the "unspeakably pleasant" experience of "straight lines," but found himself unable to translate the full experience of sound intersecting with print into his diagrams. Man Ray emphasizes the two-dimensional interplay of sound and print in traditional verse by making us wonder if his line breaks would cut into or reflect the sequential continuity of the hidden language.

cummings's "57" stands at the border of the sliding scale, because although in practical terms the poem is unrecitable, it also preserves a memory of the techniques of Wordsworth and Milton, where sequential language and visual juxtaposition, sound and silence, maintain a condition of conflict. In the poetry to be discussed in the rest of this chapter, it will become clear that the technique that Morgan regards as "halfway between being a guide to the ear and a pleasure to the eye" is a kinetic function of poetic language. It is undocumentable in the abstract terms of formalism or literary linguistics because it can only operate when apparently parallel coordinates of language, its material and its meaning, its graphic condition and its oral form are brought into contact. These effects evade the deterministic poetics of criticism because they are unpredictable: to appreciate them we are only required to realize that our understanding of language can be continuously disrupted by seeing what we might not hear, and hearing what we might not see.

William Carlos Williams

From "Spring and All"

> By the road to the contagious hospital
> under the surge of the blue
> mottled clouds driven from the
> northeast—a cold wind. Beyond, the
> waste of broad, muddy fields
> brown with dried weeds, standing and fallen
>
> patches of standing water
> the scattering of tall trees
>
> All along the road the reddish
> purplish, forked, upstanding, twiggy
> stuff of bushes and small trees
> with dead, brown leaves under them
> leafless vines—
> Lifeless in appearance, sluggish,
> dazed spring approaches

John Hollander has observed of this poem that it is "put together from fragments of assertion, it has virtually no rhetorical sound" (*Vision and Resonance*, p. 287). What he seems to mean by this is that when read aloud many of its most complex and subtle effects are lost. For instance, "the surge of the blue / mottled clouds" is an exact reenactment of the unresolved tension between substance and adjective in Milton's "clear / smooth lake," and Wordsworth's "whole / Harmonious landscape": in each case we can hear the words, but the double pattern is frozen in the silent configurations of the page.

The colloquial, localized reference to the "contagious hospital" signals a degree of idiomatic informality, which at one point enters a state of conflict with the poem's status as a formal artefact. When the persona contemplates the,

>   small trees
> with dead, brown leaves under them
> leafless vines—

the moment is a perfect synthesis of Poundian technique and unreflecting slang. Destroy the visual format and we have,

> with dead, brown leaves under them leafless vines.

"Them leafless vines" echoes the earthy and ambiguous idiom of the title, "Spring and All." The point is that one oral reading would convey this rough colloquialism, but when read with the eye it is preserved and also complemented by a poised, precise visual juxtaposition that recalls "In a Station of the Metro."

> with dead brown leaves under them
> leafless vines—

"Spring and All" is a brilliant synthesis of the unstructured patterns of speech and the almost clinical precision of poetic technique, and it succeeds in this improbable merger by silencing and uniting the disparate identities of these expressive elements.

The conventional critical opinion on how poetry can recreate a development of awareness is firmly anchored in the belief that it is speech that provides the genuine point of access to experience prior to the process of reflection and stylistic tinkering. But to simply "hear" Wordsworth organizing his emotional responses to the landscape or to merely listen to Williams's persona moving through unfocused levels of consciousness is to experience only part of a very complex process of experience, becoming thought, becoming language. In visual structures such as "Spring and All" we find that the movement, the continuous progress of language is preserved in the same way that a painting can allow us to experience a sense of vibrancy, agitation *within* the stillness of the visual configurations. And we should recall how Sheridan celebrated the positioning of "Worse" which for the silent reader "paints" the desperate state of Satan, and how Benson claimed that the "effect of the Painting would be lost" if the visual format were changed.

Williams himself offers the most vivid demonstration of this process of perceptual and aesthetic merger in "The Corn Harvest," section VII of *Pictures from Brueghel*.

> Summer!
> the painting is organised
> about a young
>
> reaper enjoying his
> noonday rest
> completely
>
> relaxed
> from his morning labors
> sprawled
>
> in fact sleeping
> unbuttoned
> on his back
>
> the women
> have brought him his lunch
> perhaps
>
> a spot of wine
> they gather gossiping
> under a tree
>
> whose shade
> carelessly
> he does not share the
>
> resting
> center of
> their workaday world

The acknowledged point of inspiration is Brueghel's *The Harvesters* (1565). By responding to another level of artistic representation Williams tacitly signals that his poem is a direct engagement with the process of seeing and recording, and his practice of excluding traditional punctuation is here effectively replaced by the conventions of visual art.

In Brueghel's painting the reaper is sleeping to the left of a tree, and on its right a group of women sit, eating, drinking, and talking. One of them, while still seated in the circle, has turned around and is either lifting something from or placing something in a basket that occupies a point in front of the tree exactly halfway between the sleeping man and the group. This series of juxtapositions prompts a bewildering variety of interpretive possibilities. Why is the man not seated with the women? Has he been invited to share, or been excluded from, their food and drink? Is the placing of the basket an accident, which only *appears* to be a symbolic point of separation?

The series of possibilities, of unresolvable conflicts of circumstance, is the result of juxtaposed visual images, and Williams recreates this mystery of unfinalized relations in linguistic form.

> the women
> have brought his lunch
> perhaps
>
> a spot of wine

We can never be sure if "perhaps" refers back to the syntax preceeding it and reflects Williams's uncertainty as to the man's relation with the women ("his lunch perhaps"), or forward to the possibility that "perhaps a spot of wine" has resulted in his conspicuously unconscious condition. An oral reading can never convey both effects. It is the visual position of "perhaps" that invites the eye of the reader to move back and forth along separate syntactic tracks. Williams has succeeded in creating in language the sense of unresolvable questioning that is conveyed by the prelinguistic juxtapositions of the painting.

Later in the poem does "carelessly" refer to the condition of the reaper who has chosen the least comfortable place to rest, or is it a more complex reference to Brueghel's intention to grant him a degree of carefree individuality, outside the "centre of / *their* workday world"? Again, it is the visual detachment of this single word that recreates the series of unanswerable questions offered by the compositional positionings of the painting.

When Kames recognized that the silent reader of Milton could "take the action to pieces and consider it first with relation to the agent, and next with relation to the patient," he sensed a threat to the order, the consecutive stability of linguistic relations. This, as he saw it, would lead to uncertainty, and we find in Williams a celebration of uncertainty as something human, something magically individual that transcends the tyranny of sequential logic.

Williams's poetry provides us with a far more eloquent guide to his technique than anything in his *ex cathedra* statements. His most notorious contribution to critical confusion is the "variable foot." No one has fully established how this enigmatic phenomenon relates to the traditional terminology of prosodic studies, and the most honest and intriguing acknowledgment of this threat to convention occurs in the *Princeton Encyclopedia of Poetry's* definition of free verse, written by one William Carlos Williams . . . "the bracket of the customary foot has been expanded so that more syllables, words or phrases can be admitted into its confines. The new unit this created may be called the 'variable foot,' a term and a concept already widely accepted as a means of bringing the warring elements of freedom and discipline together." One might ask how such an infinitely "variable" unit can establish any kind of "discipline"? Elsewhere in the essay Williams offers a clue: "The irregularity involves both eye and ear. Whether the measure be written down with a view to the appearance of the poem on the printed page or to the sound of the words as spoken or sung is of no consequence so long as the established irregularity is maintained."[1] The implication is that there might well be a tension between what we see and what we hear; in which case any equation of form and meaning will have to be determined by the recipient of both media, the reader. We might recognize a precedent here, because three centuries earlier another experimental poet offered an equally enigmatic account of visual/oral flexibility: the "variable foot" is an echo of "sense variously drawn out from one verse into another."

T. S. Eliot

If one is to regard Williams as part of a technical legacy that has maintained the essentially experimental, antitraditional tendencies of early modernism, then it would not stretch the generalization to locate his contemporary, T. S. Eliot, at the head of an opposing, and mostly British, strategy of compromise between formal precedent and individuality. This ideal of a balance between the old and the new is central to "Tradition and the

Individual Talent" and it is extended to the more specific field of prosody in his "Reflections on 'Vers Libre.'"

> We may therefore formulate as follows: the ghost of some simple metre should lurk behind the arras even in the "freest" verse; to advance menacingly as we doze, and withdraw as we rouse. Or freedom is only truly freedom when it appears against the background of an artificial limitation.[2]

For "limitation" and "freedom" one might read "mask" and "voice" (Hollander), "underlying tension of the line" and "speech rhythms" (Attridge), or "deep structure" and "surface structure" (practically any post-1956 prosodist). But unlike the later theorists, Eliot did not substantiate his model of formal tension by suggesting what exactly constitutes a point of stability and how the reader is supposed to respond to a degree of instability that might threaten it. Clues can however be found in his essays on Milton, "Milton II" (1947):

> It seems to me also that Milton's verse is especially refractory to yielding up its secrets to examination of the single line. . . . It is the period, the sentence and still more the paragraph, that is the unit of Milton's verse. . . . It is only in the period that the wave-length of Milton's verse is to be found.[3]

Eliot seems reluctant either to fully endorse Johnson's judgment of "verse only to the eye" or to grant the individual line a formal status outside the movement of a broader pattern. It is presumably the line that represents "limitation" and "the period, the sentence, and still more the paragraph" that exude "freedom"; but he does not state how the presence of both can contribute simultaneously to their beauty. An awareness of the influence of the visual lingers tantalizingly in the margins of this statement, but in an obscure TLS article in 1928 he acknowledges that something would be lost if the shape of the verse were changed: "Verse, whatever else it may or may not be, is itself a system of *punctuation*; the usual marks of punctuation themselves are differently employed."[4] One might ask how we can differentiate poetic punctuation from the "usual marks," unless of course we can see patterns that we might not be able to fully appreciate in the oral medium.

One could continue to speculate on these remarks and still never establish a degree of certainty as to their precise application, but a more intriguing chain of connections emerges when we compare them with Eliot's poetry. Consider the opening sequence of what must be the presiding monument to modern poetic writing, *The Waste Land*.

> April is the cruellest month, breeding
> Lilacs out of the dead land, mixing
> Memory and desire, stirring
> Dull roots with spring rain.
> Winter kept us warm, covering
> Earth in forgetful snow, feeding
> A little life with dried tubers.

These lines are significant, first because they serve to remind us that our appreciation of poetic effects can be severely limited by our conventions of reading. In two of the most substantial recent studies of free verse by Gross and Hartman, the two critics enter into a debate on what system of prosodic analysis can best establish the dominant metrical structure of each line.[5] This may well be a creditable exercise, but it effectively clouds our awareness of a formal effect that is far more central to their structure and meaning.

When confronted with these lines, even the most unsophisticated reader will be struck by the way in which each verbal termination operates as an axis between the words preceding and following it. To argue, as Gross and Hartman do, over whether the third line, with only three major stresses, disrupts the consistency of the more general four-stress movement, is to draw our attention away from the fact that lines operate as visual "punctuation marks," reordering our awareness of the sequential movement of language. An eighteenth-century theorist such as Rice would argue that they are not lines at all and that the visual record of their true oral identity would have them broken *before* "breeding," "mixing," "stirring," "covering," and "feeding," and Sheridan would no doubt argue that it is the pause after these words that contributes to the complex effect of progress and hesitation. The point is that the structure of this sequence is dependent not upon the internal prosody of each line but upon the isolation of key syntactic components of change between a grammatical pause and the white space of the line ending; their visual placing controls the thematic and rhythmic identity of the passage.

We have moved to the opposite end of the sliding scale of visual effects from the one occupied by cummings, but there is still a sense of typography imposing upon sound and sequence. For instance, the visual isolation of "mixing" allows a moment of subjectivity to disturb what would otherwise be a rather flat catalogue of seasonal changes. The gap between "mixing" and "Memory" adds an almost melancholy note to the series of connectives and recalls Wordsworth's emotive isolation of "connect" from the "landscape with the quiet of the sky." Both poets achieve the effect of dispersing the single authoritative voice of the speaker among the resistances and diversions of the visual medium, and Eliot goes on to use the silent text in a similar way, but with more disorientating results, in *Ash Wednesday* and *The Four Quartets*.

The opening sequence of section V in *Ash Wednesday* has raised a good deal of critical controversy.

> If the lost word is lost, if the spent word is spent
> If the unheard, unspoken
> Word is unspoken, unheard;
> Still is the unspoken word, the Word unheard
> The Word without a word, the word within
> The world and for the world;
> And the light shone in darkness and
> Against the Word the unstilled world still whirled
> About the centre of the silent Word
>
> O my people, what have I done to thee.
>
> Where shall the word be found, where will the word
> Resound? Not here, there is not enough silence

The patterns of assonance and internal rhyme are so closely interwoven with syntax that any direct causal relationship between effect and meaning seems almost to be forbidden. Gross regards it as in "marked contrast to the rest of the poem." "The rhetorical clammer. . . . The onomatopoeic bustle of harmonic punning . . . is finally tedious" (p. 202).

But there is a key to this complexity. The points at which the sound patterns seem to displace any sense of continuity and order are when they intersect with semantic distinctions. Thus, paradoxically, the eye of the silent reader is granted the only point of stability within this apparently chaotic tissue of effects: we can distinguish the "unstilled world" from the "still whirled," the "Word" from the "word" because we can see them. The moment at which this sense of tenuous stability becomes most apparent is intrinsically and self-consciously poetic: the break between the second and third lines offers the,

>   unspoken
>   Word

Is this "Word" of greater significance than the lower case "unspoken word" (l. 4) because of the convention of capitalizing line openings; or does the visual space that breaks into the continuity of language remind us that the final "Word" must remain "unspoken"? The question is unanswerable, but its significance becomes more vivid when we find that it can only be addressed from within the silent realm of understanding. The "centre of the silent Word" is, to borrow a metaphor from chaos, literally, the eye of the storm: the unstilled world still whirls about the center of the silent Word.

Eliot moves on to ask the question of how any sense of stability or assurance is ever attainable, and we are reminded again of how poetic structures are capable of vividly encompassing such issues.

> Where shall the word be found, where will the word
> Resound?

Why does he disrupt the rhythmic and rhyming symmetry of this sequence by ending the line with "word"? Because only by allowing the visual text to disrupt the apparent stability of the acoustic pattern can he fully demonstrate the illusion of purely linguistic meaning—and, appropriately enough, we can "see" that the unreliable "word" is granted the lower case. What would almost have been the assured parallelism of the couplet is broken by its visual material: the acoustic perfection of "word be found" and "word resound" is offered to the silent reader as shattered perfection. What we see challenges the comfortable patterning of what we hear. There may well be "not enough silence" to adequately cope with the search for the lost word, but there is enough to grant the reader an uncomfortably stable perspective upon its elusive nature. Milton was the first to disrupt the balance between the arbitrary categories of writing and speech, silence and sound; Eliot takes the reader even deeper into the illusion of linguistic transparency.

William Kenrick's "two distinct types of language," the "vocal," which speaks to the ears and the "written," which speaks to the eyes, were predicated upon his experience of the printed poem, and Eliot in "Burnt Norton" reminds us that the poetic line can provide a tangible axis between these two experiences.

> Footfalls echo in the memory
> Down the passage which we did not take
> Towards the door we never opened
> Into the rose garden. My words echo
> Thus, in your mind.

It is the visual rather than the metrical identity of these lines that controls the movement of the passage: the reader is drawn literally "Down," "Towards," and "Into" the rose garden. But what of the final half-lines? The visual/syntactic pattern has not changed, but we are suddenly forced into a reflexive contemplation of the technique and our participation in it. The,

>   echo
> Thus

is a silent echo. The visual resonances echo in the "mind" but not in the ear. We might here recall James Beattie on the power of the written text: "Words spoken make an immediate impression, but depend for their permanence, upon the memory." Eliot: "Footfalls echo in the memory."

This anxious concern with the interplay of the permanent and the ephemeral is more vividly realized in section V of "Burnt Norton."

> Words move, music moves
> Only in time; but that which is only living
> Can only die. Words, after speech, reach
> Into the silence. Only by the form, the pattern,
> Can words or music reach
> The stillness, as a Chinese jar still
> Moves perpetually in its stillness.

The first part of the passage evokes the fragile condition of spoken language—words might "move" us, but like music the effect is threatened by the temporal evanscence of the medium. We find the acoustic sequence of "speech, reach" placed precipitately at the line ending, which leads "Into Silence"; and Milton's "Wings / Of Silence" and Wordsworth's "lengthened pause / Of silence" are tantalizingly invoked.

But the tone changes and we are offered a "form," a "pattern," in which "words and music" can achieve a state of permanence, can "reach / The stillness." This frozen condition is to be found in the tension between movement and stillness:

> a Chinese jar still
> Moves perpetually.

The eye of the reader is caught in a faint double movement. Is the "Chinese jar still" or must it "still move perpetually in its Stillness"? The syntax, the music, might move on "in time" but the eye of the reader can trace patterns, tracks of meaning, back and forth "perpetually" in the silent text.

Williams and Eliot, poets who are often seen as standing at opposing poles of modernism, are united in this moment.

Rhyme, Silence, and Modernism

In the tracing of correspondences between the eighteenth-century theories of form, modern poetry, and criticism, rhyme presents a number of problems. The eighteenth-century critics, whether they approved or disapproved of its use, were united in their reluctance to treat rhyme as anything more than an accident of literary history—useful as a substitute for classical ideals of lineal closure but far too redolent of randomness and coincidence to be seriously regarded as an independent source of poetic effects. The most ingenious and productive readings of rhymed poetry have come from twentieth-century critics, and this sense of historical reversal holds the key to our understanding of the eighteenth to twentieth century correspondences.

Rhyme plays a relatively small part in the broader development of modern formal techniques, but in a curious way its more adventurous deployments echo the fears and anxieties of the eighteenth-century critics. The latter found rhyme to be an acoustic threat to language's stability, a threat that was much more disturbing than that offered by visual space; and, as we shall see, it is in the acceptance of this double challenge of silence and sound that modern poetry, particularly that of Auden, answers these fears.

In the early manifestoes of modernist form, emphasis was given to the restricting and stylistically limiting effects of traditional prosodic and stanzaic formulae, and it was difficult to detach rhyme from its status as a token concession to well-established precedent. Even the promotion or use of irregular rhyme and meter would inevitably evoke the conventions and the idiom of the ode form and such respectable accentual experiments as *Christabel*. There seemed to be practically nothing technically new that could be done with rhyme, and to have appended it to an Imagist lyric would have been to draw attention away from the economy and concentration of effects and towards patterns and conventions that evoked tradition and the established poetic canon—early Imagist deployments of rhyme are rare.

The most self-consciously experimental use of rhyme will be found in Marianne Moore's bizarre chiming shapes, such as "You Are Like the Realistic Product of an Idealistic Search for Gold at the Foot of the Rainbow"

> Hid by the august foliage and fruit
>   of the grape vine,
>   twine
>   your anatomy
>   round the pruned and polished stem,
>   chameleon.
>   Fire laid upon
>   an emerald as long as
>   the Dark King's massy
>   one,
> Could not snap the spectrum up for food
>   as you have done.

Moore does with rhyme what cummings was to do with typography, or to be more accurate, she adds the extra dimension of a sound pattern to a visual structure. The effect is precisely the opposite to that achieved by Walker's rewritings of enjambed couplets. What Walker attempted to hide within the syntactic and rhythmic movement, Moore establishes as the structural axis of the entire poem—Walker's shape disguised what Moore's shape actually is.

Moore's rhymed poems were eccentricities, and, like her neo-mathematical experiments with syllabism, they were engagements with the nature of artifice itself. Form, in this case the sound pattern of rhyme, is thrown into the center of the expressive movement as a challenge to individuality and meaning. But Moore also sets a somewhat exaggerated standard for later deployments of rhyme in modernist forms, as a tentative and ambivalent reference point both to the structures of tradition and to the arbitrary illogic of formal structure itself.

The most diverse and unpredictable manifestations of this will be found in the poetry of W. H. Auden. The title poem of *Look Stranger* (1936) involves a consistent avoidance of metrical regularity, with traditional rhythmic patterns emerging briefly and disappearing again into more extended prosaic movements. Juxtaposed with this is an equally irregular use of rhyme. It will emerge into the internal pattern of the second line, "The leaping light for your delight discovers," or impose itself not only as foregrounded enjambment but in the middle of a word,

> Oppose the pluck
> And knock of the tide,
> And the shingle scrambles after the suck-
> -ing surf,

Such writing might seem to be as far from the formal concerns and protocols of the eighteenth-century critics as it is possible to go. But Auden transforms their sense of anxiety into his structural principle. Those eighteenth-century writers, who paused to consider how the presence of rhyme reflects and exposes the arbitrary nature of language itself, turned away from what Cockin termed "the accidental blemishes of a different style," from a system of uncontrollable, impersonal relations. Auden takes up this same challenge and juxtaposes this "different style" with what would otherwise be a calm, unadventurous reflection upon the inexplicable nature of the sea.

His most remarkable technical achievement in this poem is that his challenge to the arbitrary, unpredictable nature of sound pattern is matched by a similarly explicit engagement with the phenomenon of silence and shape. Our suspicions are aroused by the conflict between what we hear and what we see at the lines ending with "pluck" and "suck / ing," but even more intriguing are those lines that exclude themselves from the rhyme-line ending pattern. In the first two lines:

> Look, stranger on this island now
> The leaping light for your delight discovers,

the visual format, assisted by the absence of conventional punctuation, leaves the silent reader wondering if he is being urged to "Look ... now" or "Look" only "now the leaping light ...

discovers." Tentative echoes of Wordsworth's perceptual uncertainties achieve greater clarity with,

> Here at the small field's ending pause
> Where the chalk wall falls to the foam, and its tall ledges
> Oppose the pluck.

These lines operate, silently, in two ways. The field's pause is also, as we see, the line's pause, but the isolated substantive sense is transformed into a more active verbal invitation to the reader to "pause where the chalk wall falls." The uncertainties continue when the eye reaches "Oppose." It would seem to be the cliffs that "oppose the pluck and knock of the tide," but the dominance of a single sequential pattern of meaning is threatened as the unstable condition of "pause" seems to infect "oppose" with the subtle resonance of an order to the reader.

The effect is very similar to Wordsworth's merger of personal identity and objective fact in the silent texture of *Tintern Abbey's* opening lines, and for further confirmation, if not of influence then at least of intertextual agreement, we could consult *The Prelude*, V, 380–83.

> when a lengthened pause
> Of silence came and baffled his best skill
> Then sometimes, in that silence while he hung
> Listening.

Auden's interconnected uses of rhyme and shape represent a kind of double-edged challenge to linguistic assurance and transparency. In poem XV of the *Look Stranger* collection, he employs an impressively complex stanza pattern but throws this concession to orthodoxy into a state of imbalance by the use of such pararhymes as "town—alone," "fallow—shallow," "forces—faces." The ghost of Isaac Watts seems to have returned with a vengeance.

In "In Memory of W. B. Yeats," the structure of the poem traces, appropriately enough, the shape of a cone, with the recent history of formal technique reversed. The first section is diffuse, metrically irregular and unrhymed; the middle section exhibits traces, but only traces, of iambic movement and employs irregular pararhyme—the most thematically significant of which must be "decay"—"poetry"; and the final section consists of precise, regular octosyllabic quatrains. The poem is both an exercise in technical brilliance and subtle comment on the changes in poetic technique that had taken place in the life of Yeats. And we should note that the two media of sound and shape exert a form of control over the poem's structural changes: the visual format of the first section interweaves with, but does not disrupt, the linear sequence, but in section two we find the influence of visual shape being gradually displaced by a more dominant pattern of sound in meter and rhyme, and this development reaches its ultimate form in the concluding sequence of quatrains, whose tight metrical and rhyming structure seems, implicitly, to celebrate a victory of the poem as sound.

His most subtle yet at the same time most adventurous engagement with the conflicting patterns of sound and visual shape occurs in "Musée des Beaux Arts." Correspondences with Williams are immediately signalled because the poem invites the reader to compare the apparently coincidental patterns of life with the way in which they are presented in the visual arts, both as accidents and as part of an aesthetic design.

Rhythmically, the poem seems to represent the ultimate form of free verse with unstructured, discursive movements hardly disturbed by any trace of metrical continuity. Because of a very irregular rhyme scheme we have to concentrate hard to notice that the lines end when and where they do. This method itself evokes Rice's dismissive reference to rhyme as "something that we might fall into in common conversation," since Auden seems to have isolated the rhymes almost as if they do occur at random in a prose sequence—no attention is given to line-length or metrical structure and the rhyme scheme itself is unpredictable. The result of this apparent abandonment of a coherent structural principle is, paradoxically, to draw the reader's attention to the way in which our use of language involves us in a very delicate balancing act between our control of and our submission to an arbitrary system. Comparisons can be made between this experiment with sound and the more familiar debate on the influence of shape, since Auden seems to be challenging the view that poetic structures that do not satisfy an explicit and predictable criterion of pattern and form exclude themselves from their traditional role as intended components of meaning.

The most impressive moment in this challenge occurs in the second section, when Auden, like Williams, creates a linguistic structure analogous to the juxtaposed relations of visual art.

>   the ploughman may
> Have heard the splash, the forsaken cry,

> But for him it was not an important failure; the sun shone
> As it had to on the white legs disappearing into the green
> Water; and the expensive delicate ship that must have seen
> Something amazing, a boy falling out of the sky,
> Had something to get to and sailed calmly on.

Auden succeeds in disclosing the peculiarly ironic condition of an art form that seeks to represent, but effectively freezes, the complex interplay of sound and movement of the physical world. The passage is dominated by a curious mixture of equivocation and certainty—"the ploughman *may* / Have heard," "the sun shone / *As it had to*," the ship "*must* have seen"—and creates the impression that Brueghel has, by imposing the silence and stillness of art upon a series of violent events, made the unpredictable seem strangely ordained and inevitable. The most intriguing linguistic equivalent of this effect occurs with the line break at "green / Water." Again, we are reminded of Milton's "clear / Smooth lake," Wordsworth's "whole / Harmonious landscape," and Williams's "blue / mottled clouds"; in each case the visual format traces out conflicting adjectival and substantive patterns. But Auden creates an even greater degree of textual depth by allowing the language to resonate with the reader's image of a painting. The boy's "white legs" do literally disappear into "the green" of the painting, and when our eye connects "the green" with what it represents, the water, we realize that the materiality of language is being used to create an effect very similar to that achieved with the materials of visual art. When we reach the end of the next line we find that the conflict between what we see, both in the printed poem and the painting, and what both media attempt to represent, is further intensified by the acoustic echo of "green" in "seen." We do not need Wimsatt or Kenner to speculate on how the illogic of rhyme imposes an extra dimension of meaning upon the logic of syntax, because Auden signals his own complex intention. The visual reader, has "seen" how structural components of language can be juxtaposed in a way that defies the logic of conventional grammar, and the rhyming confirmation of this silent effect establishes that Auden invokes, yet controls, the arbitrary nature of his linguistic material.

In chapter 6 I argued that the eighteenth-century critics did not follow their modern counterparts in tracing a double pattern of sound and meaning in the rhymed couplet, because such readings assumed the poet to be at the mercy of an impersonal system of coincidences and relations, and thus promoted the critic to the role of casuist and mediator in the resultant tension between logic and illogic. Auden's achievement is to have effectively displaced the critic from this role by releasing and confronting the arbitrary, illogical potentialities of rhyme. He systematically strips the poem of all concessions to formal structure apart from the visual isolation of rhyme words, so that, unlike the couplet poet, his confrontation with the randomness, the materiality of language is not limited by an attendant allegiance to formal order and logic. He chooses to deploy his rhyme words in the same way that he decides where to place his visual spaces: no concessions to abstract form are made, and this freedom with linguistic material also takes his creative range beyond the equally deterministic structures of traditional syntax. The "idle particles" that the *Monthly Review* satirist found to be a weakness of the enjambed couplets of Churchill have been put to work by the hand of Auden.

I stated at the beginning of this chapter that the last word would be given to the poem. And so it has. Milton, Wordsworth, Eliot, cummings, Williams, Auden . . . have produced verse that disrupts those distinctions between linguistic reference and linguistic material, between sound and silence, that are vital to the stability of critical analysis. These poems tell us more about criticism than criticism is capable of telling us about them. Criticism and literary history can sharpen our readerly focus, but they also have an unfortunate tendency to narrow and limit our expectations. In the final chapter I shall argue that we do not need to develop a new critical method to deal with the conflict between silence and sound—we can experience this without needing to measure it—but we do not have to accept that such verse is itself capable of challenging the widespread, if tacitly held, assumption that all poetic writing can be codified in relation to an abstract system of conventions.

Codebreaking:
Conclusions for Criticism

In his essay on "The Poem in the Eye" John Hollander considers the absence of a critical methodology with which the intersecting media of writing and speech might be dealt with by readers— "a theory of graphic prosody" (p. 277). He echoes Barthes's more extravagant plea for a "linguistics of the written" and both are redolent of a tendency, endemic to criticism, for the anatomist, the analysist, to effectively desecrate the object of study. "Demystification" is a term that has recently acquired the status of an ideal in the current literary-academic world, but as I shall argue, it is the maintenance of mystification, of tantalizing uncertainty, that holds the key to our appreciation of the poetics of silence and sound.

"Visual Poetry" has been granted a subcategory in the poetic canon, and the semioticians and grammarians of this phenomenon have, naturally enough, been drawn primarily to work in which shape has replaced sequential pattern at the structural center of the text,[1] but it is clear that in such relatively traditional poems as *The Waste Land* and *Paradise Lost*, visual structure enters a state of tension with the oral medium. We can hardly recategorize Eliot and Milton as incipient concretists, but neither can we exclude an awareness of how silence and writing operate within their work as part of a broader plenitude of effects. And in my opinion the graphic, the visual, the silent dimension of poetic writing creates the most striking intensities of meaning only when it works alongside, often in conflict with, the sequential oral medium.

Do we need a grammar, a semiotic, of silent poetics? No. Because silent poetics is probably the final point of resistance to the process by which critical writing has systematically catalogued and colonized the "language of poetry." The printed page is the ultimate refuge of formal originality, because it is there that the poet can disrupt, subvert, intensify the orderly and predictable relations of sequential language. Sequential grammar is predictable: the "deep structures" identified by transformational linguistics underpin, and to a depressing degree explain, the apparent freedom of being able to say what we like. Everything we say will be built upon these shared monoliths of signifying convention, and every departure from the correct codes will be equally conspicuous and classifiable. But silent poetics can threaten not only the surface patterns of language but also the stability of the relationship between linguistic rules and individual statements. The most eloquent spokesman for this form of tension was also one of its most vehement opponents; Lord Kames realized that the ordered regularity of sequential grammar could be thrown into a state of uncertainty when the eye of the reader is invited to shift priority back and forth, horizontally and vertically, through adjectives, nouns, subjects, objects.

The most obvious objection to my claim that silent poetics is and should remain in the realm of unpredictability would be that it is impossible for us to understand anything that is not based upon a classifiable system of codes and conventions; in currently fashionable Saussurean language, how can there be a *parole* without a *langue*? In basic terms the instance must indeed be dependent upon the system, but let us consider the nature of codes and systems. Most semioticians and structuralists would agree that the linguistic system of a particular language provides a vast framework from which other subsystems—literary poetics, the semiotics of advertising, the rhetoric of political language—draw their material. Different signifying systems exist in a kind of mechanical symbiosis—rather like the mechanism of a clock. They may have different ideological, aesthetic, or social functions but they necessarily share the same formulaic relation of system to event, *langue* to *parole*. To construct a "graphic prosody" or in broader terms a grammar of visual poetry we would, in theory, add yet another subsystem of predictable codes to the already burgeoning repertoire.

But silent poetics is not a system. It is a state of awareness of how systems work and it manifests itself in individual texts by preying upon and disrupting our sense of expectation. It is a perfect realization of individuality because instead of creating effects from within the poet's and reader's shared awareness of the impersonal structures of a grammar, it allows the poet and the reader to share in the uncreation, the subversion, of these deterministic formulae.

I have already referred, in chapter 6, to how Roman Jakobson's model of poetic language represents an example of how systems interrelate. His notion of how the poet emphasizes the tension between the syntagmatic, metonymic dimension and the associative, metaphoric relations between words is a perfect example of how literature is regarded as one element of the broader linguistic system. But when we find poets creating multidimensional effects that when "heard" will remain metonymic, but when seen will discharge metaphoric intensities, we experience not an alternative system but a condition of awareness through which the poet is capable both of exploiting and subverting the system's signifying conventions. Effects are generated not from within a single system but from the points of contact, or rather conflict, between systems. This sense of the poet disrupting the stability of the code becomes vividly evident in Geoffrey Hill's account, in a 1981 radio interview, of how, in the printed poem the predictable relation of the horizontal grammar of metonymy and the vertical axis of metaphor can literally collapse into one another. Hill never mentions Jakobson or his linguistic model, but his language cuts deeply into the latter's assumptions.

> The true realisation of the poets voice comes from a blending or a marriage of the silent and the spoken forms. If we put this into the shape of a figure of speech, if we conceived of the voice as it reads the poem as being on the horizontal plane, and if we thought of the text on the page, as it were, going down vertically, then I think that the listener should follow the spoken poem in the way that a listener follows a string quartet with a score. I think only by being most keenly sensitive to that moment when the horizontal of the spoken voice comes into contact with the formalities, with the restraints, with the restrictions that are there printed in the text, only by recognising with immediate sensitivity those moments of contact, or harmony or of hostility, only then can the reader, the listener, truly appreciate how the poets voice is being realised in the most minute, intimate, and yet profoundly rich, prosodic forms.[2]

This is a restatement of Thomas Barnes's 1785 notion of how "reading with the eye only" is an experience quite different from hearing the poem. Hill, the poet, knows that to regard the experiences of seeing and hearing certain poems as parallel coordinates of the same effect will cloud our awareness of how "harmony" can be matched by "hostility," and that a unique experience of intimacy can be granted by the reader's experience of the oral as separate from the silent medium. His claims extend far beyond critical polemic, because in the "Funeral Music" sequence of *King Log* (1968) we find tangible evidence of how silent poetics can best be understood in poetry itself, and not in the abstract "grammar" of critical method.

"Funeral Music" is a sequence of eight rhymeless sonnets, but I am only able to make this statement because I can see them on the page; the fact that these poems are fourteen lines long and that each of their lines traces out the rough equivalent of an iambic pentameter would be lost to anyone who could not see as well as hear the verse. Hill reminds us of the peculiar sense of convention in conflict with variation that faced the eighteenth-century critics of the Miltonic pentameter. The codes, the conventions, of formal regularity exist in the mind of the reader before the experience of the poem, but in that experience, tradition, with its attendant expectations, becomes an elusive and fragile phenomenon—what Barnes called the "shadow" of the music. We are able to contemplate this uneasy "moment of contact" because the silent printed poem both invokes the code, the recognition of the sonnet, and displaces it as a final determinant of effect and meaning.

Hill, like Milton, draws the silent reader into the communicative circuit, because just as Woodford and Sheridan recognized the ghost of the pentameter in the printed format and then allowed their eyes to seek out intensities and resonances, so the reader of Hill's "sonnets" is similarly caught in that moment between recognition and expectation.

2

> For whom do we scrape our tribute of pain—
> For none but the ritual King? We meditate
> A rueful mystery; we are dying
> To satisfy fat Caritas, those
> Wiped jaws of stone. (Suppose all reconciled
> By silent music; imagine the future
> Flashed back at us, like steel against sun,
> Ultimate recompense.) Recall the cold
> Of Towton on Palm Sunday before dawn,
> Wakefield, Tewkesbury; fastidious trumpets
> Shrilling into the ruck; some trampled
> Acres, parched, sodden or blanched by sleet,
> Struck with strange-postured dead. Recall the wind's
> Flurrying, darkness over the human mire.

In a note on these poems Hill states that, 'the sequence avoids shaping these characters and events into any overt narrative or dramatic structure." This is something of an understatement, because the identity and temporal presence of a single voice or perspective is ruthlessly disrupted. Phrases such as "our tribute of pain" are both retrospective and immediate; and the broader shift from the present tense of "We meditate" and "we *are* dying" to "*Recall* the cold" confirms this sense of disorientation. But, as with Eliot's similar evocation of chaos, it is possible to find a form of order, particularly if we follow Hill's advice to both listen to *and* look at the poem. An oral performance would accentuate Hill's self referential notion of "heartless music punctuated by mutterings, blasphemies and cries for help," but if we also examine the visual format of the poem we come upon breaks such as,

>   we are dying
>   To satisfy fat Caritas

which recalls Williams's,

>   them
>   leafless vines.

Are they deliberately "dying to," wanting to, satisfy fat Caritas or is this process part of a deterministic pattern? The mystery is frozen in the printed text. Similarly, with

>   some trampled
>   Acres

we need the printed text to capture the hesitant fluctuation of "some [men] trampled" and "trampled Acres."

In oral performance these intensities are lost, but, in Hill's words, "when the horizontal of the spoken comes into contact with the restrictions that are there printed in the text," we experience a productive collision of two separate, appreciative dimensions.

The silent sonnet has also been used by Gavin Ewart and, almost obsessively, by Robert Lowell. It is a form that captures the reader within an unresolvable and continuous movement between familiarity and surprise, convention and disruption and, most significantly, between sound and silence. The rhymed sonnet involves some of the most disciplined and intense coordinations of sound and sense, and our recognition of the visual token of this structure invites silent participation: the arbitrary coherence of the rhymed form is replaced by the silent reader's intervention in the communicative circuit. And we are reminded again of the effect caused by Milton in the eighteenth century. The pentameter is *there* but it only begins to operate as an instrument of form and meaning when the reader can see it. Separate codes of expectation are invoked, but meaning only emerges from their point of contact.

If, as I argue, silent poetics is neither a predictable and documentable technique of composition nor a verifiable system of interpretation, then what is it? It is a phenomenon unprecedented in literary history: poetry has succeeded in disrupting the stability of analysis and has found itself capable of clarifying linguistic issues that for criticism will remain unresolved and contingent. Consider the following case of what has come to be known as critical controversy.

In *Ferocious Alphabets* (1981) Denis Donoghue mounts an attack upon the post-Derridean promotion of writing over speech. He adapts Derrida's notion of a "graphic poetics" to his own conception of the new modes of analysis: "From GREEK *graphos*, writing. Hence the graphireader deals with writing as such and does not think of it as transcribing an event properly construed as vocal or audible." Donoghue compares graphireaders with epireaders, who "read and interpret—the same act—in the hope of going through the words to something that the words both reveal and hide. Epireaders say to poems: I want to hear you. Graphireaders say: I want to see what I can do, stimulated by your insignia" (pp. 151–52). This might seem to be a somewhat simplistic polarization of recent processes of reading, but its general accuracy would not be disputed by practitioners within each category. For instance, Donoghue's notion of "going through the words" to something "heard" echoes Hollander's endorsement of epireading as, "the mask through which the voice sounds." And most graphireaders, or deconstructionists, would, alternatively, regard writing not as a stage in the communicative circuit but as a level of signification through which any final meaning is continuously dispersed and deferred. But this distinction only presents a problem for critics, because in poems that deploy silent poetics we are obliged to become graphireaders *and* epireaders. Ricks, Hollander, Davie, and Gross all practice a form of graphireading, in the sense that they deal with effects that could only be generated from the silent printed text, but they fail to acknowledge this dimension of their interpretive experience, because to do so would also involve a radical revision of the phonocentric model of communication. The most honest acceptance of the merger of graphi and epireading came from Sheridan, who acknowledged that he was experiencing conflicting dimensions of the written and the spoken.

To recognize that graphireading and epireading interrelate is not merely a matter of critical self-awareness; it involves an acceptance of poetic writing as capable of preempting and superseding the techniques of analysis. Consider, for example, the widely practiced techniques of "close reading" and of giving attention to "the words on the page." A critic might draw the reader's attention to how the semantic distinctions between rhyme words add to the density of the verse or how the rhythmic movement of the fifth line might echo the sense of instability in the title: he is able to gather, sift, distinguish, and reassemble elements of structure in a way that is quite different from hearing a *sequential* pattern. The close-reading practices of New Criticism allow the critic to dispossess the poet of the widely celebrated status of vocal authority. A critic exerts a degree of power over the written text that allows him to emphasize and foreground elements of structure and then codify them as germane to some greater thematic intention. Donoghue would probably regard New Critics as exemplary epireaders, but what they "hear" from the poem is very often a consequence of their own visual perspective. Silent poetics allows the poet to redress the balance, because the critic's sense of control is matched and displaced by effects that actually *force* the reader to pause and contemplate the multidimensional effect of silence in conflict with sound. The poet can manipulate the codes and practices of reading to his own satisfaction. It would be wrong to assume that this is merely a case of poetry entering a reflexive realm of linguistics already occupied by analysis, because as critics such as Sheridan showed, techniques of close reading existed two centuries before their official birth, and they were generated not by abstract protocols of interpretation, but by the presence of a poem that required the reader to adjust his expectations of how the eye coordinates with the ear.

At the other end of the modern interpretive spectrum, that which Donoghue regards as occupied by graphireaders, a similar victory of poetry over theory can be seen to take place. There is a striking connection between the silence/sound conflict in *Paradise Lost* and the categories of certainty considered in a recent debate between Derrida (graphireader) and John Searle (epireader) on the theory of speech acts. In his book *Speech Acts: An Essay on the Philosophy of Language* (1969) Searle argues that the illocutionary force, or the truth, of an utterance can be guaranteed by the intention of the speaker and by the context of the utterance. He says that as one of the conditions of promising, "if the purported promise is to be nondefective, the thing promised must be something the hearer wants done, or considers to be in his interest" (p. 59). Derrida has pointed out that if unconscious desire on the part of the listener is also part of these conditions, then the status of certain promises is actually threatened by their context.[3] Both theoretical positions are preempted and displaced by Milton, because when Eve gives her account to Adam it is impossible to establish exactly what *is* the context of the utterance or *who* is being addressed. The reader of the text can choose to disclose betrayals and uncertainties that are denied to Adam, or he can recreate Adam's experience by reading the text aloud and closing down the silent resonances. Thus Searle's, the epireader's, notion of intention and certainty and Derrida's, the graphireaders, notion of the continuous deferment of meaning are both present within the conflicting textual patterns of the poem. Neither is given prominence, but the poetic experience of silence and sound grants us an illuminating perspective upon both.

It should now be evident that the eighteenth-century work on silence and sound has a significance far beyond its contribution to the map of literary history. Critics such as Sheridan, Steele, and Walker are, in the best sense of the word, revolutionary, because they were able to admit that their preconditioned notions of what poetic form is, what it could be, and how it operates within the communicative circuit were unable to accommodate their own experiences of reading. They found that the poet could transcend the code. The fact that in the case of *Paradise Lost* they came to conflicting, contradictory conclusions further attests to their value, since, by implication, they found that poetic writing could both displace and synthesize distinct conceptions of language and meaning. Their message to us is that codes, systems, grammars provide us with a language through which we can document and address the technicalities of poetic writing, but that the best poetic writing will always challenge the individual components of this interpretive format. The Miltonic pentameter both invoked the memory of metrical form as a record of the oral poem, and created the unprecedented phenomenon of a visual structure that could disrupt the sequential continuity of oral language. This unpredictable merger of codes, of silence and sound, preempted what has become one of the unanswerable questions of modern writing: what is the poetic line? The only answer available is that it is whatever the poet wants it to be, its identity is a condition of its function. It might coordinate patterns of rhythm or rhyme or it might throw the sequential movement and the controlled echoes of language into a state of chaos by inserting itself into these same patterns. The term silent poetics is similarly flexible: the poet might operate at the Miltonic end of the sliding scale or move toward the pure silence of cummings and the concretists, but in each instance "form" emerges from the point of contact between separate codes and dimensions of writing and reading. The grammar, the prosody, of silent poetics is already present within our methodology of poetic structure. To document and address this phenomenon we do not need to rewrite the codes, but only recognize that the poet creates a uniquely poetic meaning by breaking, merging, and transcending them.

Notes

Chapter 1. The Prosodic Background

1. Speculation as to whether J. D. is actually Dryden is based upon purely circumstantial evidence. See Hugh Macdonald, *John Dryden: A Bibliography of Early Editions and Drydenia* (London, 1939), p. 180. The *Parnassus* was published in the period between *Upon the Death of Lord Hastings* (London, 1649) and the *Heroic Stanzas* to Cromwell (London, 1659) when very little is known about Dryden's life. J. D. and Dryden share attitudes on "measure and rhyme," the structure of the couplet, and the irrelevance of quantitative meter, but so did many of their contemporaries. The principal distinction is between J. D.'s notion of blank verse as the ideal dramatic idiom and Dryden's long-held belief that heroic plays should embody the formal conventions of rhymed nondramatic poetry.

2. For the best account of how the quantity-accent conflict was dealt with in the sixteenth century, see Derek Attridge's *Well-Weighed Syllables: Elizabethan Verse in Classical Metres* (Cambridge, 1974).

3. Ruth Wallerstein, "The Development of the Rhetoric and Metre of the Heroic Couplet. Especially in 1625–1645." *P.M.L.A.* 50 (1935): 166–209.

George Williamson, "The Rhetorical Pattern of Neo-Classical Wit." *Modern Philology* 33 (1935): 55–81.

4. Rymer's *The Tragedies of the Last Age* (London, 1678) is reprinted in Spingarn, III pp. 181–208. For other contemporary engagements with the couplet-blank verse debate, see: The Earl of Mulgrave, *Essay on English Poetry* (London, 1682), reprinted in Spingarn, III p. 289. Francis Atterbury, Preface to the *Second Part of Mr. Waller's Poems* (London, 1690), sigs. A5v–A6r; sig. A8r. In the *Athenian Mercury* (16 Jan. 1691–92) the questions of "whether *Milton* and *Waller* were not the best English poets? and which the better of the two?" were posed. The answers are vague and unspecific.

Chapter 2. Visualist Reading: Woodford to Sheridan

1. "Life of Milton," in *Lives of the English Poets*, ed. Birkbeck-Hill (Oxford, 1905), p. 193.

2. "We in the Modern Languages have Rhythm, or a coincidence of Sound in a single Termination, to compensate for the disuse, ... of the Trisyllable Foot" (sig. B5r). Woodford probably wished to suggest a link between classical "rhythmus" and the new structural function of rhyme.

3. These lines are also discussed by Sheridan in the *Lectures*, II, p. 268.

Chapter 3. The Critical Debate: The Eighteenth versus the Twentieth Century

1. George L. Trager and Henry Lee Smith, "An Outline of English Structure," *Studies in Linguistics: Occasional Papers* 3 (Norman, Oklahoma, 1951).

2. "Robert Frost's 'Mowing': An Inquiry into Prosodic Structure," *Kenyon Review* 18 (1956): 421–38. These articles are acknowledged as the starting point of the linguistic analysis of meter. Contributors include Harold Whitehall, John Crowe Ransom, and Arnold Stein. An excellent bibliography and commentary may be found in T. V. F. Brogan, *English Versification 1570–1980* (Baltimore, 1981), pp. 290–318.

3. Both were originally actors and both performed at Drury Lane and Covent Garden in London and at Crow Street and Smock Alley in Dublin—Sheridan in the 1750s, Walker in the 1760s. Sheridan's educational venture, the Hibernian Academy, failed in 1759, and a similar enterprise by Walker, in partnership with James Usher at Kensington, collapsed ten years later. Both gave public lectures at Oxford and Cambridge on elocution and the value of studying English literature, and both proceeded upon profitable lecture tours and poetry recitals in the 1760s and 1770s. Their respective connections with the Johnson-circle are recounted in Boswell's *Life*, ed. G. B. Hill (Oxford, 1950), IV, pp. 206–7; I, pp. 374, 388, 385–86, 453; II, pp. 88, 256; III, p. 322. See also E. K. Sheldon, *Thomas Sheridan of Smock Alley* (Princeton, 1967), and W. Benzie, *The Dublin Orator: Thomas Sheridan's Influence on Rhetoric and Belles Lettres* (Leeds, 1972).

4. Ferdinand de Saussure, *Course in General Linguistics*, trans. Wade Baskin (London, 1960). First published in French, *Cours de linguistique generale* (Paris, 1916).

5. See above, chapter 6, pp. 136–37.

6. It is worth noting that most of Sheridan's directions for reading verse were adopted by Lindley Murray in his *English Grammar* (London, 1795), the most widely used pedagogical work of its type in the subsequent century (see R. C. Alston, *A Bibliography of the English Language from the Invention of Printing to the Year 1800*, pp. 95; 112–13). Unfortunately, the full textual and interpretive implications of his pause of suspension are excluded from Murray's guide.

Chapter 4. Shape and Identity: Milton, Wordsworth, and Literary History

1. Jacques Derrida, *Of Grammatology*, trans. Gayatri Chakravorty Spivak (Baltimore and London, 1977). First published in French, *De la Grammatologie* (Paris, 1967).

2. "The wind shifted . . . accompanied with a clear" (*Naval Chronicle*, 11, 1804, p. 168).

3. "On the stage, where the appearance of speaking in verse should always be avoided, there can, I think, be no doubt, that the close of such lines as make no pause in the sense, should not be rendered perceptible to the ear" (*Lectures on Rhetoric and Belles Lettres*, London, 1783, pp. 215–16).

4. See, for instance, R. D. Havens, *The Influence of Milton on English Poetry* (Cambridge, Mass., 1922).

5. Enfield's *The Speaker, or, miscellaneous pieces selected from the best English Writers . . . to which is prefixed an Essay on Elocution* (London, 1774) is clearly influenced by Sheridan's earlier elocutionary work.

6. Coleridge: *The Friend*, vol. II, pp. 239–40, in *The Collected Works of Samuel Taylor Coleridge*, ed. B. E. Rooke (Princeton, 1969).
Wordsworth: *The Prose Works of William Wordsworth*, ed. W. J. B. Owen and J. W. Smyser (Oxford, 1974), I, p. 91.

7. Wordsworth, *Selected Prose* (Oxford, 1988), pp. 377–78.

8. *The Poetical Works of Mark Akenside and John Dyer*, ed. Robert A. Willmott (London, 1855), p. 69.

9. "Edward Bysshe and the Poet's Handbook," *P.M.L.A.* 63 (1948): 858–85. See p. 880.

10. See chapter One of Fussell's *Theory of Prosody in Eighteenth Century England* on "The Codification of Syllabism and Stress Regularity." Because of his decision to exclude theories of rhyme and the pause from his study, his notion of the eighteenth-century conception of the pentameter lacks any reference to the crucial debate on seeing and hearing the line.

11. Joseph Priestley, *A Course of Lectures on Oratory and Criticism* (London, 1777), pp. 300–305; Hugh Blair, *Lectures on Rhetoric and Belles Lettres* (London, 1783), pp. 327–31. William Mitford, *An Essay Upon The Harmony of Language* (London, 1774), pp. 142–43.

12. "To Mitio," part II of *Horae Lyricae*, p. 274.

13. *Rambler 90*, Bate and Straus, IV, pp. 109–15.

Chapter 5. The Voice of Form

1. William Coward, *Licentia Poetica* (London, 1709), sig. B8v; Henry Pemberton. *Observations on Poetry, Especially the Epic: Occasional by the Late Poem Upon Leonidas* (London, 1738), p. 130; John Mason. *Essay on the Power of Numbers, and the Principles of Harmony in Poetical Compositions* (London, 1749), p. 10; *An Essay on the different nature of accent and quantity, with their use and application in the pronunciation of the English, Latin and Greek languages* (London, 1762), pp. 60–61.

2. First edition unknown. By 1793 the book had reached its fifty-fourth edition. Quotations taken from the 1740 edition.

3. See A. P. Davis, *Isaac Watts: His Life and Works* (London, 1943). Hughes's "Minutes for an Essay on the Harmony of Verse" was eventually published in *Letters by Several Eminent Persons Deceased*, ed. J. Duncombe (London, 1772).

4. The belief that Milton wished to distinguish, by spelling, between "rhyme" or "rhime" meaning the metrical structure of the verse line and "rime" meaning "the jingling sound of like endings" created a minor debate in the eighteenth century. The Richardsons suggested this distinction (*Explanatory Notes*, p. cxxxi) and the issue resurfaces in Say's work and in John Mason's *Essay on the Power of Numbers . . .* (London, 1749), pp. 13–15; Temple's "Of Poetry" (London, 1690), Spingarn, III, pp. 92–101; and Richard Bentley's *Milton's Paradise Lost, A new Edition* (London, 1732), p. 2. And in *The Manuscript of Milton's Paradise Lost Book I* (London, 1931), pp. 52–53, Helen Darbishire points out that the horizontal stroke through of "h" in the *Lycidas* M.S., may be evidence of Milton's awareness of a distinction.

I do not believe that Milton intended two meanings. The inconsistency in spelling was merely the result of the unreliability of seventeenth-century orthography and printing custom. When he announced that his endeavour was as yet "unattempted" in "Prose or Rhyme," he meant that it was unattempted in English prose or English poetry as it was understood prior to his note on "The Verse"—that is, poetry that rhymed. His new form transcended the traditional conceptions of poetry (rhymed) and prose (unrhymed).

5. The 1775 edition was called *An Essay* . . . and the more familiar *Prosodia Rationalis* or prefix was added to the 1779 edition. Page references are from the 1775 edition.

6. See chapter 3, pp. 51–52.

7. See M. H. Abrams, *The Mirror and the Lamp: Romantic Theory and the Critical Tradition* (London, 1953), pp. 83–84; 104–5. Blackwell quoted by Abrams, pp. 80–81.

8. Essay XII of his *Essays Philosophical and Moral, Historical and Literary* (London, 1789), p. 221.

9. *The Poetry and Prose of William Blake*, ed. G. Keynes (Oxford, 1961), p. 434.

10. *The Collected Writings of Walt Whitman*, ed. G. W. Allen and S. Bradley (New York, 1965), V, p. 714.

11. Preface to *Lyrical Ballads* (London, 1800). In *Literary Criticism of William Wordsworth*, ed. P. M. Zall (New York, 1966), pp. 56; 58.

12. *Biographia Literaria* (London, 1817), ed. G. Watson (London, 1975), II, ch. XVIII, p. 216.

13. *Selections for the illustration of a course of instructions on the rhythmus and utterance of the English language* . . . (London, 1812), pp. 55–56.

14. Partly reprinted in *Romantic Criticism 1800–1850*, ed. R. A. Foakes (London, 1968), pp. 180–81.

Chapter 6. Rhyme

1. See chapter 1, p. 27.

2. See chapter 4, pp. 89–94.

3. *Miscellaneous Reflections* (London, 1711). In *Characteristics of Men Manners* . . . etc. ed. J. M. Robertson (London, 1900).

4. *English Romanticism in the Eighteenth Century* (London, 1899), p. 111.

5. *Monthly Review* 30 (1764): 152.

6. Anon., *The Patriot Poet, a Satire* (London, 1764).

7. See also William Coward's *Licentia Poetica discuss'd* (1709). "And for the Liberty these *Ancient Great Poets* take in ending a Verse with *et, que, on, dum* and such Particles, its plain no Man can without ridicule expect to do the same in *English* v.g. *For, And, The, why, when* etc. would be accounted but *Botches* in our Poems" (sig, B4v).

8. The copy is in the Bodleian Library, shelf mark 8° Rawl, 173 a.b. Pasted onto p. 42 is a handwritten note, "E libris Isaaci Watts ii . . . 1693," and on the interleaf between pages 42 and 43 is a similar insertion in another hand, "The additions in this work are the handwriting of Isaac Watts a dissenting Teacher. R+R."

9. "Closing statement: linguistics and poetics," in *Style and Language*, ed. Thomas A. Sebeok (London, 1960), pp. 122–23.

10. *Fundamentals of Language* (The Hague, 1956) pp. 95–96.

11. The Preface is reprinted in *Dryden and Howard 1664–1668*, ed. D. Arundell (London, 1929), p. 10.

Chapter 7. Fenollosa and the Silence-Sound Conflict

1. References from reprint in *Prose Keys to Modern Poetry*, ed. Karl Shapiro (New York, 1962), pp. 136–55.
2. Laszlo Gefin's *Ideogram: Modern American Poetry* (London, 1982) traces the influence of Pound and Fenollosa through American poetry up to the present day, but there is hardly any reference to how, in practical terms, the visual juxtapositions of the ideogram can be transferred to sequential grammar.
3. Pound to Harriet Monroe, January 1915, reprinted in *Imagist Poetry*, ed. Peter Jones (London, 1972), pp. 141–42.
4. Preface to *Some Imagist Poets 1916*, references from reprint in Jones's *Imagist Poetry*, pp. 138–39. See also "Some Musical Analogies in Modern Poetry," *Musical Quarterly* 6 (1920): 127–57.
5. See Jones, pp. 139–40.
6. Letter to Hubert Creekmore, February 1939, in *Ezra Pound*, ed. J. P. Sullivan, Penguin Critical Anthologies (London, 1970), p. 192.
7. Interview with Amy Lowell "How Does the New Poetry Differ from the Old?" *New York Times Magazine*, 26 March (1916), p. 8.
8. "A Lecture on Modern Poetry" reprinted in Michael Roberts' *T. E. Hulme* (London, 1938), p. 8.
9. References from reprint in Jones's *Imagist Poetry*, pp. 129–34.
10. First published in *Poetry New York* III (New York, 1950). References from reprint in *Selected Writings of Charles Olson*, ed. Robert Creeley (New York, 1959), pp. 15–26.
11. *Of Grammatology* pp. 7–8.
12. *Word for Word: Essays on the Arts of Language* (Santa Barbara, 1977) vol. I.
13. "Letter 27," *Maximus Poems* IV, V, VI (New York, 1968).

Chapter 8. The Spoken Word Unheard: Silence and Sound in Modern Poems

1. "Free Verse," *Princeton Encyclopedia of Poetry and Poetics*, ed. Alex Preminger et al., (Princeton, 1974) pp. 288–90.
2. Reprinted in *To Criticise the Critic* (London, 1965), p. 187.
3. Reprinted in *On Poetry and Poets* (London, 1957), p. 157–58.
4. *T. L. S.* 27 September (1928), p. 687. Eliot objects to the notion of printing blank verse as prose, and thus seems to acknowledge the influence of the visual format.
5. See Gross's *Sound and Poetry* (Michigan, 1964), pp. 37–38 and Charles O. Hartman's *Free Verse: An Essay on Prosody* (Princeton, 1980), pp. 43–44.

Codebreaking: Conclusions for Criticism

1. Essays such as Jarrald Ranta's "Geometry, Vision and Poetic Form" *College English* 39 (1978): 707–24; Aaron Marcus's "An Introduction to the Visual

Syntax of Concrete Poetry," *Visible Language* 8 (1974): 333–60, and Janet McHughes's "The Poesis of Space: Prosodic Structures in Concrete Poetry," (1959) *Quarterly Journal of Speech* 63 (1977): 168–79 share a desire to codify and document a particular grammar of visual form as separate from the codes and conventions of oral, sequential language.

2. From the BBC Radio 3 program "The Composed Voice," 14 July 1981. First quoted in Eric Griffiths's *The Printed Voice of Victorian Poetry* (Oxford, 1989), pp. 66–67.

3. See Derrida's "Limited Inc.," *Glyph* 2 (1977): 162–54, p. 215, and Searle's "Reiterating the differences: a reply to Derrida," *Glyph* 1 (1977): 172–208.

Bibliographical Essay—Further Reading

To construct a bibliography of works that relate specifically to issues raised in this study would involve a degree of self-contradiction, because it has been my intention to show how the poetic intersections of silence and sound, of visual format and oral, sequential structure disrupt and sometimes invalidate the codes and categories of interpretation that tend to regulate and cloud our awareness of poetic meaning. But the reader who might wish to compare my readings with critical work not referred to above should consult T. V. F. Brogan's *English Versification 1570–1980. A Reference Guide with Global Appendix* (Johns Hopkins University Press, 1981). Brogan provides separate categories for studies of "Blank Verse," "Free Verse," "Visual (Typographic) Structures," and "The Poem in Performance," but it should have become clear that from Milton to Hill, poetry is capable both of merging and transcending these separate conceptions of technique and interpretation. The work that comes closest to my notion of merger is Hollander's *Vision and Resonance* (Oxford, 1975); and J. J. A. Mooij's "On the Foregrounding of Graphic Elements in Poetry," in *Comparative Poetics*, edited by D. W. Fokkema et al., Amsterdam: Rodopi, 1976), notes the reluctance of poets and critics to accept that visual shape can compromise the transparency of the oral medium.

Since the publication of Brogan's guide the interpretive category of "Visual (Typographic) Structures" has expanded considerably. However, many of these works either concentrate exclusively upon forms that are purely graphic, such as concrete poetry, or attempt to establish a specific code of interpretation, a "grammar" of visual reading. Willard Bohn's *The Aesthetics of Visual Poetry 1914–28* (Cambridge University Press, 1986) is an example of the former and Mieke Bal's "Introduction: Visual Poetics," *Style* 22 (1988): 177–82 a case of the latter. Interesting explorations of how modern poems that explicitly employ visual structure can generate a dimension of meaning distinct from oral form will be found in Stephen Cushman's *William Carlos Williams and the Meanings of Measure* (Yale University Press, 1985);

Richard Cureton's "Visual Form in e. e. cummings, 'No Thanks'" *Word and Image* 2 (1986): 245–78; Henry Sayre's *The Visual Text of William Carlos Williams* (University of Illinois Press, 1983); and Eleanor Berry's "Williams's development of a new prosodic form: Not the 'Variable Foot,' but the 'Sight Stanza,'" *William Carlos Williams Review* 7 (1981): 21–30. For a survey of recent theorists and practitioners of visual form see "A symposium on the theory and practice of the line in contemporary poetry," *Epoch* 29 (1980): 161–224.

Two journals, *Visible Language* and *Word and Image*, maintain a consistent interest in the graphic material of poetic language, and the most recent *Visible Language*, special issue (vol. 13, no. 1, 1989) called, "The Printed Poem and the Reader" (edited by Richard Bradford), contains essays on visual shape in French and English poetry from the seventeenth century to the present day.

A study by Eric Griffiths, *The Printed Voice of Victorian Poetry* (Oxford, 1989) explores the ways in which a tension between oral and written forms operates in the poetry of Tennyson, Browning, and Hopkins. Griffiths employs this as a new way of reading this work within a broad social and aesthetic context, and very little attention is given to the technicalities of prosodic form.

No one has previously examined the relation between the visual and the oral in eighteenth-century criticism. Some issues and themes from this study have been considered from slightly different perspectives in my own essays: "'Verse Only To The Eye?,' Line Endings in *Paradise Lost*," *Essays in Criticism* 3, XXXIII (1983): 187–204; "Milton's Graphic Poetics," chapter 8 of *Re-Membering Milton. Essays on the Texts and Traditions* ed. M. Nyquist and M. Ferguson (Methuen, 1987) pp. 179–97; "Criticism and the Visual Format of Poetry," *Word and Image* vol. 5, no. 2 (1989): 198–205, and "The Visual Poem in the Eighteenth Century," *Visible Language* special issue, "The Printed Poem and the Reader," vol. 13, no. 1 (1989): 6–27.

Bibliography

First editions are cited where possible; and notes on later editions or reprints refer to the edition used in the text.

Abrams, M. H. *The Mirror and the Lamp: Romantic Theory and the Critical Tradition*. London: 1953.

Addison, Joseph. *The Spectator*. Edited by Donald F. Bond. 5 vols., Oxford: 1965, nos. 39, 58–63, 285, vols. 1 and 3.

Adler, Jacob H. "Pope and the Rules of Prosody." P.M.L.A. 76 (1961): 218–26.

Akenside, Mark. *The Poetical Works of Mark Akenside and John Dyer*. Edited by The Rev. Robert A. Willmott. London: 1855.

Alston, R. C. *A Bibliography of the English Language from the Invention of Printing to the Year 1800*. Leeds: 1965, vols. 1, 6.

Armstrong, Isobel. "'Tintern, Abbey': From Augustan to Romantic." *Augustan Worlds: Essays in Honour of A. R. Humphreys*. Edited by J. C. Hilson, M. M. B. Jones, and J. R. Watson. Leicester: 1978, pp. 261–79.

Ascham, Roger. *The Scholemaster*. London: 1570. Reprinted in Smith, I, 1–45.

Athenian Mercury, The. January, 1691–92.

Atterbury, Francis. Preface to *The Second Part of Mr. Waller's Poems*. London: 1690.

Attridge, Derek. *Well Weighed Syllables: Elizabethan Verse in Classical Meters*. London: 1974.

———. *The Rhythms of English Poetry*. London: 1982.

Auden, W. H. *Collected Works*. Edited by Edward Mendelson. London: 1976.

Barnes, Thomas. "On the Nature and Essential Character of Poetry as Distinguished from Prose." *Memoirs of the Manchester Literary and Philosophical Society* 1 (1785): 54–71.

Barthes, Roland. "Style and Its Image." In *Literary Style: A Symposium*. Edited by Seymour Chatman. Oxford: 1971.

Beattie, James. *Essays*. Edinburgh: 1776.

———. *The Theory of Language*. London: 1788.

Beatty, J. M. "Charles Churchill's Treatment of the Couplet." P.M.L.A. 34 (1919): 60–69.

Beers, H. A. *English Romanticism in the Eighteenth Century*. New York: 1899.

Belsham, William. *Essays Philosophical and Moral, Historical and Literary*. London: 1789.

Benson, William. *Letters Concerning Poetical Translations, and Virgil's and Milton's Arts of Verse*. London: 1739.

Bentley, Richard. *Milton's Paradise Lost: A New Edition*. London: 1732.

Benzie, W. *The Dublin Orator. Thomas Sheridan's Influence on Rhetoric and Belles Lettres.* Leeds: 1972.

Between Poetry and Painting. I.C.A. London: 1965.

Blackwell, Thomas. *Enquiry into the Life and Writings of Homer.* London: 1735.

Blair, Hugh. *Lectures on Rhetoric and Belles Lettres.* 2 vols. London: 1783.

———. *Dissertations Moral and Critical.* London: 1783.

Blake, William. *The Complete Writings.* Edited by Geoffrey Keynes. London: 1966.

Blount, Thomas Pope. *De Re Poetica: or, Remarks upon Poetry.* London: 1694.

Boswell, James. *The Life of Samuel Johnson LLD.* 2 vols. London: 1791. Edited George Birkbeck Hill, 6 vols. Oxford: 1887. Revised by L. F. Powell. Oxford: 1934–50.

Bradford, Richard. " 'Verse Only To The Eye?' Line Endings in *Paradise Lost.*" *Essays in Criticism* 33 (1983): 187–204.

———. "Milton's Graphic Poetics." *Remembering Milton. Essays on the Texts and the Traditions.* Edited by M. Nyquist and M. Ferguson. London: 1988.

———. "Criticism and the Visual Format of Poetry." *Word and Image* vol. 5, no. 2 (1989): 198–205.

———. "The Printed Poem and the Reader," *Visible Language,* special issue vol. 13, no. 1 (1989).

Bridges, Robert. *Milton's Prosody with a chapter on Accentual Verse and Notes.* Oxford: 1921.

Brightland, John. *A Grammar of the English Tongue, With Notes, Giving the Grounds and Reason of Grammar in General, To which are now added, The Arts of Poetry, Rhetoric, Logic etc. . . . .* London: 1711.

Brogan, T. V. F. *English Versification. (1570–1980). A Reference Guide with a Global Appendix.* Baltimore and London: 1981.

Brown, Wallace Cable. *The Triumph of Form: A Study of the Later Masters of the Heroic Couplet.* Chapel Hill, N.C.: 1948.

Bysshe, Edward. *The Art of English Poetry. Containing I. Rules for making VERSES. II. A Collection of the most Natural, Agreeable, and Sublime THOUGHTS, viz. Allusions, Similes, Descriptions and Characters, of Persons and Things, that are to be found in the best ENGLISH POETS. III. A Dictionary of RHYMES.* London: 1702. Reprinted 2 vols. 1714.

Chatman, Seymour. "Robert Frost's 'Mowing': An Inquiry into Prosodic Structure." *Kenyon Review* 18 (1956): 421–38.

———. "Linguistics, Poetics, and Interpretation: The Phonemic Dimension." *Quarterly Journal of Speech* 43 (1957): 248–56.

———. "Comparing Metrical Styles." *Style in Literature.* Edited by T. A. Sebeok, pp. 149–72. Cambridge, Mass.: 1960.

———. *A Theory of Meter.* The Hague: 1965.

———. "Milton's Participial Style." *P.M.L.A.* 83 (1968): 1386–99.

———. *Literary Style: A Symposium.* Oxford: 1971.

Churchill, Charles. *The Poetical Works.* Edited by Douglas Grant. Oxford: 1956.

Cockin, William. *The Art of Delivering Written Language; or, an Essay on Reading . . .* London: 1775.

Coleridge, Samuel Taylor. *Biographia Literaria*, 1817. Edited by George Watson. London: 1975.

———. *The Friend*. Edited by B. E. Rooke. 2 vols. Princeton: 1969.

———. *The Complete Poetical Works*. Edited by E. H. Coleridge. Oxford: 1912.

Conrad, Philip. "Visual Poetry." *Poetry* 32 (1928): 112–14.

Corman, Cid. *Word for Word: Essays on the Arts of Language*. Santa Barbara: 1977.

Coward, William. *Licentia Poetica discuss'd: or, the True Test of Poetry. Without Which It is Impossible to Judge of, or Compose a Correct English Poem . . .* London: 1709.

Cowper, William. *Poetical Works*. Edited by H. S. Milford. London: 1905. Revised N. H. Russell, 1967.

Culler, A. Dwight. "Edward Bysshe and the Poet's Handbook." *P.M.L.A.* 63 (1948): 858–85.

Culler, Jonathan. *Structuralist Poetics*. London: 1975.

———. *On Deconstruction. Theory and Criticism After Structuralism*. London: 1983.

cummings e. e. *73 Poems by e. e. cummings*. London: 1964.

Daniel, Samuel. *A Defense of Rhyme*. London: 1603. Reprinted in Smith, II, pp. 356–84.

Darbishire, Helen, ed. *The Manuscript of Milton's Paradise Lost Book I*. Oxford: 1931.

Davie, Donald. *Articulate Energy: An Enquiry into the Syntax of English Poetry*. London: 1955.

———. "Syntax and Music in *Paradise Lost*." *The Living Milton: Essays by Various Hands*. Edited by Frank Kermode, pp. 70–84. London: 1960.

Dennis, John. *The Critical Works*. Edited by Edward N. Hooker. 2 vols. Baltimore: 1939.

———. *Select Works*. 2 vols. London: 1718.

De Quincey, Thomas. *The Collected Writings of Thomas De Quincey*. Edited by David Masson. 14 vols. London: 1889–90, vol. X.

Derrida, Jacques. *Of Grammatology*, trans. Gayatri Chakrovorty Spivak, Baltimore and London: 1977. First published in French, *De la Grammatologie*. Paris: 1967.

———. "Limited Inc." *Glyph* 2 (1977): 162–254.

Diekhoff, John S. "Terminal Pause in Milton's Verse." *Studies in Philology* 32 (1935): 235–39.

Dilworth, Thomas. *A New Guide To The English Tongue. In Five Parts . . .* First edition unknown. Thirteenth edition. London: 1751.

Donoghue, Denis. *Ferocious Alphabets*. London: 1981.

Dryden, John. *Essays of John Dryden*. Edited by W. P. Ker. 2 vols. Oxford: 1926.

———. *Poems*. Edited by James Kinsley. 4 vols. Oxford: 1958.

Duff, William. *Essay on Original Genius*. London: 1767.

Duncombe, John, ed. *Letters of Several Eminent Persons Deceased including the correspondence of John Hughes . . . and several of his friends, with notes.* 3 vols. London: 1772.

Dyche, Thomas. *A Guide to the English Tongue. In two parts* . . . London: 1707.

Dyer, John. *The Poetical Works of Mark Akenside and John Dyer*. Edited by The Rev. Robert A. Willmott. London: 1855.

Easthope, Antony. *Poetry as Discourse*. London: 1983.

Eliot, T. S. Letter in *T. L. S.* 27 September 1928.

———. "Milton." *Proceedings of the British Academy* 33 (1947): 61–79. Reprinted in *On Poetry and Poets*, pp. 146–61. London: 1957.

———. "Reflections on Vers Libre," *To Criticise the Critic*. London: 1965.

———. *The Complete Poems and Plays*. London: 1969.

Enfield, William. *The Speaker or, miscellaneous pieces selected from the best English Writers . . . to which is prefixed an Essay on Elocution*. London: 1774.

Fenollosa, Ernest. *The Chinese Character as a Medium for Poetry* translated by Ezra Pound, London 1919. Reprinted in *Prose Keys to Modern Poetry*, edited by Karl Shapiro. New York: 1962.

Fish, Stanley. *Is There a Text in this Class?* Cambridge, Mass.: 1980.

Fletcher, Harris. "A Possible Origin of Milton's 'Counterpoint' or Double Rhythm." *Journal of English and Germanic Philology* 54 (1955): 521–25.

Fogg, Peter Walkden. *Elementa Anglicana*. 2 vols., London: 1792–96.

Forde, William. *The True Spirit of Milton's Versification developed in a new systematic arrangement of the First Book of 'Paradise Lost', with an introductory essay on Blank-Verse*. London: 1831.

Forrest-Thomson, Veronica. *Poetic Artifice: A Theory of Twentieth Century Poetry*. Manchester: 1978.

Foster, John. *An Essay on the different nature of accent and quantity, with their use and application in the pronunciation of the English, Latin, and Greek languages*. Eton: 1762.

Fowler, Roger. " 'Prose Rhythm' and Metre." In *Essays on Style and Language: Linguistic and Critical Approaches to Literary Style*, edited by Roger Fowler, pp. 82–99. London: 1966.

———. "Structural Metrics." *Linguistics* 27 (1966): 49–64.

———. "What is Metrical Analysis." *Anglia* 86 (1968): 280–320.

———. "Three Blank Verse Textures." *The Languages of Literature* London: 1971.

Freedman, Morris. "Dryden's 'Memorable Visit' to Milton." *Huntington Library Quarterly* 18 (1955): 99–108.

———. "Dryden's Reported Reaction to *Paradise Lost*." *Notes and Queries* 203 (1958): 14–16.

———. "Milton and Dryden on Rhyme." *Huntington Library Quarterly* 24 (1961): 337–44.

Fussell, Paul. *Theory of Prosody in Eighteenth Century England*. New London, Conn.: 1954. Reprinted Hamden, Conn.: 1966.

Gascoigne, George. "Certayne Notes of Instruction concerning the making of verse or ryme in English, written at the request of Master Edouardi Donati." In his *The Poesies of George Gascoigne* . . . London: 1575. Reprinted in Smith, I, pp. 46–57.

Gefin, Laszlo K. *Ideogram: Modern American Poetry*. Milton Keynes and Austin, Texas: 1982.

Gildon, Charles. *The Complete Art of Poetry*. 2 vols. London: 1718.

———. *The Laws of Poetry As Laid down by the Duke of Buckinghamshire in his Essay on Poetry, By the Earl of Roscommon in his Essay on Translated Verse, and by the Lord Lansdowne on Unnatural Flights in Poetry, Explain'd and Illustrated*. London: 1721.

Griffiths, Eric. *The Printed Voice of Victorian Poetry*. Oxford: 1989.

Gross, Harvey. *Sound and Form in Modern Poetry: A Study of Prosody from Thomas Hardy to Robert Lowell*. Ann Arbor: 1964.

Guest, Edwin. *A History of English Rhythms*. 2 vols. London: 1838.

Halle, Morris, and Samuel J. Keyser. "Chaucer and the Study of Prosody." *College English* 28 (1966): 187–219.

———. *English Stress: Its Form, Its Growth, and its Role in Verse*. New York: 1971.

———. "Illustration and Defense of the Theory of the Iambic Pentameter." *College English* 33 (1971): 154–76.

Hamer, Enid. *The Metres of English Poetry*. London: 1930.

Hartman, Charles O. *Free Verse: An Essay on Prosody*. Princeton: 1980.

Havens, Raymond D. *The Influence of Milton on English Poetry*. Cambridge, Mass.: 1922.

Hein, Hilde. "Performance as an Aesthetic Category." *Journal of Aesthetics and Art Criticism* 28 (1970): 381–86.

Herries, John. *Analysis of a course of lectures on the theory and practice of speaking . . . To be delivered (by permission) at the Great-Room, at The Mitre, Oxford*. Oxford?: 1773.

———. *The Elements of Speech*. London: 1773.

Hill, Geoffrey. *King Log*. London: 1968.

Hollander, John. *Vision and Resonance: Two Senses of Poetic Form*. New York and London: 1975.

Hough, Graham. *Image and Experience: Studies in a Literary Revolution*. London: 1960.

Howard, Robert. Preface to *Four New Plays*. London: 1664. Reprinted by Dennis Arundell in *Dryden and Howard, 1664–1668*, pp. 8–9. Cambridge: 1929.

Hulme, T. E. "A Lecture on Modern Poetry." Reprinted in Michael Robert's *T. E. Hulme*. London: 1938.

Ing, Catherine. *Elizabethan Lyrics: A Study of the development of English metrics and their relation to poetic effect*. London: 1951.

Jakobson, Roman. "Closing statement: linguistics and poetics." In *Style and Language*, edited by Thomas A. Sebeok. London: 1960.

———. *Fundamentals of Language*. The Hague: 1956.

Jameson, R. D. "Notes on Dryden's Lost Prosodia." *Modern Philology* 20 (1923): 241–53.

Johnson, Samuel. *The Rambler*. Edited by W. J. Bate and A. B. Straus. Vols. III–V of the *Yale Edition of the Works of Samuel Johnson*. New Haven: 1969. Vols. III and IV.

———. *The Lives of the English Poets*. London, 1779, 1781. Edited by George Birkbeck Hill, 3 vols. Oxford: 1905.

Jones, Peter, ed. *Imagist Poetry*. London: 1972.

Kames, Henry Home, Lord. *Elements of Criticism*. 3 vols. London: 1762. Reprinted 2 vols. 1785.

Kenner, Hugh. "Pope's Reasonable Rhymes." *ELH* 4 (1974). Reprinted in *Pope: Recent Essays*, edited by M. Mack and J. A. Winn, London: 1980.

Kenrick, William. *New Dictionary of the English Language*. London: 1773.

———. *A Rhetorical Grammar of the English Language . . .* London: 1784.

Ker, W. P., ed. *Essays of John Dryden*. 2 vols. New York: 1961.

Keyser, Samuel J. "The Linguistic Basis of English Prosody." In *Modern Studies in English*, edited by D. A. Reibal and S. A. Schane. Englewood Cliffs: 1969.

Kiparsky, Paul. "Stress, Syntax and Metre." *Language* 51 (1975): 576–616.

———. "The Rhythmic Structure of English Verse." *Linguistic Inquiry* 8 (1977): 189–247.

Koehler, G. Stanley. "Milton on 'Numbers,' 'Quantity' and 'Rime.'" *Studies in Philology* 55 (1958): 201–17.

Lanz, Henry. *The Physical Basis of Rime: An Essay on the Aesthetics of Sound*. Stanford, 1931.

Lawler, Justus G. "Enjambment: A Structure of Transcendence." *College English* 39 (1978): 725–37.

Levin, Samuel R. "The Conventions of Poetry." In *Literary Style: A Symposium*, edited by Seymour Chatman. Oxford: 1971.

Loesch, Katherine T. "Literary Ambiguity in Oral Performance." *Quarterly Journal of Speech* 51 (1965): 258–67.

Lowell, Amy. "The Rhythms of Free Verse." *The Dial* 64 (1918): 51–56.

———. Preface to *Some Imagist Poets 1916*. Reprinted in *Imagist Poetry*, edited by Peter Jones. London: 1972.

———. "Some Musical Analogies in Modern Poetry." *Musical Quarterly* 6 (January 1920): 127–57.

MacDonald, Hugh. *John Dryden: A Bibliography of Early Editions and of Drydenia*. Oxford: 1939.

McHughes, Janet. "The Poesis of Space: Prosodic Structures in Concrete Poetry." *Quarterly Journal of Speech* 63 (1977): 168–79.

Marcus, Aaron. "An Introduction to the Visual Syntax of Concrete Poetry." *Visible Language* 8 (1974): 333–60.

Mason, John. *An Essay on Elocution. Intended chiefly for the assistance of those who instruct others in the Art of Reading And those who are often called to speak in Publick*. London: 1749.

———. *An Essay on the Power of Numbers, and the Principles of Harmony in Poetical Compositions*. London: 1749.

———. *An Essay on the Power and Harmony of Prosaic Numbers*. London: 1749. All three essays reprinted and bound in one volume, 1761.

Milton, John. *The Complete Poems*. Edited by J. Carey and A. Fowler. London: 1968.

Mitford, William. *An Essay upon the Harmony of Language*. London: 1968.

———. *An Inquiry into the Principals of Harmony in Language and the Mechanisms of Verse, Ancient and Modern.* London: 1804.

Monboddo, James Burnett, Lord. *Of the Origin and Progress of Language.* 6 vols. Edinburgh: 1773–92. Vol. II.

Monthly Review, The. 1762, 1764, 1776.

Moore, Marianne. *Collected Poems.* London: 1951.

Mulgrave, John Sheffield, Duke of Buckinghamshire, Earl of. *An Essay upon Poetry.* London: 1682. Reprinted in Spingarn, II, pp. 286–98.

Murray, Lindley. *An English Grammar adapted to the different classes of learners.* York: 1795. Reprinted 1799.

Newbery, John. *The Art of Poetry Made Easy.* London: 1746. Later revised (possibly by Oliver Goldsmith), *The Art of Poetry on a New Plan.* London: 1762.

Newton, Thomas. *Paradise Lost. A Poem in Twelve Books. The Author John Milton. A New edition with Notes of Various Authors.* London: 1749.

North, J. N. "Visual Poetry." *Poetry* 31 (1928): 3.

Odell, J. *An Essay on the Elements, Accents and Prosody of the English Language.* London: 1806.

Olson, Charles. *Projective Verse.* First published in *Poetry New York.* 3. 1950. Reprinted in *Selected Writings of Charles Olson,* edited by Robert Creeley. New York: 1959.

———. *Maximus Poems IV, V, VI.* London, 1968.

Omond, Thomas. *English Metrists: Being a Sketch of English Prosodical Criticism from Elizabethan Times to the Present Day.* Oxford: 1921.

Oras, Ants. *Milton's Editors and Commentators from Patrick Hume to Henry John Todd 1695–1801. A Study in Critical Views and Methods.* Estonia and London: 1931.

Parnell, Thomas. *An Essay on the Different Stiles of Poetry.* London: 1713.

———. *Preface to Homer's Battle of Frogs and Mice, with the Remarks of Zoilus, to which is prefix'd the Life of the said Zoilus.* London: 1717.

Parrish, Stephen M. "Wordsworth and Coleridge on Meter." *Journal of English and Germanic Philology* 59 (1960): 41–49.

Patriot Poet, The: A Satire. Anonymous. London: 1764.

Pemberton, Henry. *Observations on Poetry, Especially the Epic; Occasioned by the Late Poem upon Leonidas.* London: 1738.

Philips, John. *The Poems of Mr. John Philips.* Edited by M. G. Lloyd Thomas. London: 1927.

Phillips, Edward. Preface to *Theatrum Poetarum, or a Compleat Collection of the Poets.* London: 1675. Reprinted in Spingarn, II, pp. 256–72.

Pinto. V. de Sola. "Isaac Watts and his Poetry." *Wessex* 3 (1935): 27–36.

Piper, William B. *The Heroic Couplet.* Cleveland: 1969.

Poole, Joshua. *The English Parnassus: Or, a Helpe to English Poesie.* London: 1657.

Pope, Alexander. *The Twickenham Edition of the Poems.* General Editor J. Butt. 11 vols. London: 1939–69.

Pound, Ezra. "A Few Don'ts by an Imagiste." *Poetry* 1 (1913): 200–206. Reprinted in *Imagist Poetry*, edited by Peter Jones, London.

———. *Selected Letters*. Edited by D. D. Paige. New York: 1971.

———. *Selected Poems*. Edited by T. S. Eliot. London: 1928.

Priestley, Joseph. *A Course of Lectures on Oratory and Criticism*. London: 1777.

Princeton Encyclopedia of Poetry and Poetics. Edited by Alex. Preminger. Enlarged edition. Princeton: 1974.

Puttenham, George. *The Arte of English Poesie*. London: 1589. Original reproduced by Scolar Press microfiche. *English Linguistics 1500–1800*.

Ranta, Jarrald. "Geometry, Vision and Poetic Form." *College English* 39 (1978): 707–24.

Rice, John. *An Introduction to the Art of Reading with Energy and Propriety*. London: 1765.

Richardson(s) Jonathan. *Explanatory Notes and Remarks on Milton's Paradise Lost. With the Life of the Author as a Discourse on the Poem by J. Richardson Father and son*. London: 1734.

Rickert, William E. "Structural Functions of Rhyme and the Performance of Poetry." *Quarterly Journal of Speech* 62 (1976): 250–55.

Ricks, Christopher. *Milton's Grand Style*. Oxford: 1963.

———. "Wordsworth: 'A Pure Organic Pleasure from the Lines.'" *Essays in Criticism* 21 (1971): 1–32.

Roscommon, Wentworth Dillon, Earl of. *An Essay on Translated Verse*. London: 1694. Reprinted in Spingarn, II, pp. 297–309.

Rymer, Thomas. *The Tragedies of the Last Age Consider'd and Examin'd By the Practice of the Ancients and by the common Sense of all Ages*. London: 1678. Partly reprinted in Spingarn, II, pp. 181–208.

Saintsbury, George. *A History of English Prosody From the Twelfth Century to the Present Day*. 3 vols. London: 1906–10.

Saussure, Ferdinand de. *Course in General Linguistics* trans. Wade Baskin. London: 1960. In French, *Cours de linguistique generale*. Paris: 1973.

Say, Samuel. *Poems on Several Occasions: and Two Critical Essays, viz. The First, on the Harmony, Variety, and Power of Numbers, whether in Prose or Verse. The Second, On the Numbers of 'Paradise Lost'*. London: 1745.

Searle, John. *Speech Acts. An Essay on the Philosophy of Language*. Cambridge: 1969.

———. "Reiterating the differences: a reply to Derrida." *Glyph* 1 (1977): 172–208.

Shaftsbury, Anthony Ashley Cooper, Earl of. *Characteristics of Men, Manners, Opinions, Times and Miscellaneous Reflections on the preceding Treatises, and other Critical Subjects*. London: 1711. Edited by J. M. Robertson. 2 vols. London: 1900.

Sheldon, E. K. *Thomas Sheridan of Smock Alley*. Princeton: 1967.

Sheridan, Thomas. *British Education: or the Source of the Disorders of Great Britain. Being an essay towards proving that the immorality, ignorance and falst taste, which so generally prevail, are the . . . consequences of the present defective system of Education*. London: 1756.

———. *A Discourse delivered in the Theatre at Oxford, in the Senate House at Cambridge, and at the Spring Garden in London.* London: 1759.

Sheridan, Thomas. *A Course of Lectures on Elocution together with two dissertations on language and some other tracts relative to these subjects.* London: 1762.

———. *Lectures on the Art of Reading, in Two Parts. Containing Part I. The Art of Reading Prose. Part II. The Art of Reading Verse.* London: 1775.

———. *A Complete Dictionary of the English Language.* London: 1780.

Sidney, Sir Phillip. *An Apologie for Poetrie* (1583? Later entitled *The Defense of Poesie*). London: 1595. Reprinted in Smith, I, pp. 148–207.

Smart, George, K. "English Non-dramatic Blank Verse in the Sixteenth Century". *Anglia* 61 (1937): 370–97.

Smith, Alexander. "The Philosophy of Poetry." Published in the *Blackwood Magazine* (December, 1835). Partly reprinted in *Romantic Criticism 1800–1850*, edited by R. A. Foakes. London: 1968.

Smith, G. Gregory, ed. *Elizabethan Critical Essays.* 2 vols. Oxford: 1904. Reprinted 1937–71.

Spingarn, J. E. *Critical Essays of the Seventeenth Century.* 3 vols. London: 1909. Reprinted 1957.

Sprott, S. E. *Milton's Art of Prosody.* Oxford: 1953.

Stankiewicz, Edward. "Poetic and Non Poetic Language." In *Poetics—Poetyka—Poetika*, edited by Donald Davie. Warsaw: 1961.

Steele, Joshua. *An Essay Towards Establishing the Melody and Measure of Speech, to be Expressed and Perpetuated by Peculiar Symbols.* London: 1775.

———. *Prosodia Rationalis: or an Essay Towards Establishing . . .* London: 1779.

Sterne, Lawrence. *The Life and Opinions of Tristram Shandy.* London: 1759–67. Reprinted Oxford 1983, ed. Ian Campbell Ross.

Temple, Sir William. "Upon Ancient and Modern Learning." Part I of the second part of *Miscellanea*. London: 1690. Reprinted in Spingarn, III, pp. 32–72.

———. "Of Poetry." Part IV of the second part of *Miscellanea*. London: 1690. Reprinted in Spingarn, III, pp. 73–109.

Thelwall, John. *Selections for the illustration of a course of instructions on the rhythmus and utterance of the English language with an Introductory Essay on the application of rhythmical science to the treatment of impediments.* London: 1812.

Thomson, James. *The Complete Poetical Works.* Edited by J. L. Robertson. London: 1908.

———. *The Seasons.* Edited by James Sambrook. Oxford: 1981.

Thompson, John. *The Founding of English Metre.* London: 1961.

Trager, George L. and Henry Lee Smith. *An Outline of English Structure. Studies in Linguistics Occasional Papers* no. 3. Norman: Oklahoma: 1951.

Walker, John. *A Dictionary of the English Language, Answering at Once the Purposes of Rhyming, Spelling and Pronouncing.* London: 1775.

———. *Elements of Elocution; being the substance of a course of Lectures on the Art of reading delivered at Several Colleges . . . in Oxford.* 2 vols. London: 1781.

———. *Hints for Improvement on the Art of Reading.* London: 1783.

———. *A Rhetorical Grammar or course of lessons on elocution.* London: 1785.

———. *The Melody of Speaking delineated; or, elocution taught like music by visible signs.* London: 1787.

Wallerstein, Ruth. "The Development of the Rhetoric and Metre of the Heroic Couplet, Especially in 1625–1645." *P.M.L.A.* 50 (1935): 166–209.

Wasserman, Earl R. "The Return of the Enjambed Couplet." *English Literary History* 7 (1940): 239–52.

Watts, Isaac. *Horae Lyricae. Poems chiefly of the Lyric Kind.* London: 1706. Revised and enlarged 1709.

———. *The Art of Reading and Writing English.* London: 1721.

———. *Relinquiae Juveniles: Miscellaneous thoughts in Prose and Verse. To which is added, Remnants of Time, employed in Prose and Verse.* London: 1734. Reprinted Boston, Mass.: 1796.

Webb, Daniel. *Remarks on the Beauties of Poetry.* London: 1762.

———. *Observations on the Correspondence between Poetry and Music.* London: 1769.

Wesley, Samuel. *An Epistle to a Friend Concerning Poetry.* London: 1700.

Whaler, James. *Counterpoint and Symbol: An Inquiry into the Rhythm of Milton's Epic Style.* Anglistica, vol. VI. Copenhagen: 1956.

Whitman, Walt. *The Collected Writings of Walt Whitman.* General editors G. W. Allen and S. Bradley. 9 vols. New York: 1965. Vol. V.

Whitehall, Harold. "From Linguistics to Criticism." *Kenyon Review* 13 (1951): 710–14.

Williams, William Carlos. *Selected Poems.* Enlarged edition. New York: 1968.

———. *Pictures from Brueghel and other poems.* New York: 1962.

Williamson, George. "The Rhetorical Pattern of Neo-Classical Wit." *Modern Philology* 33 (1935): 55–81.

Wimsatt, W. K. "One Relation of Rhyme to Reason: Alexander Pope." *Modern Language Quarterly* 5, (1944): 323–38. Reprinted in his *The Verbal Icon.* Lexington, Kentucky: 1954.

———. "Rhetoric and Poems: Alexander Pope." In *English Institute Essays, 1948,* edited by D. A. Robertson. New York: 1949, pp. 179–207. Reprinted in his *The Verbal Icon.* Lexington, Kentucky: 1954.

Wimsatt, W. K., and Monroe C. Beardsley. "The Concept of Meter: An Exercise in Abstraction." *P.M.L.A.* 74 (1959): 585–98.

———. "The Intentional Fallacy." *Sewanee Review* 54 (Summer 1946). Reprinted in *The Verbal Icon.* Lexington, Kentucky: 1954.

Winters, Yvor. "The Influence of Meter on Poetic Convention." In *Primitivism and Decadence: A Study in American Experimental Poetry.* New York: 1937.

———. "The Audible Reading of Poetry." *Hudson Review* 4 (1951): 433–47.

Woodford, Samuel. *A Paraphrase upon the Psalms of David.* London: 1667.

———. *A Paraphrase Upon the Canticles, and some Select Hymns of the New and Old Testament, With other occasional Compositions in English Verse.* London: 1679.

Wordsworth, William. *Poetical Works.* Edited by E. de Selincourt. 5 vols. Oxford: 1940.

———. *The Prose Works.* Edited by W. J. B. Owen and J. W. Smyser. 3 vols. Oxford: 1974.

———. *The Literary Criticism of William Wordsworth.* Edited by P. M. Zall. New York: 1966.

———. *Selected Prose.* Edited by J. O. Hayden. Oxford: 1988.

Young, Edward. *The Complete Poetry and Prose.* Edited by John Doran. 2 vols. London: 1854.

Young, Walter. "An Essay on Rhythmical Measures." *Transactions of the Royal Society of Edinburgh* 2 part 2 (1790).

Index

Abrams, M. H., 122
Addison, Joseph, 33, 34, 143
Akenside, Mark, 87–88
Armstrong, Isobel, 82
Arnold, Matthew, 141
Atterbury, Francis, 149
Attridge, Derek, 55–56, 60
Auden, W. H., 196–200

Bal, Mieke, 216
Barnes, Thomas, 63, 85, 182, 203
Barthes, Roland, 50, 56, 201
Beardsley, Monroe, 156
Beattie, James, 67–68, 193
Belsham, William, 123
Benson, William, 47–48, 84
Berry, Eleanor, 217
Blackwell, Thomas, 122
Blair, Hugh, 80, 92, 122, 137
Blake, William, 42, 92, 122–27, 131, 168, 175
Blank verse, 20–30, 33–49, 52–56, 65–68, 74–98, 106–14, 103–32
Blount, Sir Thomas Pope, 27, 125
Bohn, Willard, 216
Boswell, James, 211
Bradford, Richard, 217
Brightland, John, 106
Brogan, T. V. F., 211, 216
Brooks, Cleanth, 56
Brueghel, Pieter, 186–87
Bysshe, Edward, 89–90, 149

Chatman, Seymour, 51
Chomsky, Noam, 54
Churchill, Charles, 146–47, 200
Cockin, William, 63–64, 144–45, 196
Coleridge, Samuel Taylor, 82, 127–29, 172, 195
Concrete poetry, 181–83
Corman, Cid, 176–77
Coward, William, 38–39, 106, 149

Cowper, William, 87–88
Creeley, Robert, 59, 161
Culler, A. Dwight, 89
Culler, Jonathan, 38, 56–57, 70, 157
cummings, e. e., 59, 180–81, 184, 200
Cureton, Richard, 217
Cushman, Stephen, 216

Daniel, Samuel, 19
Davie, Donald, 43, 45, 99, 161, 206
Dennis, John, 29, 30, 103–6, 121, 123, 131, 135, 149, 179
De Quincey, Thomas, 105
Derrida, Jacques, 72–73, 76, 174, 176, 206–8
Dilworth, Thomas, 106
Donne, John, 147
Donoghue, Denis, 206–7
Dryden, John, 21–25, 28, 34, 89, 103, 104, 105, 133, 141, 172
Duff, William, 122
Duncan, Robert, 59, 161
Dyer, John, 88

Easthope, Antony, 82
Eliot, T. S., 119, 188–94, 200, 201, 205
Enfield, William, 83
Ewart, Gavin, 205

Fennollosa, Ernest, 161–68, 175
Fish, Stanley, 57–59, 70, 115, 157, 173
Fletcher, John Gould, 172
Flint, F. S., 163
Fogg, Peter Walkden, 64–66, 140, 183
Forde, William, 130
Foster, John, 106
Fowler, Alastair, 37
Fowler, Roger, 51–52, 60
Free verse, 159–200; eighteenth-century origins of, 103–31
Fussell, Paul, 13–14, 39, 89

Gascoigne, George, 21
Gaudier-Brzeska, Henri, 165
Gefin, Laszlo, 214
Gray, Thomas, 123, 162
Grimald, Nicholas, 21
Gross, Harvey, 166–68, 190, 191, 206
Guest, Edwin, 131

Halle, William, and Samuel Keyser, 115, 117
Havens, R. D., 211
Hayley, William, 64–65
Hill, Geoffrey, 203–5
Hollander, John, 45, 53–54, 60, 62–63, 72, 74–76, 91, 96–98, 99, 111, 114, 126, 132, 165, 184, 201, 206, 216
Hooker, E. N., 9
Howard, Sir Robert, 23, 157–58
Hulme, T. E., 172–73

Imagism, 161–74
Ideogram, 161–68

"J. D.," 19–21
Jakobson, Roman, 154–55, 202–3
Johnson, Samuel, 33, 34, 40, 48, 91, 93, 128, 129
Jones, William, 122

Kames, Henry Home, Lord, 40, 69, 91, 94–96, 128, 136–37, 141, 152–53, 187–88
Keats, John, 177
Kenner, Hugh, 150–58, 161, 199
Kenrick, William, 61–66, 86, 108, 163, 193
Ker, W. P., 9
Kiparsky, Paul, 115–18

Levin, Samuel, 57–58
Linguistics and metrical studies, 115–17
Lowell, Amy, 38, 169–71, 174, 175
Lowell, Robert, 205
Lowes, John Livingstone, 38, 170, 173

Macpherson, James, 123
Man Ray, 182–83
Marcus, Aaron, 214–15
Mason, John, 39, 106, 143

McHughes, Janet, 215
Meredith, George, 38, 170
Milton, John, 14, 24–30, 36–49, 52–55, 61–67, 71, 74–81, 85, 86, 93, 94–98, 103, 106, 107, 108, 110–13, 116, 118–19, 123, 124, 125, 140, 155, 160, 164, 165, 170, 181, 184, 185, 186, 189, 192, 193, 199, 200, 204, 208
Mitford, William, 92
Mooij, J. J. A., 216
Monboddo, Lord, 109
Monroe, Harriet, 168
Moore, Marianne, 195
Morgan, Edwin, 182

Odell, J., 129–30
Olson, Charles, 42, 59, 161, 175–79
Omond, T. S., 13, 39
Owen, Wilfred, 150

Pemberton, Henry, 106
Phillips, Edward, 27
Phillips, John, 28
Piper, W. B., 139
Poole, Joshua, 19–21, 149, 150
Pope, Alexander, 115, 117, 133–35, 137, 138–40, 141, 145–46, 152–53, 155–58
Pound, Ezra, 42, 161–68, 173–74, 185
Priestley, Joseph, 92, 143–44, 149, 153
Puttenham, George, 19, 66

Quine, W. V. O., 56–57

Ranta, Jarrald, 214
Reader-response theory, 56–60, 177–78
Rhyme, 13, 19–30, 103–4, 107, 112, 116, 117, 133–58, 194–200
Rice, John, 38–42, 79, 103, 114, 120–22, 147, 170, 190, 198
Ricks, Christopher, 45, 47, 54–55, 60, 82–83, 84, 99, 114, 132, 165, 206
Roscommon, Earl of, 27
Romanticism, 122–31
Rymer, Thomas, 28

Saintsbury, George, 13, 110
Saussure, Ferdinand de, 62–63, 72, 120–22, 202

Say, Samuel, 106–9
Sayre, Henry, 217
Searle, John, 207–8
Shaftsbury, Earl of, 143
Shakespeare, William, 115, 119
Shelley, Percy Bysshe, 161
Sheridan, Thomas, 14, 42–49, 52, 66–67, 70, 77–78, 83, 84, 85–86, 95–96, 98, 99, 109, 111, 114, 126, 137, 138–42, 157, 165, 186, 190, 208
Sidney, Sir Philip, 19, 161
Smith, Alexander, 130
Smith, G. Gregory, 9
Speech act theory, 207–8
Spingarn, J. E., 9
Sprat, Thomas, 104
Spenser, Edmund, 21
Steele, Joshua, 14, 69, 109–14, 117, 129, 131, 169, 175, 208
Stankiewicz, Edward, 145
Sterne, Laurence, 68–70
Surrey, Earl of, 21

Thelwall, John, 129

Thomson, James, 88, 92–94, 123, 147, 181
Thomson, Veronica Forrest, 57
Trager, George L., and Henry Lee Smith, 51

Walker, John, 52–53, 79, 84–85, 98, 103, 111, 117–22, 145–46, 171, 195, 208
Wallerstein, Ruth, 20
Wasserman, Earl R., 139
Watts, Isaac, 90–93, 97, 147–50, 197
Whitman, Walt, 127
Wilkens, John, 104, 151
Williams, William Carlos, 59, 96, 119, 161, 163, 184–88, 194, 198, 199, 200, 205
Williamson, George, 20
Wimsatt, W. K., 133–35, 139, 142, 143
Woodford, Samuel, 14, 30, 33–38, 70, 77, 98, 104

Young, Edward, 88, 93, 181
Young, Walter, 60, 98